TRANSACTIONS OF THE

AMERICAN PHILOSOPHICAL SOCIETY

HELD AT PHILADELPHIA

FOR PROMOTING USEFUL KNOWLEDGE

VOLUME 73, PART 1, 1983

P.-L. Roederer: Political Thought and Practice During the French Revolution

KENNETH MARGERISON

Associate Professor of History, Southwest Texas State University

THE AMERICAN PHILOSOPHICAL SOCIETY

INDEPENDENCE SQUARE: PHILADELPHIA

1983

Library of Congress Catalog
Card Number 81-71030
International Standard Book Number 0-87169-731-9
US ISSN 0065-9746

To Patty

CONTENTS

Gravure of P.-L. Roederer by Bonneville. Reprinted with permission from Collection Viollet, Paris.

ACKNOWLEDGMENTS

I am indebted to Frances Acomb of Duke University not only for suggesting that I undertake a study of Roederer's political career during the French Revolution but also for guiding that study through the preliminary stages which led to its completion as a doctoral dissertation. Her firm grasp of the biographer's task and her continual attention to both the form and substance of the project taught me much about historical research and writing. I was fortunate to have had Harold Parker and Charles Young, also of Duke, as critics of my early work. I am deeply grateful to George Taylor of the University of North Carolina who, while I was an undergraduate, first sparked my interest in the field of the French Revolution and introduced me to the serious study of history.

The process of expanding and revising my work on Roederer was aided considerably by the staffs of the Archives Nationales, the Bibliothèque Nationale, and the Southwest Texas State University Library. The late Julian Boyd of the Thomas Jefferson Papers graciously allowed me to make use of a microfilm copy of the documents on the tobacco issue found in Roederer's papers in the Archives Nationales. Sandra Caillens and Jill Bourdais de Charbonnière have from time to time procured for me copies of documents from various French repositories. The Organized Research Committee at Southwest Texas provided generous financial support which aided considerably the completion of my work. My colleagues in the Department of History at Southwest Texas and especially Everette Swinney, who as chairman maintained faith in the abilities of a young faculty member at a crucial point in his career, have been supportive of my project throughout the period of its development. Terry Jeffries, a departmental assistant, typed the bulk of the manuscript.

The final version of my biography has benefited from the criticism and suggestions of a number of individuals. Jeremy Popkin, whose knowledge of the press during the Directory is unsurpassed, read the entire manuscript and provided me with a number of useful suggestions. I am grateful to Martin Staum both for his continued encouragement and his critique, based on his own deep understanding of the *idéologues*, of the chapter on Roederer's social science. R. R. Palmer, whose contribution to the study of the Revolution is universally recognized, read the final version of the manuscript and provided valuable comment on and support for my work. Of course I assume all responsibility for any errors of fact or interpretation.

Finally I owe my greatest debt of gratitude to my wife Patty, who in addition to performing the duties of typist, proofreader, and critic has endured that exacting experience associated with research and publication that only academic spouses can fully appreciate. Without her continued support and encouragement this biography could not have been completed, and for this reason I have dedicated it to her.

San Marcos, July 1982

ABBREVIATIONS

AN   Archives Nationales

AP   *Archives parlementaires de 1787 à 1860.* l^e serie (1787–1799). Ed. M. J. Mavidal and M. E. Laurent. 86 vols. Paris, 1879.

JEP *Journal d'économie publique, de morale et de politique*

JP   *Journal de Paris*

MU *Moniteur Universel. Réimpression de l'ancien Moniteur.* 32 vols. Paris, 1847–1850.

OR *Oeuvres du comte P.-L. Roederer.* Ed. A.-M. Roederer. 8 vols. Paris, 1853–1859.

INTRODUCTION

The recent interest in the career of P.-L. Roederer by such historians as J. F. Bosher, Jacob Price, Sergio Moravia, Jeremy Popkin, Michael James, Thomas Kaiser, and Jean Roels would not have surprised Georges Bourgin,[1] who argued forty years ago that there was much to be learned from studying Roederer's life. Traditionally Roederer has been known principally for his role in escorting the king to the Legislative Assembly on 10 August 1792 and for assisting in the coup d'état of brumaire. Recent historians, however, have come to discover that Roederer's career was long, varied, and significant. This study of Roederer's political thought and practice during the decade of the French Revolution places some of these recent findings of particular aspects of his career in the broader context of his life and provides new insights into his motivation and ultimate political significance.

Roederer's political career is not easily characterized. From his youth he was highly ambitious and willing to use all the tools available to him in the last years of the *ancien régime* to achieve personal advancement. At the same time he was intrigued with the possibilities that enlightened reform offered to France. This fascination with reform was perhaps natural to a highly intelligent youth maturing in the last decade of the ancien régime, an era dominated by interest in theoretical and practical ideas of reform. As an advocate of reform Roederer was as capable of writing persuasive *mémoires* as he was of pulling all the political strings at his command in order to achieve his goals. This combination of innovative, analytical, and reflective political thought with practical political activity remained an essential feature of Roederer's political career up to 1800.

Because he chose to make a career from both the exposition of political theory and the practice of politics, Roederer often laid himself open to charges of opportunism and inconsistency. Since his ambition was not well disguised, his political ideas could always be thought of as simply a means to achieve his own advancement. Similarly, when he revised his ideas during the course of the Revolution, his actions could be interpreted as mere bending with the prevailing political winds for personal advantage. There were certainly many among his contemporaries who saw Roederer precisely in this light. In Metz his opponents accused him of adopting the mantle of democracy in order to gain political power, and the Jacobins in 1792 thought he had abandoned democracy in order to retain and perhaps even increase his power under the Constitution of 1791. After

---

[1] Georges Bourgin, "Un Témoin de la Révolution: Roederer," *Revue historique*, 188 (1940): 259–270.

Roederer conducted Louis XVI to the Legislative Assembly on 10 August 1792, neither republicans nor royalists trusted him. Thus during the Thermidorian Reaction and the era of the Directory, Roederer was a frequent target for attack by the right and the left, and he did not hold elective office after 1792.

While the historical record verifies Roederer's ambition and his willingness to engage in the give and take of practical politics, he could not be classified as an unprincipled political thinker or actor. Roederer's great interest in political theory and analysis demonstrated his firm conviction in an ultimate political truth that must lie behind all political activity. As he practiced politics from his youth in Metz through the decade of the Revolution, he continually refined his political ideas to conform with reality. Naturally a political thinker whose views were based to a large extent on personal experience and astute observation was not likely to develop theories which were not subject to modification or highly impractical. Roederer's concerns with the financial condition of the glass industry during the 1780s led him to develop his economic theories. These in turn led to the creation of his democratic ideas on the eve of the Revolution. His work as a deputy to the National Constituent Assembly and in the department of Paris was based largely on this concept of democracy until the *journée* of 10 August and subsequent events proved the futility of establishing reform during revolutionary turmoil. After 10 August Roederer turned to the theories of social science developed by Condorcet as the means of providing enlightened government for France. He abandoned his belief in democracy and shunned the political turmoil that it spawned, but he continued to believe in the Revolution's ability to bring vast improvement to the government of France. He now thought, however, that such a government must be based on scientific truth rather than the mere will of the majority or parliamentary parties. He participated in the conspiracy of brumaire which led to the advent of Bonaparte and the institution of the Constitution of the Year VIII in the belief that this seizure of power would lead to the best approximation of the type of government he desired.

Roederer's political thought and practice from his youth through the coup d'état of brumaire will be explored in an effort to analyze and understand the interaction of events and ideas that shaped his political career. With this in mind, we shall examine the various aspects of Roederer's revolutionary political career including his activities as a *conseiller* in the Parlement of Metz, an advocate of tariff reform in the 1780s, the leader of the municipal revolution in Metz, a deputy to the National Constituent Assembly, *procureur-général-syndic* of the department of Paris, and conspirator in the coup d'état of brumaire. We shall also examine the origin and development of Roederer's political ideas as they were presented in his pamphlets, lectures, and articles in the journals he edited during the Directory in order to get a complete picture of Roederer's political career and its significance during the French Revolution.

I. FAMILY AND PARLEMENT IN METZ

The city of Metz, an ecclesiastical town with Roman and Carolingian backgrounds, provided the environment for the financial, social, and political rise of the Roederer family in the eighteenth-century.[1] One of the free cities of the Holy Roman Empire in the Middle Ages, Metz continued to maintain its connections with Germany into the eighteenth-century due to the trading privileges it had with the Empire and to the course of the Moselle which flowed from Metz into the Rhine. During the religious wars in sixteenth-century Germany, Henry II, upon making a favorable treaty with the German protestants, had been responsible for bringing Metz along with Verdun and Toul into France. From 1552, the date of its subjugation to France, Metz served a primary role as a heavily fortified outpost on the German border. In time it also became an administrative capital with a resident *intendant*. By 1633 the city had acquired a parlement with jurisdiction over the Trois-Evêchés, the Three Bishoprics of Metz, Verdun, and Toul. Despite its very small *ressort* the sovereign court brought Metz the prestige reserved to the handful of towns possessing this institution.

The Roederers made their fortune through the Parlement of Metz. The family had originated in Strasbourg, but Jean-George, the son of Christmann Roederer, "a merchant of hides and bourgeois" of that city, had gone to Metz where he became an *avocat* in the Parlement.[2] From the first the Roederers were conscious of improving their social and financial position in the town. Jean-George, for instance, converted from Lutheranism, acceptable in Strasbourg but not Metz, to Catholicism in 1701, and married Jeanne Lionnet whose father, Joseph, bequeathed the office of "*greffier hereditaire de la maîtrise des eaux et forêts de Vic*" to his son-in-law.[3] The eldest son of this union, Pierre-Louis, born in 1711, married Marguerite Gravelotte, the daughter of another advocat of the Parlement, Toussainte Gravelotte, seigneur of Saucy and Tronville.[4] Upon his father-in-law's death Pierre-Louis inherited these seigneuries.

The Parlement remained the major focus of family enterprise, however, and Pierre-Louis, following his father's footsteps, entered the court as avocat. Here he proved to be a man of ability. He acquired the position

---

[1] A short essay on the city can be found in Gabriel Hocquard, *Metz* (Paris, 1961).

[2] Jean-George Roederer was born in 1676. A.-M. Roederer, *La Famille Roederer* (Paris, 1849), pp. 3–5.

[3] Ibid., pp. 4–5. For an excellent study of the bourgeois desire for social advancement through inheritance and office holding see Ralph Giesey, "Rules of Inheritance and Strategies of Mobility in Prerevolutionary France," *American Historical Review*, 82 (1977): 271–289.

[4] A.-M. Roederer, *La Famille Roederer*, pp. 7–12.

3

of *substitut du procureur général et conseiller du roi*, an office which gave him personal nobility; he was entrusted by the Parlement in 1762 with the founding and staffing of a college at Metz; and he was elected five times as *batonnier* of the order of avocats. Simultaneously he served as *bailli* and *juge* of the lands of the Abbaye de Saint Symphorien and the Abbaye de Gorze.

The Maupeou Reform of 1771 provided Pierre-Louis Roederer with his greatest opportunity to be of service to the Parlement of Metz. As is well known the reform had as its purpose the suppression of the parlements and their opposition to royal reform programs.[5] Roederer spent much of his time after the suppression in Paris trying to bring about a reversal in royal policy. When the Parlement was restored upon the accession of Louis XVI, Roederer was rewarded by the *Trois Ordres* of Metz with the sum of six thousand *livres* for his efforts in behalf of the restoration.[6] By the time of his death in 1789, the Roederer family had become one of the prominent families in Metz. Through careful selection of marriage partners, they had acquired land and minor hereditary titles. Through hard work in behalf of the Parlement, Pierre-Louis Roederer had become something of a local hero. He had also become moderately wealthy, leaving an estate of 400,000 livres to his heirs.[7]

The family attachment to the Parlement continued during the early career of the eldest son of Pierre-Louis and Marguerite Roederer. Born on 15 February 1754 in the family dwelling near the town granary on the rue Chèvremont and named Pierre-Louis after his father, the young Roederer attended the newly founded college of Metz and after studying law in Strasbourg received his license to practice in June 1771.[8] In July he was admitted as avocat to the Parlement of Metz. Unfortunately for the young Roederer his admission coincided with the demise of the Parlement under the Maupeou Reform. The Parlement of Paris was suppressed in February 1771, and sometime thereafter Charles Alexandre de Calonne, the intendant for Metz, ordered the suppression of the local Parlement and the assignment of its functions to other courts.[9] The prospect of pleading cases in lower courts did not please the young lawyer. He wrote to his brother-in-law and fellow avocat, Louis Mena, that the reform "puts the seal on our annihilation."[10] He told Mena that the cases brought before the lower court would be complicated but unimportant thereby bringing no recognition to the avocats. Simple avocats like "the Rullands, the Vanniers, the Gabriels are no longer remembered by anyone."[11] With the destruction

---

[5] Jules Flammermont, *Le Chancelier Maupeou et les Parlements* (Paris, 1883) offers a complete account of the affair.

[6] A.-M. Roederer, *La Famille Roederer*, pp. 16–27.

[7] Ibid., p. 51.

[8] Emmanuel Michel, *Biographie du Parlement de Metz* (Metz, 1853), p. 460; A.-M. Roederer, *La Famille Roederer*, pp. 60, 65.

[9] Flammermont, *Maupeou*, pp. 436, 469.

[10] Roederer to Mena, 10 July 1772, in A.-M. Roederer, *La Famille Roederer*, p. 67.

[11] Ibid., pp. 70–71.

of the Parlement Roederer looked to commerce and especially foreign affairs as the only interesting careers remaining open to him. He asked Mena if his views were contrary to "my true interests" or would "displease my father."[12]

This desire for a significant career was intimately intertwined with Roederer's attitude toward his father. In a second letter to Mena he described his feelings on returning home from the study of law at Strasbourg: "After a long absence, I reentered the bosom of my family. Here, raised from my childhood, accustomed to being seen as a child, I am indignant at being again received and treated as such."[13] In the matter of securing his future by making the correct connections in society, Roederer could only see "the shadow of this same father who presents me there."[14] Furthermore his own worth would never be fairly judged "in a city and in people's homes where I am seen only as the bearer of a respected name."[15]

The elder Roederer was none too pleased with the youthful rebellion of his son. The family position in Metz so carefully established over the course of the previous seventy years might be jeopardized by his son's desire to stray from the tried-and-true formula of success. The young Roederer must have hinted at his dissatisfaction with the law before he wrote to Mena. As early as January 1772 his father had written reproaching him for his attitude: "[F]or what reason have you developed an aversion to this profession for which all the avenues have been prepared for you and [instead] displayed a taste for the dust and bondage of the Bureaux of Foreign Affairs?"[16] Later the elder Roederer became quite vexed with his son for taking his problems to Mena instead of dealing directly with him and remained perplexed at the youth's determination to leave the law:

This profession is that of your father who owes to it the public esteem, confidence, and considerations with which he is honored. He owes to it the amelioration and augmentation of the moderate fortune he enjoys and wishes to pass on to his family. Do you believe yourself degraded by following the career of your father to whom you have so many obligations, which also would be as useful and rewarding to you as to anyone, and which offers you a stability and solidity that you would be unable to find in any other station, especially the one to which you are attracted which offers only incertitude, dependence, bondage [and] a perpetually precarious existence . . .?[17]

The young Roederer acquiesced in his father's wishes and continued his career as avocat. With his submission to family duty and the subsequent recall of the Parlement by Louis XVI, the fortune of the Roederers seemed once more secure. If a suitable marriage could be arranged for Pierre-

---

[12] Ibid., p. 71.
[13] Roederer to Mena, 23 August 1772, in A.-M. Roederer, *La Famille Roederer*, pp. 78–79.
[14] Ibid.
[15] Ibid., p. 79.
[16] Father to Roederer, 4 January 1772, in A.-M. Roederer, *La Famille Roederer*, p. 86.
[17] Father to Roederer, no date, in A.-M. Roederer, *La Famille Roederer*, pp. 94–95.

Louis, the family could assume that its social and financial position in Metz would not suffer and might even improve. A marriage candidate was found through Louis Mena, the young Roederer's brother-in-law.[18] Besides his position as avocat in the Parlement, Mena was a partner with Antoine-Marie Guaita, a Frankfurt banker of Milanese ancestry, in the profitable Saint-Quirin and Monthermé glassworks. This connection led to negotiations in 1773 concerning the possibility of a marriage between Pierre-Louis and Guaita's daughter, Louise. The marriage took place in Frankfurt on 28 October 1777, with Guaita providing a dowry of 24,000 livres or an annual *rente* of 1,500 livres in addition to the invaluable family connection with an important manufacturing enterprise.[19] After such a marriage the family fortunes could hardly have looked more promising.

Having fulfilled his family obligations by remaining in the Parlement and marrying successfully, the young Roederer still had to satisfy his desire to escape from the paternal shadow by launching an independent career. Within the confines of the sovereign court this was most easily done by purchasing a more important office than that of avocat. In 1777 he tried unsuccessfully to secure the post of avocat général, one of the *gens du roi* of the court.[20] Besides bringing increased responsibilities, the office, if procured, would have given him nobility. Roederer was more successful in 1779 when he was able to secure for the price of 32,000 livres a position as conseiller in the Parlement. This office brought him hereditary nobility as well as an important role in the deliberative functions of the court.[21] While Roederer would certainly have been well known by the members of the Parlement and his background and abilities acceptable to them, a question arose as to his marriage to Guaita's daughter. Since Guaita was involved in *"un commerce de détail en épiceries"* as well as banking and manufacturing, some members of the court had reservations about allowing Roederer, with his new commercial connections, into the aristocratic Parlement. To facilitate his acceptance by the court, Roederer prepared a mémoire which argued that since his father-in-law's commerce was

---

[18] A.-M. Roederer, *La Famille Roederer*, pp. 99–100. Mena was married to the young Roederer's eldest sister, Anne. Ibid., p. 51. Roederer's dowry was well above the average of 14,300 livres received by barristers in Toulouse, which had a more important court. Lenard Berlanstein, *The Barristers of Toulouse in the Eighteenth Century (1740–1793)* (Baltimore, 1975), pp. 40–41.

[19] A.-M. Roederer, *La Famille Roederer*, pp. 99–100; AN 29AP9 "Articles de futur marriage d'entre M. P.-L. Roederer et Madesmoiselle Guaita," October 1777. Roederer divorced Louise during the Revolution and married the divorcée Madame Décrétat. Note of A.-M. Roederer in OR, 8: 501.

[20] A.-M. Roederer, *La Famille Roederer*, p. 100. Unfortunately for Roederer the post he sought did not become vacant. For a description of the post of avocat général in the parlements see Franklin Ford, *Robe and Sword: The Regrouping of the French Aristocracy after Louis XIV* (New York, 1965) p. 48.

[21] A.-M. Roederer, *La Famille Roederer*, p. 103. The Parlement of Metz, unlike some of the other sovereign courts, admitted many *roturiers* into its ranks and conferred nobility of the first degree upon them after twenty years of service. Roederer, however, received hereditary nobility because his father's office had bestowed nobility upon him after twenty years of service. Jean Egret, "L'Aristocratie parlementaire française à la fin de l'ancien régime," *Revue historique*, 208 (1952): 1–15; A.-M. Roederer, *La Famille Roederer*, pp. 10–11.

conducted outside of France "the sensibilities of the membership would not be offended by a warehouse under its eyes nor under the eyes of the citizens for whom it must preserve the dignity of the magistracy."[22] The reputation of his family and the arguments of his mémoire evidently overcame any doubts of the magistrates, and he was seated in the Parlement in March 1780.

In his new position of conseiller, Roederer took an active part in the work of the Parlement and impressed his colleagues with his diligence and ability. By 1783 he was anxious to advance his position another notch by purchasing an office of *maître des requêtes*.[23] Securing such a post would have been a major achievement for the young conseiller as he would have become a member of the Royal Council and eligible for appointment as intendant and eventually secretary or minister of state.[24] Such an advancement might have seemed a bit beyond the resources, both financial and social, of an obscure provincial magistrate. Indeed, most of the maîtres des requêtes who went on to become intendants had first been members of the Parlement of Paris.[25] Despite its relatively minor importance among the sovereign courts of France, however, the Parlement of Metz had provided many of the intendants of France during the eighteenth-century. This tradition of royal service at Metz might have emboldened the young Roederer to make a try for such a career himself.

Obtaining the office of maître des requêtes was a good deal more difficult than purchasing a counselorship in the Parlement. There were only eighty positions for all of France and the purchaser, in contrast to most venal offices, had to be approved by the crown.[26] Because of these factors, purchase was usually reserved to those with some influence in the ministry. In seeking his post Roederer, lacking ministerial support, had two of the presidents of the Parlement of Metz, Chazelles and Goussand, write letters of recommendation for him. Chazelles praised Roederer for his attention to his duties and noted that his colleagues were very much impressed with "his zeal" in undertaking the work of the court.[27] Goussand wrote that Roederer was "one of the most distinguished members of the Parlement, one of the most assiduous to the functions of the magistracy. . . ."[28] In addition to being charged with reviewing the most important criminal cases in his chamber "he is almost always chosen as commissioner in the public affairs and is very often the author of the work decreed in the assembly of chambers."[29] These testimonials were appar-

---

[22] A.-M. Roederer, *La Famille Roederer*, p. 104.

[23] Ibid., p. 125.

[24] For a description of the duties and opportunities associated with the office of *maître des requêtes* see Vivian Gruder, *The Royal Provincial Intendants: A Governing Elite in Eighteenth-Century France* (Ithaca, 1968), chapters 2 and 3.

[25] Ibid., pp. 37–38.

[26] Ibid., pp. 63, 68–69.

[27] Chazelles to le Garde des Sceaux, 26 February 1783 in A.-M. Roederer, *La Famille Roederer*, p. 127.

[28] Goussand to Roederer, no date, Ibid., p. 128.

[29] Ibid.

ently insufficient support for Roederer's candidacy as he never received the sought-after post of maître des requêtes, and any ambitions he had for royal service ended with this failure. Certainly Roederer suffered some disappointment from this experience according to his son, Antoine-Marie, who later wrote that his father had often spoken of his dream of becoming controller general, one of the posts to which the maîtres des requêtes could aspire.[30]

The Roederer family had adhered to the conventional practices of hard work, good marriages, and the purchase of offices to advance the family fortunes to the point where the young Pierre-Louis could count himself among the elite of the province, a conseiller of the Parlement. By the same token, however, as a first generation parlementaire with no influence in the king's ministry the young man had little prospect for an important career in royal administration. Roederer's practice of politics was to be limited by these circumstances to the Trois-Evêchés until the advent of the Revolution made its practice on a wider scope possible. Initially politics for Roederer meant attendance to his duties in the Parlement, which had political as well as judicial obligations. The provincial parlements understood part of their duty to lie in the defense of the interests, rights, and privileges of their ressort. This defense was made in the time-honored tradition of presenting *remonstrances* to the king's government when decrees, deemed detrimental to the provinces under the parlement's care, were made. Upon his entrance into the Parlement of Metz Roederer had undertaken the writing of a number of remonstrances for the court.[31] In these documents the young conseiller naturally accepted the role of the court as the defender of the interests and privileges of the Trois-Evêchés. His family's fortune and his own advancement depended on the maintenance of the parlementary prerogatives.

In the defense of privilege, for instance, two of Roederer's remonstrances reflected the kind of relatively trivial issues which apparently made up much of the business of the court. One dealt with claims of the Parlement of Metz to jurisdiction over the territory of Clermontois, and the other concerned the establishment of a Chambre Syndicale at Nancy with jurisdiction over the printers and booksellers of Metz.[32] The first argued that the Clermontois should be added to the ressort of the Parlement while the second contended that the Chambre Syndicale at Nancy could not establish jurisdiction over Metz as the latter city had a claim to a Chambre Syndicale of its own which antedated that of Nancy. Of more importance were the mémoires he wrote objecting to the crown's attempt to collect the *timbre*, a stamp tax on documents, on receipts for the *octroi* of Metz or to raise the revenues of the *gabelle* through the use of a surtax.

---

[30] A.-M. Roederer, *La Famille Roederer*, p. 124.

[31] These remonstrances are found in AN 29AP99–100.

[32] AN 29AP99 "Mémoire concernant la jurisdiction du Parlement de Metz sur le Clermontois et terres adjacentes." AN 29AP99 "Mémoire concernant la Chambre Syndicale de Nancy." There is no date on either of these documents.

In these cases both the government and the Parlement relied on tradition to support their respective positions. The crown wanted to increase the revenues from already overworked taxes while the Parlement defended its opposition to these taxes on the basis of tradition and privilege.

The case concerning the collection of the timbre on the receipts of the octroi, the tax on all goods entering the city, arose in late 1782 when the General Farms insisted that the *receveurs* of the octroi in Metz issue receipts to all those paying the tax and then compute the timbre on those receipts.[33] The receveurs had traditionally issued receipts only to those requesting them and thus had not collected the timbre from all of the individuals entering Metz with merchandise. The General Farms had obviously invoked the new policy of "forced receipts" to increase its revenues. The policy was rejected by the local *juge des traites*, and his decision was upheld by the Parlement's Cour des Aides on 15 January 1783. However, the Royal Council overturned the Parlement's decision on 11 February. The issues involved were clearly the General Farms' and government's desire to collect the most revenue possible from existing taxes and the Parlement's concern that the traditional method of collecting the timbre not be altered in Metz.

Roederer's remonstrance against the decision of the Royal Council traced the legal history of the timbre back to Louis XIV and argued that it was not the intent of the legislation that receipts be given to all of those paying the octroi. Furthermore, he argued that "forced receipts" had not been in use in Metz before 1770 and, therefore, even if legal elsewhere, could not now be imposed upon the city. He argued further that the Council, "considered as the *corps d'administration*," could not merely decree this new interpretation of the law.[34] When a law was registered, the interpretation of the law must be that presented to the parlements at the time of registration. If this interpretation could be altered by a simple *arrêt du Conseil*, then the concept of registration "would be illusory."[35] Only by presenting new interpretations before the court for registration was a change in the law possible. If such a procedure were followed, then "the principles of national public law are protected, [and] the laws are uniform in the Council and in the sovereign courts."[36]

In the matter of the surtax on the gabelle, Roederer's remonstrance

---

[33] AN 29AP99 "Mémoire concernant la perception du droit de quittance forcée."

[34] Ibid.

[35] Ibid.

[36] Ibid. The remonstrance was eventually found unacceptable by the king, and this message was relayed to the Parlement by the keeper of the seals on 26 September 1783. AN 29AP101 Garde des Sceaux to M. le President du Parlement. Another example of Roederer's concern that the Parlement's independence from royal interference not be diminished is to be found in his "Notice pour un mémoire sur les gouverneurs et lieutenant généraux des provinces et autres etc." Here and in a letter on the subject Roederer complained bitterly of the right of the governors of the provinces to sit in the parlements during the registration of laws. He claimed that they were "spies" on the "supreme officers of the justice of the prince" who interfered with the work of the court by their presence. AN 29AP100 "Notice pour un mémoire . . . ;" AN 29AP100 Roederer to [?], no date.

struck a note of provincial privilege even more clearly than in his mémoire on the timbre.[37] Basically he called for a repeal of the surtax of two *sous pour livre* put into effect in August 1782 as well as the retroactive repeal of all surtaxes on salt since 1760. The demand for repeal was based on the claim that Metz had become a part of France voluntarily and that a contract existed between the king and the city which "recognized clearly that the king acquired only a conventional or conditional sovereignty" over the province and which left to the people "the conservation of their freedoms."[38] This contract allowed the inhabitants of the city to "give freely" what they pleased to the king's coffers. The remonstrance also complained "of the abuse and perhaps the fraud" associated with the collection of the gabelle and demanded "the reform of the vicious and iniquitous perception [of the tax]."[39]

Roederer sent a copy of his mémoire to the Lieutenant-General of Metz, the comte de Caraman, in order to enlist his support for the reduction of the surtax and the reform in the manner of its collection.[40] Caraman expressed his concern for the rights of the Trois Evêchés in a letter acknowledging the receipt of Roederer's remonstrance: "It is unfortunate, monsieur, that the first attacks have been made on the immunity from taxes (*droits*) of the Province of the Bishoprics without the strongest and the most authentic resistance."[41] The comte promised to request a meeting with the controller general concerning the collection of the gabelle in the Trois Evêchés. A second letter from Caraman revealed that he had been negotiating with the General Farms which claimed that it was as much opposed to the surtax as the Parlement since the consumption of salt always fell when there was a rise in price.[42] However, Caraman apparently was unable to convince the government to reduce the surtax despite the objections of the Parlement and the General Farms.

A more promising tactic seemed to lie in a reform of the method of collecting the tax. Roederer had discovered that the law establishing the gabelle in the Trois Evêchés had called for all quantities of salt to be based on the measurements of Lorraine.[43] The basic measurement in this system was the "pint of Lorraine," the equivalent of a pound and one-half in weight. The unit of measure in most salt shops in Metz, however, was based on the "pint of Metz" which contained nearly a third less volume. Roederer's conclusion was that if the proper and legal measure were used the price of salt would drop by almost a third and thus offer some relief to those hard pressed by the existing high price. Caraman had indicated to Roederer that the General Farmers would be willing to accept the mea-

---

[37] AN 29AP100 "Projet de mémoire à l'occassion de l'édit d'août 1782 portant augmentation de deux sols pour livre."
[38] Ibid.
[39] Ibid.
[40] AN 29AP100 Roederer to Caraman, no date.
[41] AN 29AP100 Caraman to Roederer, 14 June 1782.
[42] AN 29AP100 Caraman to Roederer, 29 July 1782.
[43] AN 29AP100 "Mémoire pour servir de réponse au projet de M. Lavoisier."

surement of the "pint of Lorraine." However, the influential General Farmer Antoine Lavoisier had written a mémoire proposing that all salt be sold by weight in pounds which were assumed to be equal to the measure of the pint.[44] Of course this proposal would have destroyed the reform Roederer and the Parlement sought. In order to combat it, Roederer persuaded Caraman to join him in writing a counterattack on the Lavoisier plan by proving the justice and legality of the use of the pint of Lorraine as the standard for the province.[45]

Besides his defense of the legal and historical privileges of the Trois-Evêchés, Roederer became involved in the protection of the local economic interests from what was considered unnecessary interference by the royal government. In these cases Roederer's remonstrances were based more on economic than legal arguments. One such case concerned the government's attempt to end the abuses associated with the right of *transit*, the exemption from customs duties in the commerce of the Levant, the French colonies, and French Flanders. The Council believed that this right was being used as a method of escaping certain duties by those not engaged in transit but rather in ordinary foreign trade.[46] It hoped that by creating a government-sponsored monopoly, a *régie des messageries*, which would transport all goods due the right of transit, such fraud could be ended. The régie would establish warehouses at convenient places and charge fixed rates for transporting goods. Merchants and *négociants* transporting goods by means other than the régie would pay the full duties on that merchandise.

The decree was not popular in the Trois-Evêchés where the Parlement was besieged with the "unanimous complaints" of the *commerçants* of the province.[47] The remonstrance that Roederer drew up alleged that the decree would ruin the commerce of *entrepôt*, based upon the freedom from duties for goods warehoused temporarily in the province. Foreign shippers would hesitate to transport their goods with the régie because they could never depend on rapid delivery, whereas the private carriers would deliver the goods in a specified period of time or forfeit one-third to one-half of their fee. Furthermore the rates set for the régie were generally too high, thereby discouraging shippers from transporting their goods with them. The prices of the private carriers, however, were based only on "the subsistence of simple and frugal men who are employed there."[48] With these inconveniences of the decree the normal commerce of transit might be rerouted to avoid entering France, including the Trois-Evêchés which was on the trade routes to and from Germany. The decree would not even

---

[44] Ibid.

[45] AN 29AP100 Roederer to [?], 19 October 1782. In this letter Roederer said he and Caraman had written the mémoire opposing Lavoisier's project, but the mémoire conformed to Roederer's style of writing, indicating that Caraman did little more than add his name to the venture.

[46] AN 29AP99 "Arrest du Conseil d'Etat du roi," 9 August 1781.

[47] AN 29AP99 "Mémoire concernant l'arrêt du Conseil du mois d'août 1781. . . ."

[48] Ibid.

fulfill its stated intentions as there was no reason to think that a régie not controlled by the General Farms, as this one was not, would be any less likely to commit fraud than individual shippers. Finally Roederer objected to the law because it gave jurisdiction of disputes to a special tribunal thereby abridging the traditional rights of the Parlement to deal with such matters. Despite this defense of the legal privileges of the Parlement, the remonstrance was based almost entirely on the economic consequences the decree would have on the province.[49]

Similarly Roederer used an economic argument to oppose the royal regulations imposed on the cloth industry.[50] The government had issued a list of regulations to which the manufacturers of cloth had to adhere if they wanted their fabric to carry the mark of *draperie royale*. After the issuance of the regulations, the Parlement received complaints from at least one manufacturer, Bechet de Lehautcour of Sedan, who claimed that the regulations would deprive the manufacturers of "the fruit of their labor."[51] Despite the fact that his cloth would not meet the new regulations, Bechet claimed that "my fabric nevertheless will have the quality required to please the consumer," who "is a grand judge" of the value of the product.[52] He concluded that "men are motivated by self-interest, that of the manufacturer being necessarily attached to the perfection of his fabric; [and] that left to his own devices (*qu'on le laisse faire*), he will look for and find the means of making the best possible of each type [of cloth] for a particular price."[53] Roederer's remonstrance followed Bechet's argument very closely. He wrote that the manufactures of Sedan were among "the most highly regarded of Europe" and the only product from which the British textile industry feared competition.[54] This reputation had been built upon the confidence of the consumer, but the regulations, which would unfairly prejudice the consumer against these products, would only result in harming a prosperous and respected industry. The remonstrance concluded then that the manufacturers of Sedan ought to have "absolute freedom regarding [the production] of its textiles."[55]

In this period of the early 1780s Roederer read some papers at the Royal Society of Metz on the same topics, especially taxation and economics, with which he had concerned himself in his remonstrances. As one would expect, his basic assumptions remained the same, but these papers, not being written in response to legal questions, allowed the author to explore topics in which he was personally interested and demonstrated his concern

---

[49] In this case the Conseil d'Etat did revoke its original decree. AN 29AP99 Joly de Fleury to procureur général du Parlement de Metz. AN 29AP99 Arrêt du Conseil d'Etat du roi, 14 September 1782.

[50] AN 29AP99 "Projet de mémoire sur le reglement du 1er août 1780 concernant la fabrique de Sedan."

[51] AN 29AP99 Bechet de Lehautcour to Roederer [?], 16 October 1780.

[52] Ibid.

[53] Ibid.

[54] AN 29AP99 "Projet de mémoire sur le reglement du 1er août 1780 concernant la fabrique de Sedan."

[55] Ibid.

for financial and economic reform. One of these essays, *Idées sur un traité de finance*, read before the Society in August 1782, concerned the weighty problem of tax reform. In it he complained that no satisfactory studies had been written on taxation either by the *agents du fisc* or by the economists. The former were concerned only with the compilation of laws and decrees concerning the collection of revenues. Roederer observed that while "there are a hundred volumes of this type, printed in favor of the public finance, there are none of them in favor of the people."[56] For their part the economists were too concerned with "abstract ideas" for which they did not provide workable solutions. Furthermore, "they have supposed that it was possible to undermine the entire edifice of our public finance and simultaneously reestablish it anew."[57] Roederer preferred the middle course: maintain most of the system of public finance, but bring change through "partial and successive" reforms.

Before reforms in the system of taxation could be made, Roederer insisted that an inventory of the true wealth of France, landed and non-landed, had to be made. Once this inventory was completed, one would have to determine if all sources of wealth were open to taxation. In his view such could not be the case, especially when provincial privilege might be threatened: "Among the privileges of the provinces are the odious and the unjust but also the sacred; many are tied to the interests of the nation even by abstract but real conventions, by distant but important affinities."[58] Likewise he had no sympathy with administrators who demanded "absolute and mathematical uniformity" in the assessment of taxation. While recognizing that "the welfare of the greatest number ought to be the supreme law," he believed that the destruction of privilege should be carried out only if absolutely necessary for the good of the majority. What was called for first was a determination of "the needs of commerce, the interests of agriculture and natural production of each province."[59] Once this information was known, it would be possible to make reforms which would not unduly upset the existing economic situation. In addition he advocated an accurate tabulation of all taxes collected by *généralité* which would indicate where reforms might best be made.[60] Finally he supported the reduction of the number of intermediary agents who were draining the revenues collected before they reached the treasury and the creation of a budget which would enumerate the sums that needed to be collected.[61]

In another paper read before the Society, Roederer supported the proposals designed to stimulate the local economy that the former intendant of Metz and later Controller General of Finance, Calonne, had made in 1772. Basically Calonne's suggestions called for some alteration in the

---

[56] P.-L. Roederer, *Idées sur un traité de finance*, in OR, 7: 430.
[57] Ibid.
[58] Ibid., p. 432.
[59] Ibid., p. 433.
[60] Ibid., pp. 435–36.
[61] Ibid., p. 433.

structure of customs duties affecting Metz. French commerce had long suffered from the existence of innumerable internal customs barriers, but in addition to this inconvenience the Trois-Evêchés had other impediments placed upon its trade.[62] Due to the location of the province in the area known as the *provinces traitées à l'instar de l'étranger effectif* or simply the foreign provinces, goods sent from the Trois-Evêchés into the area of the *cinq grosses fermes* had to cross the national tariff boundary set up to restrict the entrance of foreign products into France proper. Of course, this situation worked to the benefit of those engaged in commerce with Germany, which was unrestricted. The commerce of the Trois-Evêchés was also burdened with numerous duties since its territory was scattered within Lorraine proper, and duties had to be paid upon crossing provincial boundaries.[63] Furthermore, Lorraine was permitted to import certain items from the cinq grosses fermes duty-free while the Trois-Evêchés were not.

Calonne had suggested some alterations in this structure of duties in an effort to improve the commercial situation in Metz, and Roederer backed these proposals in his paper. Among the recommendations were those calling for all of the foreign provinces (the Trois-Evêchés, Lorraine, and Alsace) to be considered as one in their commercial relations with the cinq grosses fermes, for the *péages* on the Moselle to be abandoned, for new, less onerous duties for entrance of goods into the cities to be drawn up, and for a tariff to be established with Germany on textiles and leather goods.[64] Most of these changes would have met with little opposition in Metz except for the proposed tariff with Germany which would have weakened the privilege of free trade then in existence. Roederer went to some lengths to defend this last proposal by arguing that French fabrics, known to be of higher quality than those of Germany, would be available to consumers while the languishing textile manufacturers of Metz, particularly flannels, would find new markets in the interior of France.[65] The German market for woolen cloth would still be open to Metz as a law of 1743 had ended duties on this cloth shipped to Germany. The goods that demanded a foreign market (wood, charcoal, wine, crockery, and glass) would still have the same advantages of free trade with Germany since the tariff would not affect those items.

Through 1783 Roederer's political activities had conformed to the traditions of his family and province. He made good use of his family's connections with the Parlement, not only to establish a career in the court,

---

[62] The complexity of the French system of customs duties in the eighteenth-century is clearly described by J. F. Bosher, *The Single Duty Project: A Study of the Movement for a French Customs Union in the Eighteenth Century* (London, 1964), pp. 1–24.

[63] P.-L. Roederer, *Avis aux messins*, in OR, 7: 591. For Calonne's original project see Robert Lacour-Gayet, *Calonne: financier, reformateur, contre-revolutionnaire, 1734–1802* (Paris, 1963), pp. 36–37.

[64] Roederer, *Avis*, in OR, 7: 592. Calonne also suggested opening canals from the Moselle to the Meuse and the Meuse to the Seine, establishing a bourse, instituting one or two fairs in Metz, and prohibiting peddling.

[65] Ibid., p. 593.

but to improve his own social position by becoming a conseiller. Furthermore he emerged as one of the outstanding members of the court by writing numerous remonstrances defending provincial privileges and interests. Roederer's defense of privilege within and outside the Parlement was a natural by-product of his social position in Metz and pervaded all of his writing in this early period. Not only was this attitude evident in his remonstrances, where one would naturally expect to find it, but it was just as pervasive in his essays read before the Royal Society. He was interested in the reform of taxation but was dubious of any radical revisions or attacks on essential privilege. In the matter of improving the economy through tariff reform, he supported only the partial changes that would bring positive economic advantages to the Trois-Evêchés. He could not support any general reform of the tariffs which might include provisions not to the liking of the province.

His views on economic development, likewise, very closely followed the interest of the province. The two economic remonstrances that he wrote on cloth manufacturing and the right of transit had both been initiated by the protests of local commercial groups. In the case of cloth manufacturing, Roederer's free trade ideas were inspired by Bechet Lehautcour, the Sedan cloth manufacturer who had corresponded with Roederer before the remonstrance was written. His support for a mild reform in the customs duties repeated Calonne's earlier proposals and were no less provincial in orientation.

In sum Roederer's early political career was very much a product of his environment and social position. While intelligently argued and thoughtfully written, Roederer's ideas conformed closely to those of the political and economic elite of the province as was perhaps befitting a young man bent on making a career for himself. While interested in reform in a general way, his concern with provincial privilege, local interests, and his own standing among the provincial elite might have precluded any allegiance to the Revolution. After 1783, however, Roederer's political assumptions underwent a transformation which altered his outlook on provincial privilege and financial and economic reform.

II. INDUSTRIAL CAPITALISM AND REVOLUTION

In 1784 Roederer was sent to Paris to plead the case of the Saint-Quirin glassworks in a legal dispute with the Royal Plate-Glass Company of Saint-Gobain, an assignment which besides developing his great interest in the glass industry, broadened his horizons considerably. From this time Roederer ceased many of his activities in the Parlement, including the writing of remonstrances, and devoted more attention to the concerns of Saint-Quirin. In the Parlement of Metz he had been primarily concerned with the preservation of the privileges of the Trois-Evêchés. The glass industry, however, had an international market for its products which required Roederer to expand his thinking. This brought him into conflict with the established interests in the Trois-Evêchés which were anxious to preserve the old provincial privileges; and in defending his attack on privilege, Roederer unconsciously prepared the foundation for his advocacy of democracy as the only means of countering the privileged elite within the Third Estate.

Roederer's industrial interests were highly unusual. First, few eighteenth-century Frenchmen, noble or bourgeois, invested in manufacturing enterprises, preferring instead to place their funds in noncapitalistic ventures such as land, offices, buildings, and *rentes*.[1] Roederer, however, now developed an interest in industrial capitalism due, at least in part, to the fact that his brother-in-law, Louis Mena, was one of the owners of the Saint-Quirin glassworks while his wife was the daughter of another.[2] Second, Saint-Quirin was hardly a common sort of enterprise. Located in the Forest of Saint-Quirin on the river Sarre Rouge just south of Abreschviller in the Trois-Evêchés, the Saint-Quirin glassworks along with those of Monthermé found just north of Charleville-Mezières in the Ardennes comprised the factories of Pierre Mena and Company.[3] In contrast to the primitive manufacturing establishments which predominated in eighteenth-century France, Saint-Quirin had all the attributes of a nineteenth-century factory: numerous employees, company houses, large buildings, power-driven machinery, and substantial sales and profits.[4] In 1788 the

---

[1] George Taylor, "Noncapitalist Wealth and the Origins of the French Revolution," *American Historical Review*, 82 (1967): 486–87.

[2] A.-M. Roederer, *La Famille Roederer* (Paris, 1849), pp. 99–100, 136–37.

[3] A map of the location of Saint-Quirin can be found in AN 29AP92 "Copie de la requête des Srs. P. Mena et Cie. à M. l'Intendant d'Alsace."

[4] For the nature of eighteenth-century capitalism see George Taylor, "Types of Capitalism in Eighteenth-Century France," *English Historical Review*, 79 (1964): 478–97. For a description of Saint-Quirin's operations see Warren G. Scoville, *Capitalism and French Glassmaking, 1640–1789* (Berkeley, 1950), pp. 40–43, 126, 147, and A.-M. Roederer, *La Famille Roederer*, pp. 136–37.

enterprise had between 600 and 700 employees, descendants of the Germans and Bohemians who had originally immigrated to the area because of their glass-making skills, and provided 90 houses for some of the workers.[5] The plant consisted of two large buildings which produced tumblers, goblets, windowpanes, sheet and plate-glass, and mirrors. Saint-Quirin was the only glassworks in France known to have used the water-powered polishing machines "de Wirtemberg," which had cost 1,000,000 livres to install.[6] The factory still used the blowing instead of the more sophisticated casting process used at Saint-Gobain in producing plate-glass, but this was due to the royal monopoly the latter had on the casting process. Between 1781 and 1785 the company had average annual sales of almost 572,000 livres and annual profits of almost 167,000 livres.[7]

Because of his family connection with Saint-Quirin it can be assumed that Roederer had developed quite early an interest in the enterprise, but only when the dispute with Saint-Gobain arose did he become seriously concerned with it. The Royal Plate-Glass Company of Saint-Gobain, the most important glass factory in France, had obtained a monopoly, renewed for thirty years in 1757, on the "casting" of plate-glass for use in the manufacture of mirrors.[8] Saint-Quirin, which had a profitable business in windowpanes reputed to be the most beautiful in France, had attempted to subvert the monopoly as early as 1769 by manufacturing its plate-glass through the more expensive "blowing" process.[9] Saint-Gobain brought complaints to the royal government, and in response the Mena Company sent Roederer to Paris in 1784 to defend its interests.[10]

From the beginning the issues were clouded by the parties which stood to lose or gain from the outcome of the dispute. The royal government had financial interests in both Saint-Gobain and Saint-Quirin so that it would not wish to see the business of either damaged.[11] Marshal Beauvau and the Chapter of Saint-Louis of Metz, whose abbess was the comtesse de Choiseul, both owned large tracts of forest land from which Saint-Quirin purchased wood to fire its furnaces, and neither was eager to see a decline in the volume of wood purchased.[12] Furthermore, the provincial interests in Metz did not care to see the profitability of Saint-Quirin disturbed; therefore, the Bishop of Metz, Laval-Montmorency, and the comte de Caraman, the Lieutenant General, both lent their support to Roederer's effort.

Roederer's principal problem after arriving at the capital was gaining an interview with the Controller General Calonne who would decide the

---

[5] AN 29AP92 "Mémoire pour les citoyens Mena et Compagnie contra le citoyen Combe."

[6] The sum of 1,000,000 livres was mentioned by Roederer to Calonne during the discussion regarding Saint-Gobain. P.-L. Roederer, Journal of 1784–85, in OR, 7: 622.

[7] AN 29AP92 Untitled memorandum on the financial condition of Saint-Quirin prepared by Roederer prior to his purchasing a share of the company.

[8] Scoville, Capitalism, pp. 9, 28–32.

[9] Ibid., pp. 9, 40, 46 n. 19; A.-M. Roederer, La Famille Roederer, p. 135.

[10] A.-M. Roederer, La Famille Roederer, pp. 136–37.

[11] The royal interest in Saint-Quirin was about one-third. Scoville, Capitalism, p. 47.

[12] A.-M. Roederer, La Famille Roederer, p. 137.

fate of Saint-Quirin. In this matter Roederer tried to make use of Caraman's influence at court.[13] Despite Caraman's efforts in early May to obtain an interview for him with Calonne, Roederer did not actually meet with the controller general until 3 July.[14] This delay caused Roederer to complain to Caraman that the government needed to be more attentive to the needs of *"grande manufacture."*[15]

When Calonne finally received Roederer, the controller general, who had earlier in his career served as intendant of Metz, seemed to be sympathetic to Roederer's case in large measure because of the high esteem in which he held the young man's father.[16] Roederer presented Calonne with Saint-Quirin's argument that it was not violating the monopoly of Saint-Gobain since a different process was used to manufacture its glass. Furthermore, he argued that an unfavorable ruling would put the 300 men who polished the glass out of work, not to mention the loss of the 1,000,000 livres investment the company had made for its polishing equipment.[17] Calonne made no immediate decision but promised to look into the matter immediately.

Further delays followed this interview, but finally in August the whole matter was turned over to the Committee of Commerce.[18] Here there was a divided opinion with one of the intendants of commerce, Montaran, favoring the argument of Saint-Gobain. Another intendant of commerce, Blondel, suggested a possible compromise which would allow Saint-Quirin to sell its polished glass to France but not allow it to introduce glass that had been silvered for mirrors. Roederer insisted, however, that Saint-Quirin had a legal right to manufacture mirrors and would not retreat from this position. Calonne finally sided with Roederer and assured him that he would speak to the entrepreneurs at Saint-Gobain to secure their agreement with this decision. The affair continued to drag on until January 1785 when it was finally settled in Saint-Quirin's favor.[19]

Despite the frustration which had accompanied his mission, Paris had proven to be an exciting place, and Roederer had taken some interest in the fads of the day: the balloon flights of Pilâtre de Rozier (a native of Metz), the discovery of the "monster" of Peru, and the work of Mesmer.[20] More important, Roederer was buoyed by his success and excited by his interaction with officials at the highest levels of government. There can be little wonder, then, that Roederer found his interests shifting from the strictly provincial concerns of the Parlement of Metz. In 1786 when Pierre

---

[13] Ibid., pp. 139–40.
[14] Roederer, Journal of 1784–85, in OR, 7: 619.
[15] Roederer to Caraman, 9 June 1784, in OR, 7: 624–25.
[16] Roederer, Journal of 1784–85, in OR, 7: 621.
[17] Ibid., p. 622.
[18] Ibid., p. 623.
[19] Ibid., pp. 623–24.
[20] Caraman to Roederer, 8 September 1784; Roederer to a journalist; Roederer to Caraman December 1784, in OR, 7: 627–28, 632–33. For a description of these fads see Robert Darnton, *Mesmerism and the End of the Enlightenment in France* (Cambridge, 1968), pp. 3–45.

Mena died, Roederer, who was now held in high regard by the other owners, was given the opportunity of purchasing one-quarter share in Saint-Quirin and Monthermé for a price of nearly 500,000 livres.[21] Borrowing 50,000 livres from a friend, Victor Colchen, for the initial payment, Roederer quickly accepted this offer. His father-in-law A.-M. Guaita, who was one of the other owners, believed that the firm's management should remain in the hands of "interested" parties and was eager for Roederer to share some of the management duties. Roederer, however, was reluctant to sever completely his connections with the Parlement, so he arranged to give one-quarter of his share to Chamot of Frankfurt in exchange for the latter's undertaking Roederer's management duties.

Once the dispute with Saint-Gobain was resolved, the most pressing issue for Saint-Quirin was the tariff situation in the Foreign Provinces which made shipping their merchandise into or through the cinq-grosses-fermes so expensive. Saint-Quirin, which relied heavily on the luxury trade, sent most of its products to Paris with some then going through Rouen and on to London.[22] A tariff reform which would provide Saint-Quirin with free trade within France would be preferable to the existing situation which only allowed the company free trade with Germany. In the early 1780s Roederer had favored the limited tariff reform suggested by Calonne in 1772, but this plan had explicitly excluded glass from the items to be allowed into France duty free. With his new-found interest in the glass industry, however, Roederer was now eager for a general tariff reform which would create a truly national tariff corresponding to the true boundaries of the realm and the simultaneous abolition of all internal customs barriers.

Plans for such tariff reform had been circulating within the government since 1778 and were presented to the Assembly of Notables when it convened in 1787.[23] Marshal Beauvau, whom Roederer had first impressed during his Parisian mission of 1784, knew of his interest in the reform and urged him to prepare his ideas on the matter in time for Beauvau to present them to the Notables.[24] In response to this plea as well as in an effort to build public support for the plan in the foreign provinces where it was likely to meet its stiffest opposition due to the issue of free trade with Germany, Roederer wrote *Observations sur les interêts des Trois-Evêchés et de la Lorraine relativement au reculement des barrières des traites*. The pamphlet, enumerating the advantages that a single, national tariff would have for the foreign provinces, argued that the numerous duties

---

[21] A.-M. Roederer, *La Famille Roederer*, pp. 178–80.

[22] AN 29AP92 "Mémoire pour les citoyens Mena et Compagnie contre le citoyen Combe;" AN 29AP92 "Renseignement sur les caisses de glaces expediées à Rouen." Naturally the London market was much smaller than that of Paris.

[23] J. F. Bosher, *The Single Duty Project: A Study of the Movement for a French Customs Union in the Eighteenth Century* (London, 1964), pp. 105–121.

[24] AN 29AP10 Beauvau to Roederer, 19 January 1787. Beauvau's role in the Saint-Gobain affair is not known, but he was obviously very interested in it as Roederer made a special point of discussing its conclusion with him. Roederer, Journal of 1784–85, in OR, 7: 634.

levied on goods entering France from the foreign provinces were a great burden on the manufacturers.[25] Furthermore, not being included within the national tariff boundary meant that they were denied the protection from foreign competition enjoyed by the rest of France. According to Roederer the royal plan would benefit the manufacturers by encouraging increased circulation of goods within France, by restricting the exportation of raw materials, and by reducing the importation of foreign merchandise. For the foreign provinces in particular he predicted the opening of a "vast market" in the rest of France.[26]

A national tariff, by fostering industry and thereby increasing the size of the local population which would be employed in these enterprises, would be beneficial to agriculture.[27] Cultivators would be able to sell their agricultural produce locally instead of having to bear the expense of shipping it out of the province as they were currently doing. This analysis led Roederer to the conclusion that "the interest of the landowner is then manifestly that which favors the manufacturer."

The growth of manufacturing due to the reform would also end the employment crisis in the provinces which was characterized by "many more workers than work."[28] The low level of wages paid workers was due primarily to the "languor of the factories" the result of which was that "idleness and even mendicity are preferred to employment in Lorraine." Roederer was firmly convinced that "the existence of flourishing manufactures would not only rouse *le bas peuple* of the two provinces from their torpor but also would soon multiply the number of workers there."[29] In short the economic prosperity of the foreign provinces depended on developing thriving industries which could only exist with the creation of a single, national tariff.

Modern practice seems to confirm Roederer's argument that a national tariff union would benefit all elements of the economy, but the truth of his contentions was not universally accepted in the foreign provinces. In a society where privileges were highly prized, there were interest groups which viewed the creation of a national tariff only as a threat to the well-established, provincial privilege of free trade with Germany. The manufacturers of the provinces certainly welcomed Roederer's pamphlet. One letter that he received after the publication of his *Observations* made it clear that some manufacturers believed "the liberty of interior commerce is not only necessary in order to augment our activity, it is also required for our continued existence."[30] However, in the Assembly of Notables the First President of the Parlement of Metz, L.-C.-F. Hocquart, insisted that the foreign provinces "lose all and gain nothing" from a national tariff

---

[25] P.-L. Roederer, *Observations sur les intérêts des Trois-Evêchés et de la Lorraine, relativement au reculement des barrières des traites,* in OR, 7: 438–40.

[26] Ibid., p. 440.

[27] Ibid., p. 437.

[28] Ibid., p. 441.

[29] Ibid., p. 442.

[30] *Entrepreneurs* to Roederer, 19 July 1787, OR, 7: 446.

since the destruction of internal trade barriers was of only minor interest.[31] According to Hocquart the major concern was the retention of free trade with foreign countries. Hocquart's position corresponded to that of the négociants (wholesale merchants) of the foreign provinces who had built up their business on the basis of free trade with Germany. The manufacturers who had written to Roederer believed the opposition to the reform came entirely from them. In one letter they wrote that the mémoires opposing reform had in fact been "disavowed by the most numerous and important part of the inhabitants [of the provinces], namely the cultivators and manufacturers. . . ."[32] They went on to say that the opposition to reform "was only the work of the négociants of some towns."[33] Roederer's *Observations* had in fact been written partially as a response to a pamphlet of the négociants of Nancy opposing the reform.[34]

Most of the six bureaux of the Assembly of Notables accepted Calonne's tariff proposals, but reservations were expressed by the bureau headed by the king's brother, the comte d'Artois.[35] Among other suggestions, the bureau recommended that the newly-formed provincial assemblies of the Trois-Evêchés, Lorraine, and Alsace be consulted before the new tariff was put into effect in those provinces. The assemblies were to be organized on the principle of double representation for the Third Estate and vote by head, but because the members were chosen by the king or co-opted by those so chosen, the privileged interests dominated the meetings.[36] When the assemblies of the Trois-Evêchés and Lorraine met, a conflict developed in each between the supporters of the manufacturing and commercial interests over the issue of tariff reform.[37] A general fear of losing privileges in what might prove to be an unsuccessful commercial experiment seems to have been a consideration which led the assemblies to vote their opposition to reform.

After the final deliberations, the decisions of each provincial assembly were to be carried out by a permanently functioning body, the intermediary commission.[38] Perhaps because of the divided opinion evident in the provincial assembly, the Intermediary Commission of Lorraine had called for "the opinions of all classes of citizens before forming its own" on the tariff question.[39] Roederer responded to this call with yet another

---

[31] Quoted in Jean Egret, *La Pré-Révolution française, 1787–1789* (Paris, 1962), p. 34.

[32] *Manufacturiers* to Roederer, 10 June 1787, in OR, 7: 443.

[33] Likewise, in a response to the *entrepreneurs* Roederer was very critical of the misrepresentations of the négociants regarding the proposed changes in the tariff. Roederer to the entrepreneurs, Ibid., p. 446.

[34] Roederer, *Observations*, in OR, 7: 437.

[35] Bosher, *The Single Duty Project*, pp. 121–123.

[36] Pierre Renouvin, *Les Assemblées provinciales de 1787: origines, développement, résultats* (Paris, 1921), pp. 155–60.

[37] Ibid., pp. 225–26.

[38] Ibid., p. 239.

[39] P.-L. Roederer, *Questions proposées par la Commission Intermediare de l'Assemblée provinciale de Lorraine, concernant le reculement des barrières et observations pour servir de réponse à ces questions*, in OR, 7: 448.

pamphlet on the tariff issue, *Questions proposées par la Commission Inter-mediare*. In this tract, besides reiterating the value to cultivators of being able to sell their produce locally to the employees of manufacturing enterprises, he developed the argument that capital could only be accumulated in the agricultural sector if a single, national tariff was established.[40] Most land was owned by absentee proprietors living in towns and cities, the richest of whom were to be found in Paris. The rentes of great proprietors, then, always found their way to Paris. How could these funds be returned to the provinces of origin when the proprietors basically used them to maintain a high standard of living instead of reinvesting them in the land? Roederer believed the answer lay in locating industry in agricultural areas. The products of industry would be bought by the *rentiers* in the cities with the funds spent on these products being returned to the provinces where they would be spent by the industrial workers on agricultural goods. Of course, with the existing tariff structure, the trade of Lorraine was directed toward Germany, and the industries, like glass, had a difficult time trading with French cities, especially Paris. Roederer argued that, if a single, national tariff was adopted, this situation would be corrected and the circulation of money between the capital and the provinces would be possible. Only then would agriculture be assured not only of sustaining itself but even of forming capital to provide for agricultural improvement or expansion from the increased sale of products to industrial workers. The manufacturers, themselves burdened by high rates on the raw materials they imported and the finished goods they exported, would obviously benefit from the creation of a national tariff.[41] Even the négociants, who opposed the destruction of the ancient privileges, would benefit from increased domestic trade with the elimination of internal customs barriers.[42] In short, the proposed tariff would increase the revenues of agriculture, manufacturing, and commerce thereby greatly stimulating the economy of the foreign provinces.[43] A failure to enact the reform would threaten the existence of the manufacturers and weaken the strength of agriculture.

In the end, despite Roederer's determined efforts, the privileges of the foreign provinces remained unreformed by the debilitated government of Louis XVI. The leadership of the Parlement of Metz represented by Hocquart, the representatives to the provincial assemblies, and the entrenched commercial interests of the provinces had all opposed drawing the tariff boundary back to the frontiers despite the general acceptance of the project

---

[40] Ibid., pp. 480–82.

[41] Ibid., p. 484.

[42] Ibid., p. 489.

[43] Roederer explained that a fully developed economy would mean expansion in agriculture, textiles, and commerce but that the *manufactures à feu* (industries requiring the use of furnaces) would only be able to maintain their present operations because of the restrictions on the building of new furnaces. This explanation was probably made to allay the apprehensions of those who might fear that a too vigorous glass or iron industry would result in the deforestation of the province. Ibid., p. 470.

in the rest of France.[44] Roederer had tried to undercut that opposition by suggesting that a unique tariff did not necessarily imply a uniform tariff. Instead each province on the frontier could have its duties adjusted according to its particular economic situation.[45] Yet when the provincial opposition continued, he did not hesitate to inform the provincial assembly of Metz that "the region could not have any privilege in opposition to the greatest good."[46] As Roederer had laid out his case, the greatest good could only result if manufacturing was aided by a general tariff reform.

By 1788 the tariff issue was dwarfed by the greater political struggle between the sovereign courts and the royal government. Calonne and his successor Lomenie de Brienne had been unable to obtain the support of the Assembly of Notables for their tax reform proposals, and Brienne had been forced to take the program directly to the parlements. Meeting strong opposition from this quarter as well, Louis XVI decided upon a reorganization of the courts and the creation of a supreme plenary court to register all royal edicts. A *lit de justice* was held on 8 May 1788 in order to register the decree with the Parlement of Paris. Protests from most parlements were immediately forthcoming, and Louis retaliated by exiling the members of the more insolent courts, including Metz, to various other parts of the realm.[47]

Roederer found himself in the curious position of having been a recent defender of part of Calonne's program and at the same time a member of an institution whose privileges were threatened by royal reform. Roederer was quickly caught up, nevertheless, in the spirit of the aristocratic revolt. He signed the protest from the Parlement of Metz and then somewhat defiantly refused to go into exile claiming that an error in the post had prevented his receiving a *lettre de cachet*.[48] His opposition to judicial reform in 1788 was far different, however, from that which he had expressed in 1771. At that time he was concerned about the maintenance of the privileges of the court upon which his own position was to rest so heavily. In 1788 he was much more interested in the political opportunities the dispute provided.

When Louis XVI finally called off his attack on the parlements and agreed to a convocation of the Estates General, Roederer and Marshal Beauvau, who had distinguished himself in the Notables, began corresponding about the composition of the representative assembly. As was the case over tariff reform, Beauvau was anxious for Roederer to formulate his ideas on the Estates General so that the Marshal could use his influence to achieve their acceptance. On 5 September Beauvau wrote that he had presented some of Roederer's preliminary ideas in high government circles

---

[44] Bosher, *The Single Duty Project*, pp. 129 ff.

[45] Roederer, *Questions*, in OR, 7: 496–97.

[46] P.-L. Roederer, *Réflexions sur la rapport fait à l'Assemblée provinciale de Metz, au sujet du reculement des barrières des traites au delà des provinces dites étrangères*, in OR, 7: 525.

[47] Egret, *La Pré-Révolution*, p. 261.

[48] A.-M. Roederer, *La Famille Roederer*, p. 189.

and was certain that they had made "the greatest impression" there.[49] In the same letter Beauvau informed Roederer that he thought the Assembly would be convened in January and urged him to come to Paris quickly "supplied with all the materials that you know how to assemble and choose so well in order to give the best form possible to that interesting assembly." On 5 October Beauvau asked Roederer to lose no time in sending him a plan for the Estates General that he could submit to the reconvened Assembly of Notables scheduled to meet in November.[50] Beauvau had received part of Roederer's materials after the convocation of the Notables but by that time had given up any hope of influencing that body to accept a progressive plan for organizing the Estates General.[51] Still hoping to make use of Roederer's ideas, Beauvau introduced him into the Society of Thirty which met for the first time in early November at the home of Adrien Duport.[52] Here Roederer made contact with others interested in political reform including Mirabeau, Lafayette, Talleyrand, Condorcet, and La Rochefoucauld. On 8 November 1788 Roederer published 500 copies of his first revolutionary pamphlet *De la Députation aux Etats Généraux*.

Roederer's pamphlet differed from the great majority of revolutionary works published during this period which had called for the doubling of the Third Estate and a vote by head instead of order. *De la Députation aux Etats Généraux* clearly demonstrated that his thinking had been strongly influenced by his frustrating experience with the tariff question. In the provincial assemblies of the foreign provinces, despite the doubled representation of the Third Estate and a vote by head, privilege still had managed to prevent reforms that would have benefited, in the view of the manufacturers, the entire population of the provinces. There was a definite feeling among the manufacturers, evident in the letters Roederer received and the texts of his pamphlets, that the opposition to reform was coming from a small minority of the Third Estate itself, the négociants, determined to thwart the will of the majority. To avoid a repetition of this experience in the Estates General, a much more complete and democratic reform of the organization of that body was needed than that called for by most of the reformers. Roederer's pamphlet offered a plan for such an organization.

The problems that Roederer envisioned were the creation of an Estates General that allowed inordinate power to the first two estates and the likelihood of a deputation from the Third Estate representing only the interests of a narrow group within that order. One possibility that seemed very real to him was the exclusion of all but landed property owners (by which he meant primarily those living off their rentes) from the assembly.

---

[49] AN 29AP10 Beauvau to Roederer, 5 September 1788.
[50] AN 29AP10 Beauvau to Roederer, 5 October 1788.
[51] AN 29AP10 Beauvau to Roederer, 10 November 1788.
[52] Egret, *La Pré-Révolution*, pp. 326–30.

Such an exclusion might be permissible in the provincial assemblies administering taxes on landed property but would be inappropriate for a national assembly.[53] Limiting representation to landed proprietors assumed that "the interest of liberty is always united to that of property" and that "the landed proprietor would hold no views contrary to those of any other class of citizen."[54] Roederer argued, however, that this assumption overlooked the importance of non-landed property and that "diverse types of property demanded different advantages, liberty in diverse persons, in diverse circumstances is composed of different qualities."[55] As an example of his point Roederer cited the indifference of landed proprietors toward "the weight of taxes" on commerce and manufacturing, especially "the [trade] barriers and péages" which the proprietors did not believe affected their well-being.[56]

Roederer even went so far as to contend that the "institution of landed property is not necessary to political societies: their essence is only *la propriété mobilière*."[57] Such was the case because "man does not live by the land but by the fruits of the land. . . ." Repeating the theme he had developed in his pamphlets on tariff reform, Roederer argued that the wealth the land might produce could only be fully realized if capital was invested in the land, and that capital was most often found in the hands of individuals with non-landed wealth. "I ask," he wrote, "if it is not evident that he who has invested his capital and his industry in the agricultural or manufacturing enterprises of a pays . . . has as many rights to the products of the land as the landed proprietor . . . ?" Since the answer was obviously in the affirmative, that the two have an equal stake in society must follow. The stability of states such as Geneva, Frankfort, Augsburg, and Holland, all of which had a minimum of landed wealth, indicated that landed property was not essential to the creation of a strong political system. Certainly *l'homme d'industrie* with the investment of time and money in his enterprise would have a more vital interest in the area of his habitation than would a proprietor living idly on his rentes who would easily be able to sell his land to another.

The Third Estate might also be unfairly represented if the ancient custom of allowing only townsmen the right to elect or be elected to the Estates General was continued. Considering their economic function, the towns were much less important than the countryside which produced all the agricultural and most of the manufactured goods. The towns by contrast consisted only of "landed proprietors living on their rentes, office holders . . . , artisans, merchants, and craftsmen" who depended on the products of the countryside for their existence.[58] Given the economic relationship between town and country, Roederer could see only injustice in an elec-

---

[53] P.-L. Roederer, *De la Députation aux Etats Généraux*, in OR, 7: 558.
[54] Ibid., pp. 544, 555.
[55] Ibid., p. 544.
[56] Ibid., p. 546.
[57] Ibid., pp. 555–56.
[58] Ibid., pp. 549–50, 558.

toral system which gave all political influence to the unproductive segment of society. Certainly the old practice of allowing the municipal officials to represent the Third only strengthened this inequity of influences. Such procedures "formed even in the Third Estate two orders, of which the one is elevated over the other as the two superior orders are elevated over the Third Estate. . . ."[59]

In Roederer's view, society was an amalgamation of sometimes conflicting interest groups. The general interest had to evolve from balancing all particular interests in the nation. The Estates General had as its most pressing duty the obligation "to reunite the interests, to clarify them and to root out abuses."[60] This end could only be achieved if the deputies resembled as closely as possible the national plurality. All citizens must be equally represented because "if each deputy does not represent the same number of citizens . . . the plurality of these deputies does not represent the plurality of citizens. . . ."[61] Unless the plurality exercised the legislative power, the nation would be characterized "by arbitrary power and oppression on the one hand, obedience and servitude on the other."

Having made his case for the representation of the plurality of the nation, Roederer had to deal with the question of the limits of citizenship. Since he understood politics to be a conflict between economic interest groups, it was difficult for him to deny political rights to any category of individuals without compromising his basic argument. As he stated his position, if the Estates General were to undertake the project of "remaking society on the principle of justice and the eternal order, it is necessary to call to this great work all those whose rights and needs ought to be taken into consideration. . . ."[62] He did share the typical eighteenth-century aversion to citizenship for women, domestic servants, and soldiers, due to their state of dependence on other individuals.[63] However, he concluded that the poor could not be denied the political opportunity to defend their own interests "for who does not know how the rich are indifferent to the surety of the poor."[64] Roederer tried to console the more affluent classes with the thought that the common people would probably vote for deputies of a "superior" class, but he stressed that it would be voter choice, since he opposed the American and English practice of different qualifications for electing and being elected to office.[65] He waved aside objections that the rich might purchase the votes of the poor by arguing that "on a possibility or even a presumption of abuse one is not able to deprive anyone of a legitimate right. . . ."[66] Nor did he see the ignorance of the

---

[59] Ibid.
[60] Ibid., p. 545.
[61] Ibid., p. 563.
[62] Ibid., p. 545.
[63] Ibid., pp. 553, 562.
[64] Ibid., p. 546.
[65] Ibid., pp. 549, 562.
[66] Ibid., pp. 548–49.

masses as a great problem since individuals would soon learn how to exercise their rights properly.

In his search for a scheme that would permit the most accurate representation of the plurality of the nation, Roederer could hardly condone the continuation of the concept of estates. Only an "assembly without distinction of power" would permit the true will of the national plurality to be determined, and from this it followed that the "division of the national assembly by orders is contrary to the rights and interests of the nation."[67] The Patriot program which merely called for doubling the Third Estate and vote by head would be little improvement over the traditional organization of the Estates General. Roederer ignored that plan and instead insisted that elections should be held for the assembly by dividing France into districts of about 6,000 voters who would choose electors without regard to estate.[68]

Roederer's democratic point of view had been fostered by the frustration that he, as spokesman for the manufacturers of the foreign provinces, had felt during the tariff controversy. The surest method of preventing control of the Estates General by the privileged orders and the powerful elements of the Third Estate was to organize the entire assembly on the principle of democratic suffrage and abolition of representation by order. In such an assembly the manufacturers would be only one interest among many, but such a prospect was infinitely more promising than any in which they might be totally excluded. By this time, however, Roederer was not solely interested in securing a voice for the manufacturers in the Estates. He was also eager that an organizational plan, fair and equitable to all, be established. In the *Députation* he made a particularly strong case for the political rights of the lowest economic strata of the nation. Because of his own frustrating experience in defending the interests of the manufacturers against the politically powerful négociants in the matter of the tariff, he had come to have a real understanding of the necessity of the poor having an active role in the selection of their representatives. Merely allowing their betters to choose their deputies could not provide them with a satisfactory means of defending their interests.

Roederer's plan did not influence the royal government's decisions regarding the organization of the Estates General. Louis XVI opted for convoking the assembly in the traditional manner with the sole exception of allowing the Third Estate doubled representation. The electoral situation in Metz, however, was complicated by the request of the Trois Ordres, in effect the municipal council, for an additional, direct deputy to represent the city.[69] The Trois Ordres argued that the city deserved such a deputy

---

[67] Ibid., pp. 569–70.

[68] Ibid., pp. 570–74.

[69] This request was made in November 1788. *Mémoire des Trois-Ordres de la ville de Metz et du pays messin pour établir leur droit à députer aux Etats Généraux, de la même manière que les pays d'Etat*, in René Paquet, *Bibliographie analytique de l'histoire de Metz pendant la Révolution* (Paris, 1926), 1: 3.

since Metz had once sent deputies to the Diet of the Holy Roman Empire. According to the royal decree of 24 January 1789, Paris was to be the only city to send deputies to the Estates General.[70] On 6 April, however, the king succumbed to the pressure from the Trois Ordres and issued a decree permitting Metz a direct deputy who would sit with the Third Estate.[71] The election of this deputy was to be conducted according to the proce-dures established for *bailliage* elections in the decrees of 24 January and 7 February 1789. The 24 January decree required towns which were the seats of their bailliage or which sent more than four deputies to the bail-liage assembly to allow the guilds to serve as primary assemblies.[72] Those who belonged to no guild were to form their own primary assembly. The 7 February decree stipulated that Metz was both to serve as the seat of the bailliage and to send more than four deputies to the bailliage as-sembly.[73] Presumably then Metz should have assembled its voters in pri-mary assemblies consisting of the city's guilds.

The municipality did not follow this procedure in establishing the pri-mary assemblies to elect the direct deputy.[74] Instead the officers of the municipality, arguing that time did not permit assembling the inhabitants by guilds, held the primary assemblies in the parishes and claimed that the keeper of the seals had authorized this change in procedure. The parish assemblies of 14 April were stormy affairs marred by the protests and walk-outs of those, mainly guild members and lawyers, alleging the illegality of the proceedings. The secondary assembly held at the Hôtel-de-Ville on 14 and 16 April was equally tumultuous with some deputies refusing to participate in its activities. Nevertheless the assembly did draw up a *cahier* and elected Pierre Maujean, the *Maître-echevin* of Metz, as its direct deputy to the Estates General.

Roederer was naturally interested in the electoral process in Metz. In the bailliage elections he had served on the commission of the nobility which had drawn up their cahier, but he was not elected to represent the local aristocracy at Versailles—perhaps because he had argued in the com-mission for vote by head instead of order.[75] After the bailliage elections Roederer turned his attention to the controversy surrounding the direct election of the deputy from Metz and published a pamphlet attacking Maujean's election.[76] Here he argued that the election was "neither legal, legitimate, nor honest" since the royal decrees had not been followed;

[70] Armand Brette, ed., *Recueil de documents relatifs à la convocation des Etats Généraux de 1789* (Paris, 1894), 1: 78.

[71] Ibid., pp. 227–28.

[72] Ibid., pp. 76 n. 3, 77–78.

[73] Ibid., pp. 222–23.

[74] P. Lesprand, "Election de député direct et cahier du tiers état de la ville de Metz en 1789," *Annuaire de la Société d'Histoire et d'Archéologie de Lorraine*, 15 (1903): 163, 167.

[75] The list of those who served on the commission which drew up the cahier of the nobility is found in Paquet, *Bibliographie*, 1: 19. Roederer described his activities on the commission in the pamphlet *Réponse de M. Roederer à MM. Maujean et Séchehaye*, a copy of which is in AN 29AP9.

[76] P.-L. Roederer, *Observations sur l'élection d'un prétendue député de la ville de Metz aux Etats Généraux*, in OR, 7: 606–16.

and he charged that the keeper of the seals, contrary to the assertion of the municipality, had never authorized the change in procedure. Furthermore, by assembling the voters by parish, where the well-to-do were likely to dominate the proceedings, the municipality had not permitted "each class of the Third Estate [to] participate equally in the right of naming the defender of their interests" or "to register at least some lines relative to its rights in the cahiers."[77] On the other hand, election by guilds, where artisans voted among equals, would insure participation by all classes in the political process.

This attack on the electoral proceedings in Metz was not the first political dispute between the Roederers and Maujean. In 1783 the elder Roederer and Maujean had been nominated for the post of maître-echevin with Maujean emerging as the victor.[78] Young Roederer and Maujean later had differed on the establishment in Metz of a Mont-de-Piété, a public lending institution designed to provide non-usurious loans.[79] Roederer had opposed this project in the Parlement because it would require a tax of 12 per cent on wages and had as its principal object "creating lucrative places" at the disposal of the municipality and multiplying "the creatures of the *messieurs* of the *echevinage*."[80] Maujean, as in the contest with Roederer's father, prevailed and had the satisfaction of seeing the establishment of the *Mont-de-Piété*.

After the publication of his pamphlet condemning the electoral procedures, one of Maujean's supporters, Jules Séchehaye, the alternate deputy to the Estates General and *procureur-syndic* of Metz, charged Roederer with trying to avenge these old political defeats by overturning the results of the elections.[81] According to Séchehaye, since Roederer had been unsuccessful in winning election by the nobility, he had instigated the disturbances in the primary assemblies, urged sending a delegation to the Estates General to seek nullification of Maujean's election, and even provided the delegates with 50 *louis* for expenses in hopes of procuring the seat for himself. If this were not malicious enough, Séchehaye said, Roederer also hoped that reversing the election results would bring more favorable legislation for the glass industry in which he had a considerable investment. Roederer publicly denied that he was responsible for the disturbances accompanying the election, that he had paid 50 louis to the delegates to Versailles, or that he had any personal interest in the outcome of the affair.[82]

---

[77] Ibid., p. 609.

[78] Jules Séchehaye, *Mémoire pour établir la validité de l'élection du député direct de la ville de Metz*, in Paquet, *Bibliographie*, 1: 1439. The elder Roederer's name had been placed in nomination without his knowledge. AN 29AP9 Roederer, *Réponse de M. Roederer*.

[79] Séchehaye, *Mémoire*, in Paquet, *Bibliographie*, 1: 1439; AN 29AP99 P.-L. Roederer, "Réflexions sur le projet d'un Mont-de-Piété à Metz."

[80] AN 29AP9 Roederer, *Réponse de M. Roederer*.

[81] Séchehaye, *Mémoire*, in Paquet, *Bibliographie*, 1: 1437–39. The municipal officers harassed Roederer not only in print but also through rude treatment in a domiciliary visit ostensibly conducted to uncover grain hoarding. A.-M. Roederer, *La Famille Roederer*, pp. 204–08.

[82] AN 29AP9 Roederer, *Réponse de M. Roederer*.

There can be little doubt, however, that Séchehaye was correct in believing Roederer to be the leader of the opposition to Maujean's election.
Roederer made both the initial suggestion and the practical arrangements
for the sending of the delegation to Versailles to seek the nullification of
Maujean's election.[83] When the National Assembly did indeed disqualify
Maujean on 11 July, a Patriotic Committee was organized in Metz to
replace the corrupt municipality.[84] The first sixteen members of the Committee were chosen by the guilds and the rest were added by co-option.
Roederer was chosen as the Committee's president.

On 16 August the Patriotic Committee wrote to Minister of War La
Tour du Pin, who had jurisdiction over the garrison city, asking that he
recognize the Committee as the municipal government.[85] The Committee
asserted that it was the true governing body of the city, the Trois Ordres,
and promised that if given authority it could keep order in Metz. Not
content to wait for the minister's reply, the Committee called for guild
and parish elections on 18 August for the purpose of electing a new
municipality.[86] The elections elicited little interest, however, and the fate
of the municipality was still undetermined. However, the marquis de
Bouillé, the commandant of the garrison at Metz, had enough confidence
in the Committee to instruct his troops to take an oath of loyalty to it as
if it were the legitimate municipal government.[87] Finally both the Committee and the old municipality sent delegates to La Tour du Pin who sent
orders on 23 September as to how the municipality was to be constituted.[88]
This directive in effect accepted the results of the municipal revolution
which had brought the Committee into practical control of Metz. The new
municipality was to be composed of 20 members each from the clergy and
nobility and 40 members from the Third Estate who were to be chosen
by the deputies selected in the irregular August guild and parish assemblies. Those guilds and parishes which had not met in August were instructed to do so now in order to choose their deputies. On 24 and 25
September the new municipality was organized with Roederer as its president. The city authorities then moved quickly to solidify their position
by arranging for a certain supply of grain and bread and by securing the
formal allegiance of Bouillé and his troops.[89]

---

[83] Roederer, Observations sur l'élection, in OR, 7: 616; Séchehaye, Mémoire, in Paquet, 1:
1439; AN 29AP9 Roederer, Réponse de M. Roederer. Roederer did not deny Séchehaye's
allegation that he persuaded those attending a meeting on 11 May 1789 to send a delegation
to Versailles and raise a voluntary subscription to defray its expenses.

[84] Lesprand, "Election," p. 167.

[85] Ibid., p. 174.

[86] Ibid., p. 175.

[87] F.-C. Amour, marquis de Bouillé, Mémoires, Berville et Barrière, eds. (Paris, 1823), 3rd
ed., p. 82; Lesprand, "Election," p. 175.

[88] Lesprand, "Election," pp. 177–80.

[89] AN 29AP99 "Extrait des registres des deliberations des representants de la commune,"
8 October 1789; Adresse du Comité municipal de Metz aux troupes en garnison dans cette ville
à l'époque de la révolution, 4 October 1789; Lesprand, "Election," pp. 180–83.

The next order of business was drawing up a new cahier for the city and electing a replacement for Maujean. Here the municipality basically adhered to the royal decrees and convoked the primary assemblies by guilds, but as a political expedient they prohibited the guilds subordinated to the municipality, such as the officers of the *Bureau des finances* and the *sergents royaux*, from voting by guild.[90] The new primary elections thus held in October resulted in the meeting of a secondary assembly much different in composition from that of April on 23 October at the Hôtel-de-Ville. The spring assembly had consisted of forty-nine delegates of which twelve were present or former members of the municipality while only nine could be classified as artisans.[91] The autumn assembly, by contrast, consisted of no members of the municipality and thirty-eight artisans out of a total of ninety-eight representatives.[92] The proportion of artisans had increased from a little over 18 percent to almost 39 percent. In effect Roederer's Committee had ended the political power of the municipal leaders and established the artisans as a major political force in the city. In addition the new elections resulted in a reversal of the city's stand on the national tariff. The April cahier from the city, like the bailliage cahiers of the nobility and Third Estate, had been vehemently opposed to the creation of a single national tariff.[93] The new cahier, drawn up under Roederer's influence, supported a national tariff and called for simplification of taxes "notably those which restrict commerce."[94] After drafting its cahier, the assembly named Roederer as Maujean's replacement in the National Assembly.

A direct connection is evident between Roederer's role as an entrepreneur, the development of his revolutionary political position, and his election as deputy from Metz. If he had simply remained a young conseiller in the Parlement and had not defended the manufacturers' interests on the tariff question, his political concerns would have been far different. Because of his experience in the tariff controversy, he became aware of the likelihood that a traditionally organized Estates General or even an assembly with a doubled Third and vote by head would be unrepresentative of many groups within that Estate.

This link between Roederer's economic interests and his political ideas makes him something of a curiosity within the traditions of recent revolutionary historiography. Given his successful entrance into the nobility, he hardly fits the picture presented by many historians of the bourgeois resentful of unobtainable noble status and privilege.[95] His heavy invest-

---

[90] Lesprand, "Election," p. 191.

[91] Ibid., p. 201.

[92] Ibid., p. 205.

[93] AP, 3: 764, 769–70; Lesprand, "Election," pp. 192–201.

[94] Lesprand, "Election," pp. 197, 202.

[95] See especially Elinor Barber, *The Bourgeoisie in Eighteenth Century France* (Princeton, 1955), p. 144; Norman Hampson, *A Social History of the French Revolution* (Toronto, 1963), pp. 14–15; and M. J. Sydenham, *The French Revolution* (New York, 1966), pp. 25–26.

ment in the glass industry also distinguishes him from the French industrial classes described by Alfred Cobban as politically inactive.[96] Finally his career fails to confirm the Marxist view of the Revolution as a struggle between the bourgeoisie and the nobility since Roederer believed the essential political contest to be among the economic and political interests within the Third Estate.[97]

Roederer's political view was in reality more closely akin to that of the French merchant class which had similar fears that it would not be fairly represented and had sought special representation for itself in the Estates General.[98] Like the merchants, Roederer developed his revolutionary political position in order to prevent the domination of the Third Estate by the powerful interests within it. However, unlike the merchants who sought additional political privileges for themselves, Roederer hoped to overthrow the traditional leaders of that Estate through the implementation of democratic elections. As events developed he was able to do just that in the municipal revolution in Metz. This is not to argue that Roederer was unconcerned with the issue of undue representation of the privileged orders, but the main thrust of his attack was clearly against the traditional leadership of the Third Estate. For Roederer, then, the initial stage of the Revolution was a struggle for political power within the Third Estate itself.

---

[96] Cobban's theory was first presented in *The Myth of the French Revolution* in 1954 which is now available in Alfred Cobban, *Aspects of the French Revolution* (New York, 1970), pp. 90–111. A fuller treatment of the same theme is found in *The Social Interpretation of the French Revolution* (London, 1964). Cobban and other historians were unaware of Roederer's investments in the glass industry and, therefore, were unable to imagine any connection between his financial interests and his political activity. Cobban could not have known of Roederer's investments when he analyzed the deputies of the Constituent Assembly in *The Myth of the French Revolution* since he had relied on Armand Brette's *Les Constituants: Liste des députés et des suppléants élus à l'Assemblée constituente de 1789* (Paris, 1897), p. 150. Brette had described Roederer simply and incompletely as a squire, councilor of the Parlement of Metz, and a member of the municipal committee of Metz. Likewise J. F. Bosher, while well aware of Roederer's political activity in behalf of tariff reform in 1787, was not conscious of his investment in the Saint-Quirin glassworks. See Bosher, *The Single Duty Project*, p. 136.

[97] For a recent example of the Marxist interpretation of the Revolution see Albert Soboul "L'Historiographie classique de la Révolution française: sur des controverses récentes," *Historical Reflections/Réflexions Historiques*, 1 (1974): 141–67.

[98] Paul Lucas, "How 'Bourgeois' Was the French Bourgeoisie in 1789? The Political Desires of the Community of Merchants," paper read at the American Historical Association Annual Meeting in Dallas, Texas, December 1977.

III. REVOLUTIONARY FINANCE: THE TAX COMMITTEE IN THE CONSTITUENT ASSEMBLY

As a deputy in the National Assembly Roederer's greatest contribution to revolutionary reform came from the work he did on the Tax Committee. Characterized by tax farming and private accountants capitalizing on the archaic structure of the Treasury in the search for personal profit, the financial system of the ancien régime was so distasteful to Frenchmen that there was great interest in overhauling its entire structure. The main controversy in the Constituent Assembly then stemmed from the divergent views on how best to reform public finance in France. Should it be reformed in the name of efficiency and uniformity so that greater revenues could be collected for the monarchy, or should a totally new theory of the purposes and practices of finance be instituted? Within the Assembly there were numerous voices, among them that of Dupont de Nemours of the Tax Committee, clamoring for the reform of institutions based on efficiency and uniformity. These voices were opposed by the radical deputies, who, like Roederer, sought in the interest of the nation a total revolution in these institutions.

As the author of proposals on the stamp and tobacco duties, the abolition of the General Farms and the creation of tax collection agencies to replace them, and the organization of the Treasury, Roederer was not only a participant in this debate but one of its principal instigators. Roederer came to this position quite naturally. Having fought the privileged groups in Metz over economic and financial reform, he had long since concluded that these matters should be decided on the basis of national, not particular, interest and that this interest was to be determined by the representatives of the nation in the National Assembly. If the financial institutions of the monarchy were to conform to these principles, then the total demolition of the concept of public institutions based on private interest was required. Roederer managed to convince a majority of his colleagues on the Tax Committee, who at first had gravitated to the leadership of Dupont, that his approach was correct, and he eventually had similar success with much of his program in the Assembly. Roederer then became the principal advocate of totally revolutionizing rather than merely reforming France's financial structure.

The National Constituent Assembly had originally intended that financial matters be dealt with by its Finance Committee of sixty-four members, but it had come to the realization that the workload was so great that a separate, smaller committee was needed to deal strictly with the reforms of taxation. Therefore, on 18 January 1790 the Assembly created a Tax

Committee (comité d'impositions) and on 21 January named its member-ship of eleven.[1] The committee contained such well-known personalities as the duc de La Rochefoucauld, who was chosen chairman, Talleyrand, Adrien Duport, and Dupont de Nemours. Other members of the committee (Jarry, Defermon, Monneron, Dauchy, the baron d'Allarde, La Borde de Mereville, and Roederer) had lesser reputations within the Assembly.

Roederer was an early advocate of the establishment of a Tax Committee possibly believing that his verbal support for its creation would win him an assignment on it.[2] Since he had entered the Assembly after committee assignments had been made, Roederer had been without any influence on the legislative proceedings except for occasional speeches from the floor. A committee assignment, however, would provide him an oppor-tunity to participate in the actual formation of legislative proposals, and the Tax Committee in particular would handle such important legislation. There was, of course, the possibility that the more well-known individuals on the committee would dominate its proceedings thereby leaving the less prominent members with little influence. However, Duport and Talley-rand seem to have taken relatively little interest in the committee's work; and Dupont, who should have been the committee's most influential member, given his reputation as a physiocrat and a reformer within the administrations of Vergennes and Calonne, found himself at odds on many issues with the committee majority. As events developed, Roederer emerged as the real leader of the committee, a position he developed in part on the basis of a close association with La Rochefoucauld.[3] The cre-ation of the Tax Committee and his subsequent appointment to it provided Roederer with an influence in the Assembly which he could never have developed otherwise.

The committee's task was to bring about a general reform of taxation in France. However, some of this work was done by the Finance Com-mittee which abolished the gabelles and aides and by the Commerce and Agriculture Committee which reformed the customs duties. The Tax Com-mittee was left with the responsibility for providing proposals for the direct taxation of landed and non-landed property, as well as methods of levying indirect taxes through the registration of documents, stamp taxes, and the sale of tobacco and wine. It was almost a foregone con-clusion that the reform of indirect taxes would involve some change in the status of the General Farms, the great agency for their collection.

The manner in which the committee dealt with its responsibility is not entirely known as it did not seem to have any official files or records. However, the various reforms were presented to the Assembly by different committee members which indicates that individual members were re-sponsible for investigating particular types of taxation. La Rochefoucauld

---

[1] AP, 11: 232, 266.
[2] Ibid., p. 22.
[3] Gouverneur Morris, *A Diary of the French Revolution, 1789–1793*, ed. Beatrix C. Davenport (New York, 1939), 2: 147.

presented the committee proposals on the direct taxation of landed property; Defermon had responsibility for direct taxation of nonlanded wealth; Talleyrand handled the registration duties; Dupont reported on the wine tax; and Roederer was in charge of tobacco taxes and stamp duties.[4] In Roederer's case all of the committee's documents on the tobacco tax and stamp duties are to be found among his personal papers, strengthening the impression that the committee did not work as a unit at least in the preliminary stages of preparing legislation. If the committee did function in the described fashion, Roederer probably had little responsibility in the drafting of tax proposals other than those concerned with the stamp duties and tobacco. A study of his role in the formulation, defense, and execution of these proposals, however, should provide some insight into the underlying attitudes and motivations of their principal author, the workings of the committee as a whole, the attendant problems accompanying massive, fundamental reform, and the operation of the political process in the early stages of the Revolution.

Roederer's proposal concerning the stamp taxes (*droits de timbre*) illustrates some of the problems the Tax Committee had to grapple with in an effort to revolutionize the system of taxation. Stamp taxes had been a feature of taxation in the ancien régime, stamps or special paper bearing the royal watermark being required for all legal documents. Stamp sales by the General Administration of the *domaines* produced for the royal treasury about 6 million livres per year.[5] The nature of the tax and the small sums involved in its collection made it one of the least onerous of all duties before 1789. However, Calonne's attempt in 1787 to increase the royal revenues through a greatly expanded stamp tax had been one of the factors in the revolt that year of the Parlement of Paris against royal authority.

Taxation in general was a very sensitive issue in the Assembly, and the Tax Committee wanted to be careful in selecting the types of taxes it would recommend for approval. As La Rochefoucauld explained in his first report to the Assembly, the Tax Committee was anxious that all new taxes be harmonious not only with the Constitution but also "with individual liberty [and] with the welfare and tranquility of the citizenry. . . ."[6] Despite the furor caused by Calonne's 1787 proposal, Roederer, in making his report to the Assembly on the stamp tax, said that this particular duty could be collected in a manner entirely "compatible with the principles of the Constitution."[7] Yet the committee was anxious that the tax yield considerably more than the 6 million collected before 1789. Therefore, in formulating the project Roederer familiarized himself with Calonne's pro-

---

[4] AP, 28: 696; 21: 300; 20: 638.

[5] George T. Matthews, *The Royal General Farms in Eighteenth-Century France* (New York, 1958), p. 147; Marcel Marion, *Dictionnaire des institutions de la France aux XVIIe et XVIIIe siècles* (Paris, 1928), p. 536. The sum of 6 million livres included the revenues from the closely related *droit de formule*.

[6] AP, 18: 143.

[7] AP, 22: 83.

posed stamp duty which had been designed to at least triple the revenues
of the tax and investigated the system then used in Britain which produced
considerable revenues while presumably not infringing on British liber-
ties.[8] The original French stamp tax had been limited to legal documents,
but both Calonne's proposal and the British system required stamps on
a much wider variety of items including commercial transactions and
newspapers. Obviously by increasing the categories of documents requiring stamps, the revenues from the tax could be increased dramatically.
Roederer and the committee, then, accepted the concept of the tax practiced in England and suggested by Calonne.

In presenting his project on the stamp tax to the Assembly, Roederer
explained some of the features of the similar duty in England and pointed
out that the British were able to collect from it 30 to 40 million livres per
year.[9] He estimated that France should collect about 27 to 30 million from
the stamp tax itself plus 30 to 40 million from the related duties on the
registration of documents (which formed part of the British stamp duties)
for a total yield of 60 to 70 million. The national administration (*régie*) of
the registration duties was also to sell the stamped paper which would
be required for use in a large number of specified documents: all minutes
and expeditions of acts which had to be registered; all minutes of judg-
ments of justices of the peace; the registers of the municipalities which
did not concern their public functions, the registers of faculties, colleges,
hospitals, priests and bishops, notaries, factories, tax receivers, and regis-
trars and concierges of the prisons; all copies of the above registers; all
receipts for rentes paid by the public treasury; all receipts for customs
duties and indirect taxes; the registers of négociants, merchants, manufacturers, and bankers; and all letters of exchange and other commercial
paper. Newspapers were not to be taxed because of the special service
they rendered in the cause of the Revolution. If paper or parchment other
than that of the régie were to be used, it could be stamped with a *timbre
extraordinaire* which would bear the same cost as the stamped paper. Public
officials not complying with the law would be fined 300 livres for the first
offense and 1000 livres plus removal from their functions for a second
offense. Private persons failing to pay the duties would pay a fine of 20
livres. Thus constituted, the stamp tax, covering a wide variety of everyday
activities, would provide ample revenues for the nation while assessing
only minor penalties for private individuals who failed to comply. Roederer expressed the committee's hope that the moderate duties would
encourage compliance among the population. For instance a small sheet
of stamped paper would cost 4 sous and a large sheet 8 sous while a sheet
for a letter of exchange valued at less than 400 livres would cost 5 sous

---

[8] There are copies of the royal reform plan as well as a schedule of the British duties in
Roederer's papers. AN 29AP84 *Declaration du roi concernant le timbre, 4 août 1787* (Paris,
1787); *Tables de tous les droits dits du timbre dans la Grande Bretagne;* and an untitled printed
table of the British stamp duty in English.

[9] AP, 22: 83–90.

and a letter of exchange over 1200 livres would cost 1 livre. These duties were comparable to those suggested by Calonne in 1787.

The Assembly, attracted to the revenues promised, seemed basically inclined to accept the committee's proposal on the stamp tax. However, the financier Le Couteulx de Canteleu objected strongly to the requirement that letters of exchange drawn on foreigners and payable to foreigners should be subject to the tax as they were only passing through France.[10] He argued that Paris, which was "the center of a great many negociations of notes between commercial nations," would lose this advantage if notes could not be traded without the delays the stamp duty would require. Roederer dismissed this objection by saying that such notes in effect became for a short time "a veritable national property" which should be subject to the tax. He also supported his position by arguing that England followed such a practice and "there is no reason that France should not do the same."[11] The Assembly, little concerned with the problems of those dealing in the commerce of international notes, accepted Roederer's explanation and voted in the article calling for the stamping of all letters of exchange.

On 10 January Le Couteulx, supplied with new information, returned to the attack in the Assembly. Attempting to destroy Roederer's justification for the levying of the stamp tax on letters of exchange coming into France, he produced letters from two English residents of Paris who denied that such a duty existed in Great Britain.[12] Le Couteulx then went on to reiterate his assertion that such a tax would be positively harmful to the French commerce in international paper. Roederer replied with hauteur that "your committee has been guided by principles" rather than by examples but had investigated very thoroughly the English practice and found it to conform to that proposed for France. Charles de Lameth interjected that he thought Le Couteulx's objections were only those of a "particular interest which militates here against the general interest."[13] The Assembly, perhaps sharing these sentiments, once again ignored Le Couteulx's proposal.

Le Couteulx, however, did not yield to the majority opinion. He submitted to the Tax Committee one of the letters from his English acquaintances which denied the existence of the tax on letters of exchange coming into England. The writer, a certain Boyd, agreed with Le Couteulx that such a tax would interfere with the necessity of speed in such financial transactions and in addition alleged that the process of obtaining the stamp would violate "the secrecy which is indispensably necessary in the execution of this type of operation."[14] Boyd also argued that the Assembly would fail in its objective of taxing *capitalistes* if the exchange market

---

[10] Ibid.
[11] Ibid., p. 90.
[12] Ibid., p. 112.
[13] Ibid., p. 113.
[14] AN 29AP84 Boyd to Le Couteulx de Canteleu [?], 10 January 1791.

moved elsewhere due to the inconvenience of the tax. Le Couteulx reinforced his argument and clarified the British practice by writing a letter
to the committee in which he pointed out that the English term "foreign
bills" which were subject to the stamp tax referred only to those drawn
in England and payable abroad.[15] He also presented a new argument
against the tax in suggesting that it might violate the commercial treaty
between England and France.

This last effort finally brought Le Couteulx success. On 7 February Roederer admitted that there had been a translation error regarding the term
"foreign bills" and that letters of exchange originating outside of England
were not subject to the British stamp tax. Once this admission was made,
the mood of the Assembly abruptly shifted. The principles of the committee melted away before the example of the great trading nation across
the Channel. The Assembly decreed that letters of exchange only passing
through France not be subject to the stamp duty.[16] Roederer did not suggest
such a change; but by reintroducing the subject and acceding so readily
to the revision, he had obviously come to the conclusion that his first
proposal could pose a serious threat to French financial activity.

The other major attack on the stamp tax came from the paper manufacturers and merchants. Roederer's files contain a printed petition dated
26 January 1791 from the *papetiers* of Paris opposing the establishment
of a régie with the exclusive right to sell stamped paper.[17] The petition
argued that the exclusive sale of stamped paper by the régie would destroy
the commerce of private paper manufacturers and merchants by denying
them any significant market and would force fifty thousand families
into a life of poverty. They portrayed the establishment of such a régie
as a reversion to the "despotism of the ancien régime" and a denial of
the revolutionary doctrine of liberty of commerce. The petitioners desired
the revision of the stamp tax so that paper to be stamped would be supplied
by individuals. They argued that the provisions for the stamping of ordinary paper with the timbre extraordinaire was not satisfactory to their
interests because individuals had to supply their own paper and yet pay
a tax equal to that charged by the régie for the stamp and its paper.

In the Assembly the deputy Saint-Martin distributed this petition on
7 February.[18] Roederer responded to it by arguing that the exclusive sale
by the régie of stamped paper was the only method by which counterfeiting could be controlled. This was such an essential point that it was
an integral part of the English stamp duty. Without offering any supporting
evidence, Roederer consoled the paper manufacturers and merchants with
his assurance that the damage to their enterprise would not be as great
as they anticipated. The Assembly, if not the paper interests, accepted
Roederer's explanation.

---

[15] AN 29AP84 Le Couteulx de Canteleu to the Tax Committee, 17 January 1791.

[16] AP, 23: 30–32.

[17] AN 29AP84 "Petition des fabricants et marchands de papier à l'Assemblée nationale."

[18] AP, 23: 33.

Having failed within the Assembly, the papetiers attempted to marshall public pressure against the régie. They distributed throughout France a circular letter to individuals they believed to be sympathetic to their petition, without doubt primarily to manufacturers and merchants of paper.[19] In the letter they asked these individuals to persuade their district administrations to protest the establishment of the stamp tax in its present form. The papetiers apparently also included in their circular letter a printed petition to be used in dealing with the local directory.[20] The petition outlined the injustices of the new stamp tax and predicted the financial ruin of 50,000 families. Not content to urge their provincial colleagues to action, the papetiers also sent an untitled circular letter to the various district administrations charging that the new stamp tax violated the principle of liberty of commerce.[21] The letter urged the districts to send their protests to the National Assembly, the Tax Committee, the municipality of Paris, and the Jacobin Club. The paper interest was probably also responsible for the publication of an open letter to Roederer denying the validity of his arguments in favor of the régie.[22] The letter alleged that under the plan of the papetiers, counterfeiting would be less of a problem than under the Assembly's decree.

As a result of the campaign of the papetiers, a number of petitions and protests were sent to the Tax Committee. The paper merchants of Lyons wrote that they would be ruined by the exclusive sale of stamped paper by the régie.[23] The paper manufacturers of Thiers (Puy de Dôme) wrote that 3,000 workers in that town earned their livelihood in the manufacture of paper and warned that they would not "suffer tranquilly the horrors of starvation."[24] These manufacturers urged the Assembly to adopt the project suggested by the Parisian papetiers. The municipality of Dannonai (Ardèche) supported its local paper manufacturers by sending to the Assembly a protest calling for the end of the exclusive sale of stamped paper by a régie.[25] The Directory of the department of the Calvados transmitted the objections of the manufacturers of the district of Vire and the merchants of Caen regarding the stamp tax and put itself on record as an opponent of the régie.[26]

Roederer and the Tax Committee were not moved by these protests to

---

[19] AN 29AP84 Untitled printed circular letter of the papetiers.

[20] AN 29AP84 Printed petition entitled "A Messieurs les administrateurs du district du. . . ."

[21] AN 29AP84 Untitled printed circular letter to district administrators.

[22] AN 29AP84 *Lettre adresse à M. Roederer, rapporteur du comité d'impositions au sujet de son rapport sur le timbre.*

[23] AN 29AP84 Petition of the paper merchants of Lyons.

[24] AN 29AP84 "Petition sur le commerce du papier de Thiers (Puy de Dôme)," 14 March 1791.

[25] AN 29AP84 "Extrait du registre des deliberations de la municipalité Dannonay (Ardèche)," 25 March 1791.

[26] AN 29AP84 Directory of the department of the Calvados to the Agriculture and Commerce Committe and to the Tax Committee, 23 April 1791; Caen paper merchants to the Directory of the department of the Calvados, no date.

amend their law. Except for his response in the Assembly to the petition of the papetiers, Roederer is not on record as having made any statement on this issue. After obtaining possession of the various circulars of the paper interest, Roederer was well aware that the petitions he was receiving were not spontaneous. Yet he had hardly received enough of them to make creditable the claim of the papetiers that the livelihood of 50,000 families was at stake. If the campaign of the papetiers was truly a national one, why had more departmental or district administrations not participated? Obviously the papetiers had tried to use the tactics of a massive public out-cry against the stamp duty but had really failed to rouse much interest in the issue. Roederer and the Tax Committee, under no real pressure to amend their proposed law, did not do so.

The final wording of the 7 February decree establishing the stamp tax stipulated that any extracts of copies of the registers of any administrative bodies (i.e. municipalities, districts, or departments) or certificates, passports, or other acts issued by those bodies which were requested by individuals for their personal use would be subject to the stamp duty.[27] This article of the law caused considerable confusion among officials of local government, who were never quite sure how to distinguish the functions of administration which were purely public in nature from those functions which might be utilized for the benefit of particular individuals. In this state of confusion they naturally looked to the National Assembly for clarification. As the author of the stamp tax, Roederer received these queries and had to find some way to end the confusion that his law had created.

The nature of the problem was clearly expressed in the communications from the departmental administrations. For instance the department of the Seine-Inférieure asked the Tax Committee if requests and mémoires presented to the Directory concerning direct taxation and the subsequent orders the department issued in response to these requests were subject to the stamp duty.[28] The directory was particularly concerned that the taxing of these "purely administrative" acts would be unjust since such functions were a legitimate part of public administration. Furthermore, in many cases the administration would have to tax itself to fulfill the requirements of the law. The department of the Allier asked if dispatches to the districts and municipalities were subject to the stamp tax.[29] The Directory of the department of the Sarthe was confused about the proper procedures for issuing receipts to purchasers of national land.[30] The administrators complained that they were required by law to deliver without cost to the highest bidder the first copy of the paper work associated with

---

[27] AP, 23: 33.

[28] AN 29AP84 Directory of the department of the Seine-Inférieure to the Tax Committee, 28 March 1791.

[29] AN 29AP84 Directory of the department of the Allier to the National Assembly, 19 May 1791.

[30] AN 29AP84 Directory of the department of the Sarthe to the National Assembly, 18 May 1791; Directory of the department of the Sarthe to de Lessart, Minister of Finance. (This is a copy of the original letter.)

the purchasing of national land but were constrained from so doing because the law establishing the stamp tax mandated that all administrative
procedures benefiting an individual were to be recorded on stamped paper.
The department, while seeking a clarification, offered the opinion that
purchasers of national land should be exempt from the stamp duty. Even
the minister of the marine made inquiries of the committee regarding the
use of stamped paper in the registers of the treasurers of the *invalides de
la marine'* the rolls from which the *invalides* and sailors were paid, and
the receipts for their wages.[31]

Given the widespread confusion caused by the law, the Tax Committee's first reaction was to respond administratively rather than legislatively.
Roederer answered the 54 questions submitted by the department of the
Seine-Inférieure and scribbled comments on the letter from the minister
of the marine which were obviously intended to be returned to him.[32] At
some point Roederer became concerned about the extent of the confusion
and drafted a circular letter of a general sort that was designed to answer
all the questions that had been submitted to the committee.[33] That this
was ever printed and distributed to the departments is doubtful because
in early June Roederer, in an effort to establish the necessary clarifications,
went before the Assembly seeking amendments to the law of 7 February.[34]
The amended law called for any actions of local administrative bodies
which were inscribed in the margins of mémoires, petitions, or requests
of private individuals to be subject to the stamp tax. The first copy of all
paper work relating to the sale of national lands was to be delivered free
but all subsequent copies were to be on stamped paper. Various papers
given to soldiers and seamen such as *billets de subsistance* and *billets
d'hôpitaux* were not to be stamped. In addition the Assembly forced
through, against the committee's wishes, an amendment ending the tax
on receipts given in exchange for the payment of indirect and direct taxes.

Even these clarifications in the law did not end the stream of correspondence which flowed from the departments to the Tax Committee.
The notaries of the town of Romans (Drôme) were distraught with an
over-zealous tax receiver who insisted that they cease the traditional and
lawful practice of entering notarial acts *en minute* in registers in order to
collect more stamp taxes by having each act recorded on a separate sheet.[35]
The department of the Calvados insisted that it could not act in accordance
with the new amendments because it had no means of stamping the
mémoires and petitions that were brought before the Directory.[36] The dis-

---

[31] AN 29AP84 Minister of the marine to the Tax Committee, 17 May 1791.

[32] AN 29AP84 List of questions posed by the department of the Seine-Inférieure; Minister
of the marine to the Tax Committee, 17 May 1791.

[33] AN 29AP84 "Projet de circular aux differens départements concernant l'execution de
la loi du timbre."

[34] AP, 28: 100–01.

[35] AN 29AP84 "Mémoire pour les notaires de la ville de Romans." This was received by
the Committee on 19 June 1791.

[36] AN 29AP84 Directory of the department of the Calvados to the National Assembly, 20
July 1791.

trict of the Plaine inquired as to the proper procedure for levying the
stamp tax on documents associated with the purchase of national land if
that land was located in different districts.[37] Apparently seeking assurance
of the correctness of its procedures, the department of the Vosges sent
the Assembly a copy of its policy on the collection of the stamp tax within
the department.[38]

The political process which resulted in the creation of the stamp tax
reveals much about the Tax Committee. Despite Roederer's assertion that
the committee was guided by principles rather than examples, the evidence
indicates that they were forced to rely heavily on Calonne's proposals and
the experience of England in order to assure the nation a sufficient revenue
from the tax. The result of Le Couteulx's campaign to obtain a revision
of the procedure for taxing letters of exchange indicates just how dependent on the English model the committee was. In the end Roederer and
the committee were guided more by practicality than revolutionary zeal.
The entire bent of their activity was toward producing as high a revenue
as possible within the limits of the tax. Thus they were unmoved by the
public campaign of the papetiers which did not represent the interests of
a large number of citizens nor any vital revolutionary principles. At the
same time they felt keenly the responsibility of interpreting and clarifying
the law for the departmental administrations in order to insure the complete and accurate perception of the duty.

The role of Roederer and the Tax Committee in the writing of new
legislation governing the tobacco tax (the *tabacs*) offers an interesting com-
parison to their activities regarding the stamp tax. Many of the same
political components were present in each situation: a desire to conform
to revolutionary principles, a necessity for large revenues, considerable
pressure from interest groups which sought legislation favorable to themselves, and administrative problems associated with the new legislation.
Despite the great influence that Roederer exercised in the formulation of
both taxes and the apparent similarity of problems, the outcome in the
case of tobacco was the reverse of that of the stamp tax. In the latter the
Tax Committee recommended and secured the creation of a government
monopoly on the sale of stamped paper in the interest of high tax revenues.
In the matter of the tabacs, however, the committee under Roederer's
guidance supported the destruction of the government monopoly on tobacco and the high revenue associated with it in exchange for the creation
of a system of free enterprise and low public revenues. Only an examination of the political problems associated with the tobacco tax can offer
an explanation of this phenomenon.

Before 1789 the manufacture and sale of tobacco in the interest of the
royal treasury was the exclusive prerogative of the General Farms.[39] In

---

[37] AN 29AP84 Directory of the district of the Plaine to the National Assembly, 18 July
1791.

[38] AN 29AP84 "Extrait de deliberations du directoire de departement des Vosges," 12
August 1791.

[39] Jacob Price's very thorough study of the tobacco farm, *France and the Chesapeake: A
History of the French Tobacco Monopoly 1674–1791, and of Its Relationship to the British and*

order to maintain the effectiveness of the monopoly, the cultivation of tobacco was prohibited within the boundaries of the realm except for certain privileged border provinces (Flanders, Artois, Hainault, Cambrésis, Alsace, and Franche Comté). These grew a low quality tobacco, mixed this with some high quality imported leaf, and then exported the final product or smuggled it into the territory of the monopoly to compete with the higher priced tobacco of the General Farms. To prevent smuggling and the fraudulent sale of tobacco, the General Farms employed guards who had the right of search and seizure which enabled them to ferret out illicit stocks of tobacco. The monopoly was a lucrative one for the Monarchy, producing over 30 million livres in 1789. The tobacco monopoly, unlike the gabelles, the notorious salt monopoly, was not an institution despised by Frenchmen before 1789.[40] However, there was some opposition to its continuation. Foremost among this opposition were the tobacco interests of the privileged provinces who correctly saw the continuation of the tabacs as a threat to their existence. Others, opposed to the monopoly, believed its destruction would encourage greater commercial exchange between the United States and France. The principal defense of the tabacs came from within the organization of the General Farms itself.

The pro-monopoly forces bombarded the Tax Committee with mémoires extolling the value of the monopoly. One General Farmer, Desmarest, wrote that the monopoly was of all taxes *"la plus douce, la plus imperceptible"* while another, Delahante, alleged that since the tax was collected only on a luxury it was in fact "a voluntary imposition."[41] Most of those writing in favor of the monopoly stressed that the revenue of 30 million livres was essential to the welfare of the nation and could only be collected if the monopoly was preserved. There could be little doubt that the General Farms would not survive the Revolution, but the monopoly could be converted into a régie operated in the interest of the nation. Desmarest, who suggested this as early as April 1790, envisioned the régie staffed with régisseurs, almost certainly former general farmers or high officials of the Farm, knowledgeable in the affairs of the monopoly.[42] Some of the writers were indeed aware of the necessity of having the monopoly conform to constitutional principles. The General Farmer Duvaucel suggested abolishing the use of interior guards to search for contraband tobacco and lowering the price of the product itself which could be effected by ending the privileges of the border provinces and selling the monopoly there.[43]

The one point upon which all these writers agreed was that the free cultivation of tobacco could not be continued in the heretofore privileged

American Tobacco Trades (Ann Arbor, 1973), 2 vols., was of great assistance in writing this account of the abolition of the tabacs.

[40] Price, *France and the Chesapeake,* 2: 794–95.

[41] AN 29AP85 H. Desmarest, *Mémoire sur la ferme du tabac;* J. Delahante, "Observations," 22 August 1790.

[42] AN 29AP85 Desmarest to La Rochefoucauld, 30 April 1790.

[43] AN 29AP85 L.-P. Duvaucel, *Lettre adressée à M. Blancons député à l'Assemblée nationale* (n.p. 1790).

provinces.[44] The officials of the General Farms envisioned the Revolution as the perfect instrument for bringing uniformity and efficiency to the administration of the tobacco farm. The cessation of privileges in the border provinces would provide new markets for the monopoly's product and would simplify the control of illegal tobacco. All agreed that the free cultivation of tobacco could not exist in conjunction with the monopoly if fraud was to be controlled in any measure. They further justified their position by arguing that land used for the production of food should not be turned over to the production of a non-food crop. Even though some proposed an indemnity to the tobacco interests in those areas, all suggested that the affected provinces renounce their privileges for the national good.

Those individuals interested in improving Franco-American trade opposed the continuation of the monopoly. They were interested in substituting for it import duties on foreign tobacco which they believed would allow more American tobacco to be sold in France thus increasing sales of French goods in the United States.[45] Lafayette was the most well-known individual associated with this opinion even though the American chargé d'affaires in Paris, William Short, was its most vigorous supporter. This plan required the continuation of a planting ban on tobacco, but its supporters seemed unaware that an attack on the monopoly might also result in the destruction of the planting ban which would be detrimental to the American tobacco trade.

Finally the tobacco interests in the privileged provinces and their representatives in the Assembly opposed the continuation of the monopoly which would almost certainly have led to the destruction of the production and processing of their tobacco. The tobacco manufacturers of Strasbourg informed the Tax Committee that they employed 6,000 workers in the annual production of 60,000 quintals of tobacco which sold for two million livres. Their conclusion, of course, was that "this commerce procures, then, considerable advantages for old Alsace . . ." which would be lost if a régie were established.[46] In addition they argued that the retention of the monopoly violated the revolutionary principles of free commerce.[47] Under the guise of patriotism they justified the abolition of the monopoly which would have to rely totally on American tobacco while arguing that a free commerce in tobacco would consist mostly of French leaf. The tobacco interest insisted, however, that it must have access to some foreign (i.e. American) tobacco in order to make its product palatable.

---

[44] See especially AN 29AP85, Desmarest to La Rochefoucauld, 30 April 1790; "Observations sur la vente exclusive du Tabac;" and Duvaucel, *Lettre adressée à M. Blancons.*

[45] AN 29AP85 Lafayette, "Resumé de mon avis au comité du commerce avec les Etats-Unis lorsque la question des tabacs nous a été presentée;" De Moustier to La Rochefoucauld, 19 April 1790; William Short to La Rochefoucauld, 23 March 1790.

[46] AN 29AP85 "Observations sur les fabriques et le commerce de tabac du département du Bas Rhin."

[47] AN 29AP85 Députés extraordinaires du commerce de Strasbourg, "Mémoire sur la prohibition des feuilles de tabac étrangères dans le royaume," 18 October 1790; [Députés extraordinaires], "La Régie peut-elle utile à l'état?"

It was the responsibility of the Tax Committee to weigh the merits of these views and deal with the political pressures which lay behind them. The process the committee used to formulate its position was by the nature of the controversy much different from that used in the case of the stamp tax when little pressure was put on the committee until after it had made its first report to the Assembly. In the matter of tobacco, letters, mémoires, and requests began to fill the committee files in the spring of 1790, long before Roederer made even a preliminary report on the tabacs to the Assembly. William Short may have been the first to send some memoranda to the committee when he provided it on 23 March 1790 with a letter Thomas Jefferson had written to Vergennes in 1785 suggesting the abolition of the monopoly in favor of import duties.[48] This was shortly followed on 30 April with a letter and mémoire by the General Farmer Desmarest outlining the basic position of the friends of the monopoly.[49] In early May the pro-monopoly forces apparently were apprised that Roederer would be in charge of the legislation on tobacco, and the General Farmer Delahante sent Roederer a polite letter and a copy of a mémoire describing the operations of the Farm.[50] In addition Delahante urged Roederer to come dine with him if he desired further information. On 6 June the Controller-General Lambert wrote to Roederer urging prompt action on the creation of a régie on the tobacco question. Revenues from the monopoly were dwindling in the first months of 1790 due to the uncertainty about the fate of the tabacs.[51]

The committee was uncertain which direction to take. From the beginning Dupont had favored the retention of the monopoly and spoke to that effect in the Assembly on 23 April 1790.[52] However, on the same day Dupont made his speech, William Short reported that the Tax Committee seemed inclined to support the free commerce of tobacco.[53] A week later, though, Short believed the committee had decided to maintain the monopoly; and when a deputation from Alsace and Flanders met with the committee, they came away completely convinced that the monopoly would be retained.[54] The problems that existed within the committee were readily apparent in Roederer's equivocal speech of 12 June.[55] He hinted that the committee had accepted Dupont's plan but devoted most of his

[48] AN 29AP85 Short to La Rochefoucauld, 23 March 1790; "Lettre de M. Jefferson à M. le comte de Vergennes."

[49] AN 29AP85 Desmarest to La Rochefoucauld, 30 April 1790; Desmarest, Mémoire sur la ferme du tabac.

[50] AN 29AP85 Delahante to Roederer, 5 May 1790; Delahante, "Observations sur la constitution et le régime de la ferme." Actually both the letter and the mémoire were the work of Antoine Lavoisier, another General Farmer. Price, France and the Chesapeake, 2: 809.

[51] AN 29AP85 C.-G. Lambert to Roederer, 6 June 1790. In addition to his letter Lambert sent Roederer a table which illustrated the decline in revenues.

[52] AP, 15: 271. Dupont had become very familiar with the tabacs in 1787 in his capacity of commissaire général du commerce. Price, France and the Chesapeake, 2: 779–81.

[53] Short to John Jay, 23 April 1790, The Papers of Thomas Jefferson, ed. Julian P. Boyd (Princeton, 1961), 16: 375.

[54] Short to Jay, 1 May 1790, Ibid., p. 403.

[55] AP, 16: 196.

speech to an attack on the monopoly. He said the high price denied the poor the same opportunities to enjoy this luxury as the rich and taxed them in an unequal fashion if they did indulge themselves. Also the exclusive sale of tobacco was characterized by injustice since it demanded "prohibitions, inquisitions, and penalties always disproportionate to the offense."[56] Finally there were the concerns of the tobacco interests in Flanders and Alsace. Roederer did not think the Assembly could prohibit the free cultivation and commerce of those provinces without attacking their property rights nor establish the monopoly without including those areas within its jurisdiction. The deputies from Flanders opposed the monopoly and asserted that its extension into their provinces would lead to a revolt against the authority of the Assembly. The Alsatian deputies agreed to accept the monopoly only if it could be positively proven that its revenues were needed by the nation for the next year's expenses. Roederer asked and received from the Assembly a postponement of the committee's report until they had certain knowledge of the financial needs for the coming year.

Dupont's influence on the Tax Committee was probably still preeminent, but Roederer had, in his role as reporter, begun to undermine Dupont's influence. Roederer's call for delay in effect reopened the entire question of the monopoly before the committee which was at the time in favor of its continuance. His efforts gave a boost to the hopes of the tobacco interest but dampened those of the pro-monopoly forces. The American interests were totally ignored but they hardly stood to profit from the turn of events in any case.

During the summer of 1790 the Tax Committee, probably at Roederer's insistence, began to examine alternative schemes of taxing tobacco. One such plan was presented by two of Controller General Lambert's subordinates, Mollien and Mahy de Cormeré.[57] In separate treatises these men argued that the revenues of the state could be maintained and freedom of culture permitted by adopting the Prussian system of domestic tobacco production. This system operated on the careful monitoring of the quantities of tobacco grown domestically to insure that no more was produced than could be consumed. The revenues were obtained from the state monopoly on manufacture and sale of the finished product. They estimated that the nation could collect between 28.8 and 38.6 million livres with this monopoly. Both authors argued that abolition of the American tobacco trade would not injure Franco-American trade relations as Americans had continued to prefer British goods even after independence.

Roederer was sufficiently impressed with this plan to send that of Mahy de Cormeré to Vincent Magnien, a former employee of the General Farms and a well-known economic reformer.[58] Magnien reviewed Mahy's project

---

[56] Ibid.

[57] AN 29AP85. [Mahy de Cormeré], "Mémoire sur l'impot du tabac et sur les moyens d'allier la culture avec le privilege de vente exclusive;" Untitled mémoire by Mollien; Price, *France and the Chesapeake*, 2: 809.

[58] AN 29AP85 Handwritten notes by Roederer on Mollien project; Price, *France and the Chesapeake*, 2: 810.

but reported to the committee that it was too impractical to be implemented.[59] Innumerable quarrels would accompany the decisions regarding which land was to be set aside for the cultivation of tobacco. Some departments, unable to produce high quality tobacco, would have to mix theirs with the higher grade leaf of others. The free cultivation of tobacco would make the monopoly very vulnerable to the production of fraudulent tobacco.

On 11 August 1790 Magnien submitted his own plan to Roederer with the observation that it was the only one "which is able to conciliate the two parties."[60] Essentially this project called for the free cultivation and manufacture of tobacco in France and also for the creation of a régie to sell imported tobacco. Since Flanders and Alsace would not have access to American leaf and since those areas of France more favorable to tobacco cultivation could not produce any until 1793, the national régie could yield 20 million livres for three years. After that time the privileged provinces might not find free cultivation so important and a true monopoly could be restored. Even without the monopoly some foreign tobacco would be necessary and could be subject to an import tax which would yield 3 million to the treasury after customs expenses.[61] Taxes could also be levied on cultivators and manufacturers in France.

The Tax Committee, or at least Roederer's faction within it, found Magnien's scheme attractive and sent it for comment to Mahy de Cormeré as well as to the General Farmers Delahante and Lavoisier. Mahy did not believe the project would produce the 20 million livres that Magnien suggested but rather something between 8.4 million and 9.9 million depending on the prices charged for foreign tobacco.[62] Neither Delahante nor Lavoisier believed that this system would allow the régie to prevent the smuggling of foreign tobacco, and Lavoisier suggested that there would be a major problem with fraud on the part of the employees of the régie itself.[63] They supplied no figures but seemed doubtful that a régie of this type would produce any significant revenues. Roederer, determined to destroy the monopoly and seizing on the Magnien scheme as the best alternative, ignored the caveats of the general farmers and managed to convince a majority of his colleagues on the committee to reverse their previous stand on the monopoly and to vote for a project based on free cultivation, manufacture, and sale with a prohibition on the importation of foreign tobacco.[64]

---

[59] AN 29AP85 Untitled mémoire with V. Magnien's name appended.

[60] AN 29AP85 Magnien to Roederer, 11 August 1790; Magnien, "Que peut on faire de mieux dans l'état actuel pour le tabac?"

[61] Jacob Price implies that Magnien believed his project would produce 20 million livres per year indefinitely. Actually Magnien did not believe it could yield 20 million after 1793 when high quality French leaf would enter the market. See Price, *France and the Chesapeake*, 2: 811; AN 29AP85 Magnien, "Que peut on faire."

[62] AN 29AP85 Mahy de Cormeré to La Rochefoucauld, 22 August 1790; Mahy de Cormeré, "Reflexions sur le tabac."

[63] AN 29AP85 Delahante to La Rochefoucauld 22 August 1790; Delahante, "Observations;" Lavoisier to La Rochefoucauld, 25 August 1790.

[64] AP, 28: 737. Those accepting the plan were Roederer, La Rochefoucauld, D'Allarde, Dauchy, Defermon, Jarry, and Talleyrand.

Reporting for the committee on 13 September 1790, Roederer justified their decision by arguing that a tobacco monopoly was incompatible with the principles of the Revolution. It constituted an attack on property by forbidding individuals the right to utilize their property as they saw fit.[65] A monopoly was a threat to liberty with its proscription of certain types of employment and its strict measures of control such as arbitrary domiciliary visits. This assault on liberty would be a more serious blow to the residents of the former privileged provinces who "would be losing the liberty they have enjoyed than it would be for the other inhabitants of the realm not to recover a liberty of which they have so long been deprived."[66] Finally the exclusive cultivation of tobacco hurt the poor more than the wealthy. After all, "it is not the rich of the cities" who would suffer from a planting ban on tobacco, but "the people of the countryside," presumably the class "for which you have made the Revolution and the Constitution."[67] Roederer concluded that the tobacco tax which was so "unjust by its nature" and the regime of the Farms which was so "oppressive" had to be replaced by a system more suitable to the Constitution.[68]

He outlined the possible alternatives to the Assembly.[69] The cultivation, manufacture, and sale of tobacco could be absolutely free with taxes levied at various stages of production. Unfortunately this plan would raise only a few million livres in revenue for the nation. An alternative plan, actually that of Mollien and Mahy de Cormeré, would follow the Prussian practice of limited domestic production and a state monopoly on manufacturing and sales; but Roederer rejected this because of its violations of liberty and property. Therefore, the only project which offered any hope of being compatible with revolutionary principles and producing some revenue was that of the committee. The committee plan called for the free cultivation, manufacture, and sale of domestic tobacco. All foreign leaf would be imported and manufactured by a régie which could compete effectively with the domestic variety by offering a higher quality product. Roederer was unwilling to predict Magnien's estimate of 20 million livres in revenue but did not care to adopt Mahy's gloomy projection of less than 10 million either. Instead he opted for a compromise figure of 12 million livres revenue for 1791.[70] For those who had hoped that the tabacs could yield 30 million a year, Roederer offered the argument that such a revenue would be impossible even with the implementation of exclusive sale if there were no domiciliary visits. Given the amount of contraband tobacco that had

---

[65] Ibid., pp. 730–31.
[66] Ibid., p. 733.
[67] Ibid.
[68] Ibid., p. 736.
[69] Ibid., pp. 734–37.
[70] Ibid., p. 737. There is an untitled mémoire in Roederer's papers suggesting that a régie on foreign tobacco would yield 12 million livres. AN 29AP85. According to Short Roederer admitted the Committee had no idea how much revenue the plan would yield. Short to Jefferson, 27 August 1790, in *The Papers of Thomas Jefferson*, 28: 439.

filtered into France during the instability of the Revolution, 30 million could not be raised in the immediate future no matter what system was put into effect. Roederer was not entirely honest with the Assembly in the matter of the expected revenues. Magnien had said that his expectations of relatively high revenues would only hold for three years when higher quality French leaf would come into the market and cut into the sales of foreign tobacco. Delahante and Lavoisier had pointed up the very real problem of fraud for the projected régie. Roederer totally ignored these probabilities in his speech before the Assembly. The 12 million livres, then, were more of a speculation than anything else, and there was every likelihood that revenues of that dimension would never emerge from the new régie.

Discussion of the Tax Committee's project was postponed until November, but in the interim the committee came under heavy fire from both pro-monopoly forces and the tobacco interests. The pro-monopoly forces argued that the plan would be a disaster for the nation because it would sacrifice revenues of 30 million livres. In order to publicize their cause, two General Farmers, Desmarest and Duvaucel, printed pamphlets arguing their case.[71] Desmarest even questioned Roederer's competence to deal with tobacco, charging that he "did not display even the most basic understanding of this important branch of the revenues of the state."[72] For its part the tobacco interest praised Roederer's attachment to the Constitution in the matter of free cultivation but argued that they would be ruined by a régie that would deny them foreign leaf to mix with their local product.[73] A *mémoire* from the tobacco manufacturers of Strasbourg even hinted that the destruction of their business by the régie might touch off a revolt among the local inhabitants. These arguments were repeated during the Assembly debate in November.[74] Interestingly enough neither Roederer nor any other committee member spoke in favor of their project. Finally Barnave demanded that the Tax Committee produce figures demonstrating how the revenues lost from tobacco would be replaced before any decisions about abolishing the monopoly were made.

La Rochefoucauld reported on 6 December that the Tax Committee estimated the total expenses for 1791 at 560 million livres with revenues of 540 million not including the tobacco tax.[75] The remaining 20 million could be produced through a reformed tobacco tax and the sale of the stocks of tobacco and salt still in the possession of the General Farms. The Finance Committee contradicted these figures in January when Lebrun

[71] AN 29AP85 Duvaucel, *Lettre adressée à Blancon;* AN 29AP81 H. Desmarest, *Observations sur le premier rapport de M. Roederer á l'Assemblée nationale concernant le revenue public établi sur la consummation du tabac.*

[72] AN 29AP81 Desmarest, *Observations.*

[73] "Opinion de M. Schwendt," in AP, 18: 738; AN 29AP85 "Observations sur les fabriques et le commerce de tabac du Département du Bas Rhin;" Députés extraordinaires, "Mémoire sur la prohibition des feuilles étrangères," 18 October 1790.

[74] AP, 20: 404–06, 443–56, 461–71.

[75] Ibid., 21: 261–62.

presented his own estimates of expenses and revenues which demon-strated the need for the tobacco monopoly.[76]

Whatever the truth of these estimates they made little difference to the Tax Committee. Roederer and his colleagues were so anxious to appease the tobacco interest and destroy the monopoly that the revenues produced were the least of their concerns. Most probably during the November debates Roederer, influenced by the hostility to the régie of the tobacco manufacturers, had not defended his original proposal because he had already decided to alter it in order to accommodate this opposition. This attitude became obvious when the committee made its second report on the tabacs in January 1791. In his report Roederer repeated the arguments against the monopoly that he had cited in his September speech, and once again he proposed establishing a system of free cultivation, manufacture, and sale of tobacco.[77] However, the new plan called for an import duty of 50 livres per quintal of foreign leaf, an obvious concession to the tobacco manufacturers. The state revenues would come from the import duty as well as from a régie which would manufacture high quality imported tobacco, not subject to the import duty. Delly d'Agier, who had family ties to the Farms, responded to Roederer's address by charging that the tabacs would never have been destroyed "if the particular and local in-terests had not raised their voices."[78] More of a challenge to the committee, however, was Mirabeau's counterproposal, almost certainly written by the General Farmer Lavoisier, calling for the establishment of a tobacco monopoly throughout all of France with compensation to the former priv-ileged provinces.[79] According to Mirabeau, his project would produce rev-enues of 30 million for the nation without the arbitrary measures of en-forcement associated with the ancien régime. Roederer immediately challenged Mirabeau's figures, arguing that such revenues were impossible due to the existence of large stocks of contraband tobacco which had come into France during the Revolution. Even in normal circumstances these sums could not be raised without domiciliary visits by agents of the mo-nopoly. Le Chapelier also expressed concerns about continuing a tax based on "the corporal punishments of the old fiscal code" which threatened "the liberty of the citizens."[80] The Assembly decreed another postpone-ment of the discussion to allow further consideration of Mirabeau's project.

The pro-monopoly forces by this time had abandoned all hope of per-suading Roederer and his colleagues of the value of exclusive sale and did not bother to send any more mémoires to the Tax Committee, but they did produce a number of pamphlets supporting Mirabeau's proposal in hopes of influencing the Assembly at large.[81] One of these by Desmarest

---

[76] Lebrun tabulated somewhat lower revenues for certain taxes and higher government expenses. Ibid., 22: 231.

[77] Ibid., 22: 549–50.

[78] Ibid., p. 551; Price, *France and the Chesapeake,* 2: 820.

[79] AP, 22: 557–58; Price, *France and the Chesapeake,* 2: 824–25.

[80] Ibid., pp. 557–58.

[81] Price, *France and the Chesapeake,* 2: 825.

which found its way into Roederer's files, supported Mirabeau's project while denying the validity of Roederer's assertion that the existence of contraband tobacco would prevent the monopoly from raising 30 million in revenue.[82] According to Desmarest, the contraband tobacco was of such poor quality that it would never attract buyers. On the other hand those favorable to a free tobacco trade were visibly upset with Mirabeau's proposal, and they tried to pressure the Assembly into action favorable to the tobacco interest with threats of counter-revolution. The municipal officers of Strasbourg wrote to the Assembly that the maintenance of the monopoly might lead to disturbances among the peasantry already alarmed over the Assembly's attack on religion. In addition they argued that Strasbourg had suffered much from the Revolution due to the decision to create a national trade barrier which would end their free trade status with Germany. If the tobacco monopoly was instituted, "our fellow citizens, great lovers of liberty, would no longer be able to prove their devotion and love for your laws. . . ."[83] The Minister of War, Duportail, had also learned of possible disturbances in Alsace over the tobacco question and hastened to warn the Assembly about these dangers.[84]

In February discussion on tobacco was resumed. Mirabeau had been elected president of the Assembly which prevented his participation in the debate. On 11 February a report on the rebellious atmosphere in Alsace had been made.[85] On 12 February, the date scheduled for discussion of tobacco, Delley d'Agier insisted that the debate be postponed for fear that the deputies would be influenced by the events in Alsace.[86] Roederer responded that Delley degraded the integrity of the Assembly by implying that the Alsatian situation could influence their decisions. Furthermore, the revolt in Alsace was not the work of the opponents but rather the supporters of the monopoly, that is, "the ecclesiastics and their adherents." With that remark Roederer won the Assembly to his view and was permitted to make his third report on tobacco, which reiterated the opposition of the committee to the monopoly and again proposed free cultivation, manufacture, and sale of tobacco with a régie exempt from import duties that would manufacture and sell foreign leaf for the profit of the nation. This project, in the interest of providing higher revenues, did include proposals for licensing the manufacturing and sale of tobacco.[87] However, it lowered the proposed tariff duty from 50 to 40 livres per quintal as a

---

[82] AN 29AP85 H. Desmarest, *Derniers observations sur l'impôt du tabac.*

[83] AN 29AP85 Municipal officers of Strasbourg to the National Assembly, February 1791.

[84] AN 29AP85 Commissioners of the king to Duportail, 1 February 1791. The committee of commerce of Strasbourg also sent two more députés extraordinaires to Paris for lobbying purposes. AN 29AP85 "Extrait des registres du comité du commerce de la ville de Strasbourg," 1 February 1790.

[85] AP, 23: 173. Jacob Price argues that the Tax Committee was anxious to have its proposals considered with Mirabeau in forced silence and uneasiness in the Assembly due to the situation in Alsace. There seems to be no reason not to accept this interpretation of events. *France and the Chesapeake,* 2: 826–27.

[86] AP, 23: 142–43.

[87] Ibid., p. 149.

concession to the American trade interests and the tobacco manufacturers. Roederer estimated that the project would yield revenues of 8 million. He denied that Mirabeau's proposed monopoly would be able to yield over 14 million for the next two years or 20 million after that. After a lively debate the Assembly voted for the establishment of free cultivation and manufacture of tobacco.[88] In the following days the details of the new system were worked out. The Assembly lowered the import duty to 25 livres per quintal (with a 25 percent deduction for tobacco shipped in French vessels), established a régie to produce tobacco to be sold for the profit of the nation, but refused to exempt the régie from the 25 livres import duty. Also the proposal for taxing the processing and sale of tobacco was abandoned.[89] The tax monopoly was dead, and the pro-monopoly forces and the American interests were defeated.

With the defeat of the tobacco monopoly Roederer almost immediately sought the total abolition of the General Farms. Since the Assembly had voted a virtual end to all of the functions of the Farms, "you will be able from the 1st of April to terminate the appointments of the general farmers and régisseurs."[90] He realized that the Farms' accounts would have to be settled and the general farmers ought to be compensated for this activity, but "this rendering of accounts ought not to be a means of prolonging their appointments." This same attitude dominated Roederer's thinking about the stock of goods of the Farms that now became the property of the nation. Accusing the agents of the Farms of delay in the sale of the nation's property in order to perpetuate their positions, Roederer suggested that all goods in the warehouses of the Farms be sold within a year. "In immediately suppressing the warehouses," he said, "you will deny the General Farms all pretext of delay in the rendering of its accounts. As long as the warehouses remain, the warehousemen (entreposeurs) will want to perpetuate their existence."[91] In response to a query concerning the employment of the former employees of the Farms, Roederer said that the only place in the new regime for them was the position of customs agent. Furthermore, he expressed little sympathy for the plight "of this multitude of armed men who depopulated our countryside and consumed a part of our public revenues."[92] On 8 March Roederer even proposed the abolition of the régie which had been created to manufacture and market foreign tobacco.[93] The tobacco factories were to be leased and tobacco on hand

---

[88] Ibid., p. 153. On a procedural issue the Assembly voted 372 to 360 in favor of the Tax Committee. This vote indicated the slim margin of victory for the Committee on the tobacco question.

[89] Ibid., pp. 162–67, 173–75. William Short demonstrated his disgust with the results in a conversation with Gouverneur Morris where he referred to Roederer as a "Rascal." Morris, *Diary of the French Revolution,* 2: 147.

[90] AP, 23: 670.

[91] Ibid.

[92] Ibid., p. 672. Earlier Roederer had expressed more sympathy for the agents of the Farms, but this may simply have been a means of bolstering his case for a régie to manufacture and sell foreign tobacco. Ibid., p. 174.

[93] Ibid., p. 735.

was to be sold for 35 sous per pound if processed and 12 sous if unprocessed. Without an exemption from the import duties on tobacco the régie would have had little competitive advantage over the private manufacturers. Apparently Roederer and the committee decided the nation would benefit more by ridding itself of these facilities than by managing a marginal operation. When the Assembly accepted this decree, the only function remaining to the old administration of the tobacco farm was to sell its inventories.

The correspondence that Roederer received after the abolition of the Farms indicated a reluctance within the Farms to proceed as directed by the Assembly. For instance Roederer's charge that the employees of the Farms would try to perpetuate their positions was justified by the numerous mémoires of warehousemen citing reasons for the necessity of the continuation of their functions.[94] One wrote that if all tobacco were sold immediately shortages would develop and *"effervescenses populaires"* would follow. Another suggested that one or more manufactories remain in operation to provide high quality leaf for other European states. A petition from these warehousemen asked also for compensation for their losses associated with the reform. In order to justify the continuation of a régie, Lavoisier wrote Roederer that he did not think that the high prices of tobacco set by the Assembly could be maintained at auction as similar quality leaf could be had on the open market for considerably less.[95] Such prices could be charged only by retaining a régie to sell these stocks at retail as demand warranted over the course of time. Interestingly enough, the warehousemen had been arguing that the price set by the Assembly was too low for them to make a decent commission on sales.[96] Roederer seems to have been immune to these pleas. There is no record of his addressing any of these problems in the Assembly. When Lavoisier made a simple request for assurances of payment of salaries for employees of the Farms in Paris who were engaged in selling the remaining tobacco, Roederer somewhat contemptuously ignored Lavoisier's desire for "a prompt decision."[97] There is little doubt that Roederer viewed the institution of the Farms, the general farmers, and the employees with great disdain. The sooner the nation was done with the whole operation the better off it would be.

This attitude toward the General Farms provides an important clue to Roederer's motivation in striking down the proposals for a tobacco monopoly. He could hardly have favored the continuation of privileges in Flanders and Alsace after working so hard before 1789 to destroy them in Lorraine. He might have had some sympathy with fellow manufacturers

---

[94] Various mémoires from these entreposeurs are found in AN 29AP85.

[95] AN 29AP85 [Lavoisier] to Roederer, 12 April 1791; [Lavoisier], "Mémoire sur la vente des tabacs appartenu à la Nation."

[96] AN 29AP85 "Mémoire pour les entreposeurs du tabac," 12 April 1791.

[97] AN 29AP85 Lavoisier to Roederer, 27 April 1791; Lavoisier, Untitled mémoire on the salaries of employees of the Farms; Lavoisier to Roederer, 3 May 1791.

trying to maintain their existence, but he had turned a deaf ear to the pleadings of the more numerous paper manufacturers that the stamp tax would ruin them. Nor could he have found the idea of a régie in the abstract repulsive since he had brought about the creation of one for the stamp tax and had supported a limited régie for tobacco. Yet his speeches and actions do demonstrate considerable hostility to the General Farms and farmers. The monopoly would have to adopt the practices of the Farms to be successful, and the general farmers as individuals probably would have some role in the enterprise. Roederer was certainly aware of the subtle pressures the general farmers tried to exert on him in the early stages of the controversy. Even more impressive was the preponderance of material submitted to the Tax Committee in favor of the monopoly by general farmers or administrators of the Farms.[98] Very little in the way of support came from other sources. Naturally most of the mémoires and petitions opposing the monopoly came from the tobacco interests of the privileged provinces, but these frankly admitted that the decision on tobacco would have a great effect on their fortunes. The information supplied by the general farmers claimed to support the monopoly in the interest of the revenues of the nation, but it would not be unlikely for Roederer to make the assumption that they also had their own pecuniary interests at heart. These men were not well known for their selflessness.

The destruction of the tobacco monopoly was a product of the Tax Committee's efforts to revolutionize the tax structure of France by rooting out all vestiges of the despised General Farms. Jacob Price has argued that the tabacs only became a question of revolutionary principles in 1791.[99] While this assessment may have some validity for the Alsatians or Dupont de Nemours, it is not applicable to Roederer nor the majority of the Tax Committee. From the first Roederer perceived it to be an issue of great relevance to the principles of the Revolution. Price alleges that Roederer allied with the tobacco interests because he was from Lorraine, but Lorraine was not one of the privileged provinces.[100] Actually his alliance with this opposition was undertaken because it offered him the best hope of defeating the monopoly. Then by presenting the issue to the Assembly in terms of revolutionary principles of liberty and property he was able to muster a bare majority in the Assembly to accept his proposal. Clearly the revenues that the nation might derive from the monopoly could not be as valuable as the destruction of an institution, the General Farms, which was so characteristic of the past and so antithetical to the postrevolutionary future.

The financial problems of the Monarchy at the end of the ancien régime necessitated some reform of the Treasury. As J. F. Bosher has so ably demonstrated, the monarchial finances had long been handled by private

---

[98] The General Farms had demonstrated no interest in the stamp duties over which they had lost control in 1780. Matthews, *The Royal General Farms*, p. 79.

[99] Price, *France and the Chesapeake*, 2: 828.

[100] Ibid., p. 801.

accountants who, operating essentially as financiers rather than government officials, came under little administrative supervision.[101] Efforts to reform the financial system had begun during the last years of the ancien régime but had not been completed before the Revolution. Those who had been anxious to achieve such a reform before 1789 now dominated the Finance Committee and considered a plan for a reorganized Treasury able to deal efficiently with the Monarchy's financial problems.[102] An essential feature of the Finance Committee's thinking was that a properly functioning system of public finance would have to be under the direct control of the executive branch of the government. Hence, when Lebrun reported for the committee on 11 December 1790, he proposed that the control of the Treasury should lie with an *ordonnateur général* appointed by the king and responsible for all financial operations including the oversight of taxation.[103]

Roederer and the majority of the Tax Committee, however, fearing that monarchial control of the Treasury would permit too much opportunity for abuse, reacted to the plan of the Finance Committee with alarm. On 20 December Roederer presented a counter-proposal for the organization of the Treasury which would leave it independent of the executive. This project was voted out of the committee by virtually the same members (La Rochefoucauld, Dauchy, Defermon, D'Allarde, and Jary) who had supported Roederer in the tobacco question.[104] However, Talleyrand, who had voted to abolish the tobacco monopoly, now joined the more conservative members of the committee led by Dupont in refusing to support Roederer's Treasury project. While no papers on the Treasury are to be found in his files, there is no reason to doubt that Roederer was the author as well as the reporter and principal defender of this proposal.

In support of his project Roederer argued that the "financial powers are essentially distinct and separate from other political powers" and that it would not be wise to unite "the supreme administration of finance with the supreme exercise of the executive power."[105] In Roederer's view proper public finance was not a means of facilitating government operations so much as a method of conserving the Constitution. If the executive controlled the Treasury and its associated functions, the king could more easily usurp the sovereignty of the nation and the Constitution. A vital part of public finance was the collection of indirect taxes. If the executive replaced the General Farms as the collector of these taxes, abuses were likely to follow. For instance if the executive named the officials in charge of this collection, the monarch might be able to become independent of the Assembly. Through vigorous collection methods excess revenue could be collected, and the executive could utilize these funds without authorization of the legislature. Similarly if the collection procedures were too

---

[101] J. F. Bosher, *French Finances 1770–1795: From Business to Bureaucracy* (Cambridge, 1970).
[102] Ibid., p. 226.
[103] AP, 21: 378.
[104] Ibid., p. 586.
[105] Ibid., pp. 579, 583.

lax, the executive would once again be forced in a search for credit to call upon the old "crowd of financiers," those "apostles of arbitrary power." By controlling the collection of indirect taxes, the executive would in effect have control of public expenditures leaving the Assembly powerless. Furthermore, if the king named the employees of the agency controlling these taxes, he would have "at his disposition a very numerous and redoubtable army" which could be utilized to weaken the Constitution. Roederer referred to the English example where the executive had control of such offices and was able "to corrupt the legislator and even the electors" by offering administrative posts in exchange for political support. He asked his fellow deputies to consider "how the multiplicity of places of finance in France will be able to win it [the executive] votes." The result would almost certainly be a corrupt legislature which could neither control abuses nor bring about a reform of public finance.

The committee's project was designed to make public finance an agency for the defense of the Constitution. Their plan called for the creation of one or more régies for the collection of indirect taxes with the régisseurs being named by the Assembly at the end of its session.[106] The treasurer and general administrators of the Treasury were also to be elected by the Assembly at the end of its session and from outside its membership. The king's representative in the Treasury would be a *commissaire* with a consultative voice. This plan would assure the Assembly control over the Treasury and the related function of the collection of indirect taxes. The king's position allegedly would be unchanged since there would merely be a substitution of a national council and a commissaire of the king for the old royal council of finances under a minister. The new system would even increase executive power in some ways: "The orders of this minister (commissaire) will have more weight in the departments, his authority will have greater respect. The executive will only lose the power of abuse."[107]

When the discussion on the Treasury resumed in March 1791, Lebrun reported the Finance Committee opposed Roederer's project because it violated the concept of separation of powers.[108] Lebrun argued that the legislature had the duty to oversee the conduct of the executive. If the legislature assumed executive duties such as the appointment of officials, the people would have no agency to protect them from oppression. The people might forgive the monarch for making a poor choice of officials but would be less likely to forgive the legislature which was supposed to represent their interests. The project of the Tax Committee, therefore, offered a serious threat to the functioning of the Constitution. Lebrun was supported in the debate by Dupont of the Tax Committee, who argued that a minister of the Treasury would be unable to act in an arbitrary fashion under the Constitution. However, if the deputies named the ad-

---

[106] Ibid., p. 586.
[107] Ibid., p. 585.
[108] Ibid., 23: 736–37, 745, 748.

ministrators, they would create, "a political monster" free of executive control and irremovable for the two years the legislature would sit. D'André claimed that if the king did not control the Treasury there would be a confusion of powers and "there will no longer be a Constitution."

The issues that Roederer had raised in December, however, struck a responsive cord among the radicals of the Assembly who were anxious to limit the king's power, and in the March debate they made their suspicions of the king entirely clear. Roederer repeated his argument that executive control of the Treasury would open France to the same sort of corruption that existed in England where the government sold places for votes and would increase the likelihood that France would once again find itself in need of the services of the financiers. "It is to prevent the corruption of all the branches [of government]," he said, "that we do not want the revenue to leave the hands of the nation."[109] Certainly these funds should "not be accumulated in hands that are suspect." Pétion charged that the Finance Committee's plan would revive "an absolutist minister of finance." Given the "plundering committed by the minister of finance" in the past, Pétion asked his colleagues how they could again entrust a single individual with this task. The Finance Committee's plan should be defeated, according to Robespierre, because it placed too much faith in "the intrigues of the court." Despite these arguments the Assembly, apparently concerned with the constitutional issue of separation of powers, supported the Finance Committee by voting to have the king name the administrators of the Treasury. The deputies were influenced by the concerns of the radicals, however, to the point where they were unwilling to establish a Ministry of the Treasury as requested by Lebrun. Instead they created a committee of six which would be independent of all ministries and responsible to the legislature.[110]

The Tax Committee continued its efforts to limit executive influence in the collection of indirect taxes. Here Roederer was successful in convincing the combined Committees on Taxation, Agriculture and Commerce, Finance, and *Domaines* to accept the Tax Committee's views on the organization of the régies of indirect taxes. In the report that he made to the Assembly in the name of these committees he stressed the necessity of avoiding ministerial despotism in the collection of these impositions.[111] Reiterating his fear of executive abuse in the distribution of the 18,000 positions in the régies, Roederer insisted that the Ministry could not be allowed total authority over these agencies. On the other hand he clearly perceived that allowing the elected local officials to collect the indirect taxes would be dangerous since these officials, more concerned with pleasing the local electorate than fulfilling their national duty, would not be "animated by the *esprit de perception* necessary to assure the [required] revenues." The solution to this problem was to establish régies at least

---

[109] Ibid., pp. 743, 745, 746, 748.
[110] Ibid., 24: 8–14; Bosher, *French Finances,* 229.
[111] AP, 25: 255–59.

partially independent of executive control in the collection of indirect taxes and to require that all funds collected be turned over to the tax receivers of the districts. This plan would have the advantage of a professional agency to collect revenues which could then be safeguarded from executive abuse by elected officials.

In order to limit the monarchial influence and yet satisfy the Assembly's desire that all executive appointments be made by the king, Roederer introduced an ingenious scheme for the appointment of the officials of the tax collection agencies.[112] There were to be two régies, one for the collection of the stamp and registration taxes and the other for the collection of the customs duties. The king was to have the right to choose the régisseurs généraux but was limited in his choice to those already holding high administrative positions within the régie. The minister of public contributions was permitted to fill the second level of administrators from candidates named by the régisseurs, and all other employees of the régie were to be chosen by the régisseurs. The minister could propose the dismissal of the régisseurs, but this dismissal could only be effected in consultation with the six commissaires of the Treasury. The legislature was to be informed of the appointment of the régisseurs. By thus limiting the monarch's freedom of appointment and dismissal, Roederer clearly intended to limit executive control of the régies as well as to prevent the king from creating a party through the distribution of offices.

The Assembly was basically willing to accept his scheme for the nomination of the régisseurs, administrators, and employees of the régie.[113] However, Lanjuinais, Regnaud de Saint-Jean d'Angely, and Le Chapelier argued against the consultation of the commissaires of the Treasury in the dismissal of the régisseurs on the grounds that this was a ministerial responsibility. Roederer remained convinced that this provision was necessary if the executive influence was to be limited, and he tried to salvage this point by presenting it in a variety of forms. In the end, however, he had to give way and allow the king the right to remove the highest officials of the régie on the advice of the régisseurs alone.

There was also opposition to the other major provision of Roederer's project; namely, the placement of all funds collected by the régies with the tax receiver of the districts. Both Dupont and Pierre de Delley argued that these receivers were not familiar enough with the intricacies of the indirect taxes to be charged with the care of these revenues.[114] Roederer responded that the funds of the nation could not be left in "the suspect hands" of the royal appointees of the régies.[115] Placing these revenues in

---

[112] Ibid., p. 260.
[113] Ibid., pp. 666–68. The Assembly, however, did insist that the minister could not be distinguished from the king and decreed that the king would appoint both régisseurs and high level administrators.
[114] Ibid., pp. 672–74.
[115] Ibid., pp. 674–76.

the *caisse* of the district along with the direct taxes would have three distinct advantages. First, the collection of indirect taxes would be made thoroughly public as it had never been under the General Farms. Second, the tax receivers, who had made much profit from the transfer of funds by letters of exchange from their caisses to the Treasury and on the payment of funds to state creditors, would not be able to continue their *jeux de fonds*. If the funds were not transferred to the Treasury but remained in the departments, no speculation could be made on such funds in transit. Instead the state's creditors within that department would be paid from the local caisse. Also the use of assignats instead of letters of exchange would end the speculation in public finance. Third, the utilization of district receivers would complete the reform of indirect taxation as it was as necessary to employ new men as new laws in bringing about a reform in public service. Accepting this reasoning, the Assembly voted that all revenues from the indirect taxes should be placed in the district caisses.

The passage of the decree on the régies for indirect taxation ended Roederer's work on the Tax Committee. His achievement here was a solid one. He had molded the committee into an instrument of revolutionary reform, nipping in the bud Dupont's efforts merely to reform monarchial institutions. He had persuaded the Assembly to accept most of his revolutionary proposals which were responsible for much of the destruction of the financial system of the ancien régime and its transformation from a private to a public enterprise. Finally, through the organization of public finance he was able to limit the independence of the monarch in the national interest.

Roederer's achievement on the Tax Committee reinforced his view of the Revolution as an opportunity to destroy privilege and establish rational institutions designed to meet the needs of the nation. With the success he had in accomplishing his goals, he naturally believed the Revolution could eventually reach the goal of wholly reforming France. Using his own work as an example, he had every reason to think that effective political action could bring the desired result even from a diverse body like the Constituent Assembly. In sum Roederer's efforts to reform France's financial system did nothing to diminish in his eyes the promise the Revolution held for the revitalization of the nation.

IV. RADICAL POLITICS IN THE
CONSTITUENT ASSEMBLY

Roederer's faith in the possibilities for good government offered by the revolutionary political process, a fact confirmed by his success on the Tax Committee, was tested but not destroyed by the constitutional questions raised in 1791. Roederer's financial reforms had demonstrated his commitment to revolutionize totally France's institutions; and when the king's flight to Varennes dramatically increased the doubts about his trustworthiness, Roederer quickly allied himself with the radicals determined to save the Revolution. The radicals of the Assembly in 1791, caught between the Feuillants advocating compromise with the monarch and the crowds demanding dethronement, opted for defense of the Constitution as the sign of their revolutionary ardor. While this temporarily appeased the crowds and the Jacobin Club and seemed to confirm the value of parliamentary debate, the seeds of Roederer's ultimate disillusionment with the revolutionary assemblies and crowd action were sown at the very point of his greatest political popularity. We must now turn to Roederer's concern with the constitutional questions before the Assembly in order to trace the development of his radicalism and its relationship to the Revolution.

Roederer suffered from a significant political disadvantage when he entered the National Constituent Assembly in November 1789, six months after the first meetings had been held in May. The patriots had undergone a number of stiff challenges in defying the king's authority, supporting the popular revolution, and making certain basic decisions about the new Constitution. Roederer had no part in any of these early revolutionary activities. He joined the Assembly after political alliances and enemies were already formed. The patriot deputies had no idea where he stood on such important issues as the creation of an upper house, the granting of a royal veto, the degree of popular suffrage to permit the citizenry.

If Roederer was to make a mark in the Assembly, he would have to overcome this initial disadvantage. He believed that his entrance into the Assembly was "preceded by [my] reputation for citizenship and talent," a claim which may contain some truth given his role on the Committee of Thirty and in the municipal revolution in Metz.[1] Nevertheless, Roederer was anxious to identify himself quickly as a patriot on the floor of the Assembly. His opportunity came on 17 November when he joined the attack on his own sovereign court, the Parlement of Metz, which had protested the Assembly's decision to keep all the parlements on vacation

---

[1] P.-L. Roederer, *Notice de ma vie pour mes enfants,* in OR, 3: 278.

status until a new judicial system was established.[2] He believed his characterization of the Parlement's protest as "a reprehensible act" convinced his colleagues that they should consider him "among the most energetic patriots in the Assembly."[3] During the remainder of 1789 and early 1790 Roederer spoke in favor of many reforms supported by those who called themselves patriots. He suggested church reform, calling into question the continuation of the monastic orders and proposed reducing the number of bishops by combining two departments into a diocese.[4] For judicial reform, he along with Robespierre, Barnave, and Charles Lameth supported the use of jury trials in civil as well as criminal cases.[5] He opposed any royal interference in the nomination of judges which could only lead to the reestablishment of the "old despotism by the most abominable means, the corruption of justice."[6] He even recommended giving civil status to Jews and placing their lives and property under the protection of municipal authorities.[7]

More indicative of Roederer's political views were his statements on matters of suffrage and representation. In Metz he was known for his democratic opinions on these issues, but in the Assembly he was not quite so consistent. He did attack the creation of the *marc d'argent*, the heavy tax required for eligibility for election to the Legislative Assembly. This, he argued, "excludes citizens who do not have wealth, but who have talents and virtues; it excludes the fathers of truth, of justice, of liberty . . . . Rousseau [if subjected to such a tax] would not [have been] able to sit among you." In particular "your decree spurns the artisans, this species of men so useful [and] so respectable. . . ."[8] Undoubtedly many in the Assembly agreed with Adrien Duquesnoy that Roederer's remarks were full of "exaggerations."[9] Yet Roederer was not the democrat he at first appeared. His defense of the political rights of the working class did not include those who earned "only a rigorous subsistence" and who therefore should "be put outside the rank" of those eligible to vote, let alone serve in office. This attitude distinguished him from the extreme democrats like Robespierre, who in refusing to let such an opinion remain unchallenged,

---

[2] AP, 10: 70, 83–84; Edmund Seligman, *La Justice Pendant la Révolution* (Paris, 1901), 1: 220–23.

[3] Roederer, *Notice*, in OR, 3: 278.

[4] AP, 11: 575; AP, 16: 43. Interestingly enough he opposed the low salaries suggested for bishops. AP, 16: 408.

[5] AP, 12: 579–80; Georges Michon, *Essai sur l'histoire du parti Feuillant: Adrien Duport* (Paris, 1924), p. 154.

[6] AP, 15: 416–20.

[7] AP, 13: 76–77. Roederer had earlier interested himself in the plight of Jews and had organized an essay contest in the Royal Society of Metz in 1785 on the question *Est-il moyens de rendre les juifs plus utiles et plus heureux en France?* in OR, 7: 597–600; Arthur Hertzberg, *The French Enlightenment and the Jews* (New York, 1968), pp. 324, 332–33. In 1788 Malesherbes asked Roederer for his assistance in trying to ameliorate the condition of French Jews. Roederer to Father, 18 April 1788, in OR, 7: 636.

[8] AP, 10: 415.

[9] Adrien Duquesnoy, *Journal*, ed. Robert de Crevecoeur (Paris, 1894), pp. 141–42.

insisted that "the right of citizenship is a natural right which all members of a political society ought to enjoy. . . ."[10]

This disagreement with Robespierre over the nature of citizenship raises the interesting question of Roederer's place within the political alignments of the Assembly. Ever since the defeat of the *monarchiens* on the issue of the upper house and the royal veto, the leadership of the patriots had resided at the Jacobin Club under the direction of the radical Triumvirate: Alexander Lameth, Barnave, and Duport. Apparently anxious to be associated with the true patriots, Roederer had joined the Jacobins and even became one of the secretaries in June 1790.[11] From the first, however, he does not seem to have been active in the society. There is no record of his speaking there during 1789 or 1790, and in the summer of the latter year he deserted the club to join Lafayette's more moderate Society of 1789, which had been formed to counter the growing influence of the Triumvirate.[12]

Roederer's motives for entering the Society of 1789 can only be surmised. There is some indication that Roederer was not entirely happy with the leadership at the Jacobins. He once wrote that he left that club in 1790 because it "was filled with ambitious schemers," an apparent reference to the Triumvirate.[13] Roederer is known to have had some disagreements over tax policy with Duport, a member of the Tax Committee and part of the minority in that body opposed to Roederer's tax projects. It is possible that friction developed between these two in the committee and led Roederer to spurn Duport's leadership at the Jacobins. Furthermore, La Rochefoucauld, whose chairmanship of the Tax Committee made Roederer's alliance with him a necessity, had entered the Society of 1789.[14] Very likely La Rochefoucauld encouraged Roederer to join him in the new association.

Whatever benefits Roederer had expected to reap from his membership in the Society of 1789 did not materialize. As has been demonstrated, Roederer's own thinking had become progressively more radical in the matter of taxation during the course of the year 1790. In order to achieve his goals in the tobacco tax and the organization of the Treasury he would need the support of the radical element of the Assembly, which was only to be found at the Jacobins. Accordingly by 15 February 1791 he had reentered the club where he defended his tobacco project before its membership.[15]

Roederer's return to the Jacobins did not result in a reconciliation with Duport, Barnave, and Lameth. The decision of these men in the spring

---

[10] Roederer developed this point during the debate in October 1790 on the tax to be paid by active citizens. AP, 19: 771.

[11] Alphonse Aulard (ed.), *La société des Jacobins: recueil de documents pour l'histoire du club des Jacobins de Paris* (Paris, 1889–97), 1: Lxxx.

[12] Roederer to the Society of Friends of the Constitution of Metz, August 1791, in OR, 7: 602; Albert Mathiez, *The French Revolution*, trans. Catherine Phillips (New York, 1964), p. 78.

[13] Roederer to the Society of Metz, in OR, 6: 602.

[14] Mathiez, *French Revolution*, p. 78.

[15] Aulard, *Jacobins*, 2: 88.

of 1791 to accommodate the king in order to acquire his sincere acceptance of the Constitution only enhanced Roederer's distrust of them. When the Triumvirate began to advocate increasing the authority of the monarch and limiting the influence of the populace in order to make the Constitution more attractive to Louis XVI, Roederer and others in the Jacobins saw this as a crude scheme to acquire personal power. Therefore, during the spring Robespierre and Roederer sought very definite limits on the Ministry, since they feared the Triumvirate would soon be appointed to it.[16] To prevent these men from dominating the next Assembly, Robespierre proposed that no deputy to the Constituent be eligible for reelection to the Legislative Assembly.[17] Pétion, Barère, and Roederer extended this reasoning by suggesting that members of the Legislative Assembly should not be allowed indefinite reelection either.[18] Roederer was responsible for halting the Triumvirate's attempt to deny the right to serve as deputies to all those who worked for wages and were, therefore, considered dependent on another individual.[19] Thus by June 1791 the radicals were no longer associated with the Triumvirate but were now united in their desire to prevent these men from compromising the accomplishments of the Revolution in order to reach an agreement with Louis XVI. Roederer was clearly a member of this informal radical coalition.

The attempted flight of Louis XVI to the border on 20 June created problems for the moderates and radicals alike. The moderates had hoped to stabilize events and end the Revolution by putting the Constitution into effect. The radicals hoped to limit the monarchial power and potential for royal abuse by placing certain safeguards in the Constitution. Louis XVI had foiled both plans by fleeing the capital and denouncing the Revolution in the memorandum he left behind. Neither the Triumvirate nor the radicals had considered a Constitution without a monarch.[20] Barnave soon took the lead in arguing that the constitutional monarchy must be maintained to avoid anarchy. The majority of the Assembly rallied to this position basically trying to ignore Louis's flight altogether by passing it off as a kidnapping. The radicals were less willing to be tolerant of Louis but were uncertain as to exactly what path to take. Even Robespierre did not pronounce for a republic.

Roederer, caught just as much by surprise as his colleagues, only gradually and incompletely responded to the threat Louis's action had posed for the Revolution. On 22 June Roederer was able to express his indignation while remaining neutral on the king's responsibility by calling for the arrest and provisional dismissal of General Bouillé who was to have met Louis at the border with support troops.[21] On 24 June Roederer, assigned to investigate how Louis had obtained a passport in the name

[16] J. M. Thompson, *Robespierre* (New York, 1968), 1: 124–25; AP, 24: 691.

[17] Thompson, *Robespierre*, 1: 134–35.

[18] Roederer favored allowing a deputy to be reelected for one term only, the formula eventually adopted. AP, 26: 209, 214.

[19] AP, 27: 78–9.

[20] See especially Thompson, *Robespierre* 1: 156–60; Mathiez, *French Revolution*, pp. 129–30.

[21] AP, 27: 426.

of the Baroness de Korff, reported that Minister of Foreign Affairs Mont-
morin was innocent of any complicity in the affair.[22]

Roederer's attitude became clearer on 25 June when the Constitution
Committee proposed that the king be taken to the Tuileries and "provi-
sionally given a guard which, under the orders of the commanding general
of the Parisian National Guard, will attend to his safety and will be responsible for his person."[23] Malouet, claiming that the measure actually
called for the imprisonment of the inviolable person of the king, was
indignant. Roederer responded to Malouet that the inviolability of the
king had yet to be defined. Did it cover only "acts of the administration
of the state" or did it extend to personal activities such as "connivance
with enemies of the state."[24] Actually in the present circumstances Roederer argued "it is neither a question of judging nor accusing the king,
it is a question of holding him in a provisional state of arrest. . . ." He
could not finish his statement because of the turmoil that erupted in the
Assembly when he used the word "arrest." Thouret, the reporter for the
Constitution Committee, objected that it was not a question of arrest.
Many deputies demanded that Roederer be called to order, and it was
some minutes before the Assembly could be quieted. Quickly retreating,
Roederer retracted his language and somewhat lamely explained that he
had misunderstood the intention of the Committee's proposed decree.
However he insisted that the Committee's decree in calling for the protection of the king from the nation's wrath did not go far enough. "As
for myself," he said, "I ask that the decree have two purposes and at the
same time preserve the nation from the king."[25] The Assembly did agree
to accept this definition of the king's confinement.

The ultimate fate of Louis was a far thornier problem than that of his
immediate disposition. The talk of dethroning him, an idea circulating in
the Paris clubs, involved a number of imponderables. If the Constitution
was to be maintained, who would be regent during the minority of Louis's
young son? The king's brothers as émigrés were unacceptable, and the duc
d'Orleans was not entirely trustworthy. If a republic was established, what
would happen to the Constitution and how would war with the Austrians
and civil war within France be avoided? When these issues were discussed
at the Jacobins on 29 June, Anthoine charged that Louis, in leaving Paris,
had made war against the Constitution. Henceforth it would be necessary
to guard him as a prisoner, and "a prisoner is not able to be head of the
executive power of a great empire."[26] The king must be dethroned and
a regent named. Roederer suggested that a regent could be chosen from
another family, or better yet a council of regency could be formed "then
one would have a regency without a regent." In elaborating on this idea

---

[22] Ibid., p. 488.
[23] Ibid., p. 517.
[24] Ibid., p. 518.
[25] Ibid., p. 519.
[26] Aulard, *Jacobins*, 2: 566.

he said, "This system would have the advantage of soon establishing a great truth, which is that having had a very good regency without a regent it would also be possible to have a very good monarchy without a monarch."[27] Roederer assured the society that he was anxious to retain the Constitution but asked if it was possible for the Constitution to remain in existence. Charles Lameth with a ready answer to this question responded that Roederer's suggestions were a threat to the reputation of the Society of Friends of the Constitution as well as incompatible with the principle of hereditary monarchy.

Roederer's remarks at the Jacobins were symptomatic of the radical position. Reluctant to accept a consitutional monarchy with a treasonous king, they still shied away from declaring openly for a republic. Vainly wishing there were some way to maintain the Constitution but get rid of the king, the left remained ambivalent and indecisive. Robespierre, for instance, announced that he was neither a republican nor a monarchist.[28] The talk of a regency came to no conclusion, and none in the Jacobins were willing to lead the growing republican movement found at the Cordelier Club. The left searched desperately for a solution to this dilemma, but none presented itself.

With the leadership of the left uncertain as to how to proceed in light of the king's conduct, the Cordeliers began to organize popular support for the dethronement of Louis XVI. Popular petitions and demonstrations resulted in mid-July after the Assembly had exonerated Louis of all responsibility for the flight to the border. On 15 July a large crowd entered the Jacobins asking the Club to join with them in taking a petition demanding the dethronement of the king to the Champ de Mars. The Jacobin Club initially favored the petition; but upon learning that the Assembly had voted to reinstate the king upon his acceptance of the Constitution, they withdrew their support. The populace, unwilling to be bound by the decision of the Assembly or the Jacobins, presented their petitions on the Champ de Mars where they were finally dispersed with some bloodshed by the National Guards on 17 July.[29]

The events of July had serious repercussions for the Jacobins. Disassociating themselves entirely from the movement for the dethronement of the king, the Triumvirate and its followers withdrew from the club. They believed it had encouraged the populace with its initial acceptance of the petition and created a rival society meeting at the Feuillants. Only the most uncompromising radicals from the Assembly remained with the Jacobins: Robespierre, Pétion, Buzot, Royer, Coroller, and Roederer.[30] These deputies were the most distrustful of the king and his advisers in the Assembly, the Lameths, Barnave, and Duport. They were also the only deputies who might be considered true patriots by the populace of Paris.

---

[27] Ibid., p. 568.
[28] See Thompson, *Robespierre*, 1: 158–59; Mathiez, *French Revolution*, pp. 129–30.
[29] Aulard, *Jacobins*, 3: 19, 42; Mathiez, *French Revolution*, pp. 130–31.
[30] Michon, *Duport*, p. 271.

While these men were very distrustful of the king and the Triumvirate, their support of democracy was more equivocal. After the schism the major issue in the Jacobins was to clear the reputation of the club from the taint of having denounced the Assembly's decree regarding the king and fostering the popular demonstrations on the Champ de Mars. The address written by Robespierre and sent to the Assembly in the name of the society on 20 July was designed to assure the deputies of the club's respect for its decrees and to disassociate it from the events on the Champ de Mars.[31] Pétion, meanwhile, was working to bring the deputies at the Feuillants back to the Jacobins and urging action to prevent the affiliated societies from declaring for the Feuillants. Thus concerned with the preservation of the Jacobins, neither man came to the defense of the crowd of 17 July.[32]

The other deputies remaining in the club were considerably less active than Robespierre and Pétion. Coroller and Royer are on record as at least having attended the meetings of the society in the last half of July, but Buzot and Roederer did not take part in the proceedings.[33] Roederer's last known appearance at the Jacobins was on 15 July when he, Robespierre, and Pétion entered the hall to the sound of warm applause from the membership.[34] He had intended then to speak against the dethronement petition but the crowd entered the club and disrupted the proceedings.[35] His relationship with Robespierre and Pétion immediately after the schism is unknown, but apparently no contemporary observer placed Roederer among those few deputies remaining at the Jacobins. All of the evidence suggests that Roederer, uncertain of the course to follow after 17 July, merely ceased attending the Jacobins without withdrawing from the club.[36] However, by early August he decided to remain with the society. His standing in the club does not seem to have been impaired by his absence for on 1 August he was placed on a committee with Pétion, Brissot, and Buzot to help Robespierre rewrite an address he was preparing to send to the affiliated societies.

Roederer revealed his motivation for remaining in the Jacobins on 5 August when he read to the Parisian society his letter addressed to the Friends of the Constitution of Metz in an effort to prevent it from affiliating with the Feuillants. In it he described the events in the club on 15 July. He told the society of Metz that when the question of the petition for dethronement was raised he had been prepared to speak against it on the

---

[31] Aulard, *Jacobins*, 3: 23–44.

[32] Ibid. See also Thompson, *Robespierre*, 1: 161–63.

[33] Aulard, *Jacobins*, 3: 14–64. These pages cover the proceedings in the society from 15 July through 1 August 1791.

[34] Ibid., p. 16.

[35] Roederer to the Society of Metz, in OR, 6: 593–97.

[36] Roederer was not on the July list of the Feuillants. Augustin Challamel, *Les Clubs contre-révolutionnaires: cercles, comités, sociétés, salons, reunions, cafés, restaurants, et librairies* (Paris, 1895), pp. 286–93. For Roederer's reappearance at the society see Aulard, *Jacobins*, 3: 65, 70.

basis of the principle "that representative government was established to remedy the impossibility of a common deliberation between all members of a great society. . . ."[37] He was prevented from making these remarks due to the influx of the crowd demanding that the club join with the Cordeliers in presenting such a petition. Roederer argued that when the club agreed to this proposal most of the members had already left, and those present were greatly outnumbered by non-members. In effect the decision was not made by Jacobins at all but rather by the crowd which intruded on the session. If this was the case, why had so many members withdrawn from the club to form the Feuillants? Roederer argued that the schism was the work of "schemers" who wanted to compromise the goals of the Revolution in order to win favor with the king. According to this view,

One of the ways by which they expect to achieve the success of their views is to destroy the Societies of the Friends of the Constitution in the realm. . . . The blow given to the Jacobins and the creation of a new society at the Feuillants has no other object.[38]

He charged that those responsible for the schism were the followers of Alexander Lameth and the members of the Society of 1789, two opposing factions which had formed a coalition to achieve their aims. Roederer said: "It is only ambition which created the parties; it is intrigue that moves them; that is what excites the one against the other; that then is what unites them."[39]

Roederer's political concerns after 17 July were similar to those of Robespierre and Pétion. He did not rally to the defense of the club as quickly as they, but by early August he was exerting some effort to limit the effects of the schism on the network of affiliated societies. Like his colleagues he was unwilling to support the popular movement which had led to the events on the Champ de Mars. He was anxious to disassociate the Jacobins from the petition offered by the Cordeliers on 15 July. Perhaps the most interesting issue is the reluctance of these deputies to respond more radically to events. Roederer had hinted at the necessity of a republic; Pétion was one of the principal defenders of the Jacobin Club; and Robespierre was known to be a friend of the people. Yet, these men had been put on the defensive by the Assembly's decree authorizing the reinstatement of the king upon the completion of the Constitution. Was it proper for the Jacobins or the crowd to question the will of the nation as represented in the Assembly? Obviously none of these men thought so. The events from the flight of the king to the Massacre of the Champ de Mars had thrown the left into a quandary. Without having developed the idea of truly revolutionary government that was to come after 10 August 1792, they were unable to deal effectively with the crisis. To attack the monarchy

---

[37] Ibid., p. 69; Roederer to the Society of Metz, in OR, 6: 595.
[38] Roederer to the Society of Metz, in OR, 6: 600.
[39] Ibid., p. 604.

or the will of the Assembly was to attack the Constitution, the implementation of which was the goal of the Revolution.

This perplexing situation gave the left few alternatives for action.
Outnumbered in the Assembly and prevented by their scruples from an
outright attack on the Constitution or an alliance with the Parisian crowds,
Robespierre and Pétion bent their efforts to the salvation of the Jacobin
Club as the meeting place for the true friends of the Constitution. Roederer,
initially less certain of what course to follow, eventually came to the same
conclusion. His particular contribution to this effort was to develop the
theme, first advanced by Brissot in the *Patriote française* but basically ignored in the formal proceedings of the society, that the schism was the
result of a conspiracy of corrupt men anxious to appease the king.[40] A
conspiracy theory, an ever-popular explanation for events in the Revolution, permitted Roederer to help the left regain some of its lost mo-
mentum by offering an interpretation of recent occurrences that shifted
responsibility from the Jacobins to their political enemies. By attacking the
Triumvirate instead of the Constitution, Roederer could paint a picture
of unpatriotic conduct which freed the Jacobins of any liability for the
events of mid-July.

Once the Jacobins had regrouped and definitely disassociated themselves from republicanism or popular democracy, they envisioned their
role to be that of defenders of the Constitution that had gradually developed since 1789. The Feuillants, however, anxious to cajole Louis XVI
into accepting the Constitution in good faith, wanted to introduce certain
modifications which would strengthen the monarch's power. Since the
Committees of the Constitution and Revision under the influence of the
Triumvirate were in charge of presenting the constitutional decrees to the
Assembly in August, the left had no choice but to react to their proposals.
The Jacobins were united in their opposition to these revisions, but there
seemed to be little attempt made to coordinate their attacks on the committees' projects. Each member of the left responded to the decrees which
interested him most. In some cases the personal predilections of individual
members prevented the radicals from presenting a united front in the
Assembly. Roederer's principal interests were those he had developed the
previous spring; namely, setting firm limits to the executive power. The
attempt of the Feuillants to augment that power merely increased his
suspicion of their motives for action.

Roederer's initial response to the Feuillant offensive came on 10 August
when the reporter Thouret read the proposed article on the public powers
which stated that "the French Constitution is representative; the representatives are the legislative body and the king."[41] Roederer immediately
objected that the king "does not have a representative character . . . the
concepts of heredity and representation are incompatible. . . ."[42] Rep-

---

[40] Selections from *Le Patriote français* are provided in Aulard, *Jacobins*, 3: 50, 60.
[41] AP, 29: 323.
[42] Ibid.

resentatives should be chosen only by the process of election. If this process was undermined, the safeguards against "all usurpation of the legislative power" would be destroyed. Nevertheless, Roederer did think it important that representation not be limited to the deputies in the assembly. If the only representatives of the nation were those sitting in the legislature, the government would be no more representative than it had been under the ancient French or present English constitutions. It was essential that the king's administrators also have a representative character. Administrators responsible to the nation and not the king would be unlikely to undermine the Constitution. During the debates on the Treasury he had made his position clear on this issue, and it was to this example that he again referred. Tax collection should be handled by administrators elected by the people, and the activities of the Treasury should be supervised by the legislature.[43] This arrangement would prevent the king from arbitrarily interfering in the administration of public finance.

Yet the Constitution defined the executive power as that delegated to the king and "exercised under his authority by the ministers and other agents" without reference to this representative character of administrators. Was there any obstacle to the next legislature's merely revising the statutes governing the collection of taxes? Hyperbolizing, Roederer argued that the next legislature could go so far as "to re-establish the intendants or any other such magistrates for the collection of public funds" and thus remit the control of finances to the agents of the king.[44] To prevent such an occurrence, the concept of representative administration must be placed in the Constitution where it would be protected from legislative alteration. He proposed an article defining the sovereignty of the nation as lying in the "representative powers and the commissioned powers which are for the most part exercised by citizens named by the people." Within such a framework "the executive power is essentially commissioned." Murmurs emanating from the Assembly after this statement caused Roederer to remark that "it would be unfortunate if interpretations of republicanism threw disfavor on my proposal."[45] Yet there was a kind of republicanism behind this project since its intent was to prevent the king from exercising complete authority over his administrative personnel.

Roederer's project was doomed to failure. Thouret easily convinced the Assembly that the proposal was at best redundant since the Constitution provided for the election of local administrators. Even Roederer's colleagues on the left provided little support. Robespierre firmly backed the contention that the king could not be considered as a true representative of the people, but he seemed totally to have misunderstood the real intent of Roederer's project, an executive more dependent on the people than the monarch.[46]

---

[43] Ibid., p. 324.
[44] Ibid., p. 325.
[45] Ibid.
[46] Ibid., p. 326.

The radicals were more united on the issue of the qualifications needed to serve as an elector. Originally the Assembly had declared that those paying the equivalent of ten days' wages in taxes could be chosen electors. On 11 August Thouret reported a proposed revision which would require the payment of forty days' wages in taxes for electors.[47] The committees did agree to drop the payment of marc d'argent as a requirement for legislators. The democrats found this dramatic increase in the financial requirements for electors to be quite unacceptable. Pétion said he would rather retain the marc d'argent than disqualify so many from the right to serve as electors.[48] Robespierre, ever the purist, insisted on the repeal of the marc d'argent and all requirements for service as elector, while Roederer, already on record as opposing the marc d'argent, attacked the committees' project because it was an attempt to alter the already existing constitutional decrees.[49] He argued that the emphasis of the new regime on direct instead of indirect taxes would allow more individuals to qualify for the legislature even with the requirement of the marc d'argent. More willing to accept the marc d'argent than to see the Constitution altered, he thus demanded "that the Constitution remain just as it is."[50] Buzot followed Roederer's lead in arguing that the Constitution should remain unaltered and noted the irony in the situation which caused "those so long accused of republicanism [to be] the first to fight for the maintenance of the Constitution as it stands."[51] From this point the proceedings became rather tumultuous. Barnave attempting to speak was shouted down by the extreme left. Roederer proposed a point of order that "there be no more discussion on the Constitution." Barnave, finally obtaining the floor, objected that Roederer's motion was only a means of opposing the committees' project and should be ignored, advice readily accepted by the Assembly. The decree revising the qualifications for electors then won the deputies' approval.

The battle between the Feuillants and Jacobins continued on 13 August when Saint-Martin called for placing in the Constitution the 7 April 1791 decree prohibiting deputies from the Constituent Assembly from serving as the king's ministers. Thouret, speaking for the committees, opposed this suggestion since it would be "a profound error to designate executive power as the enemy of the public welfare and the national liberty."[52] Duport, offering the major defense of the committees' decision to allow former deputies to serve as ministers, told the Assembly to do otherwise would merely make the executive the foe of the Constitution. The nation would consist of supporters of the executive and those of the legislature, a division that would be disruptive to public tranquility.[53] Furthermore,

---

[47] Ibid., p. 357.
[48] Ibid., p. 358.
[49] Ibid., p. 361.
[50] Ibid.
[51] Ibid., p. 365.
[52] Ibid., p. 399.
[53] Ibid., p. 402.

allowing former elected officials to serve as ministers would bring popularity and exerience into the executive. The principal opposition to the committees on this matter came from Roederer who countered Thouret's and Duport's reasoning with the argument that the main concern was to bring to the law "the profound respect of the people who ought to obey it."[54] Only such respect, which should be "a sort of public religion," could insure the stability of the Constitution. The only way to win this respect was "to demonstrate to the people that no personal interest is able to affect or control the legislators." The people, however, will always fear that the legislators are corruptible if the executive is able to obtain from the legislators "the condescension to its views by the promise of superior and even inferior employment. . . ."

Since the previous spring Roederer had been concerned that the French political process would come to resemble that of England, where the desire for government places had helped create a court party. If the ministers were allowed to be chosen from the deputies, "it would necessarily form two parties in the legislature, the party of the opposition [and] the party of the Ministry. . . ."[55] The inevitable result in the Assembly would be that "intrigues [and] tactical maneuvers would replace wise and enlightened discussions." In England, where this system reigned supreme, "the laws made by the parties are regarded as trophies of some victory won not by truth over error, by reason over prejudice, but by Fox over Pitt or by Pitt over Fox. . . ." Since all observers agreed that England's "fall is certain" unless its constitution was reformed, Roederer saw no reason for France to follow in her footsteps. He professed to be unconcerned about the arguments of Thouret and Duport that without allowing deputies to become ministers the executive and the legislature would be in constant opposition to one another. By far the greater danger lay in "an opposition of cupidity" which would result in attacks on the Ministry by deputies anxious to achieve those places for themselves.[56] In addition the Assembly had to recall the character of Louis XVI whose activity since his flight made it even more important to preserve in appearance and actuality legislative independence from the king.[57] The constitutional exclusion of deputies from the Ministry for a four-year period was the only means of preventing the next legislature from abolishing the practice.

The concept of exclusion was by this time so well established in the Assembly that the Feuillants were unable to overcome the opposition to their proposal despite the pleas of Thouret and Duport. By themselves Roederer's arguments were enough to carry the day for the radicals. The final form of the article, however, was a compromise formula suggested by Buzot for a two-year exclusion instead of the original four.[58] Neverthe-

---

[54] Ibid., p. 404.

[55] "Observations par M. P.-L. Roederer sur le observation des comités de constitution et revision prononcées dans la séance du 14 [i.e. 13] août par M. Thouret," in AP, 29: 438.

[56] AP, 29: 404.

[57] "Observations par M. P.-L. Roederer," p. 440.

[58] AP, 29: 405.

less, the exclusion of deputies from the Ministry was one of Roederer's and the left's great victories in August 1791.

The Committees on the Constitution and Revision also hoped to strengthen the powers of the government by applying limits to the freedom of the press. On 22 August Thouret presented the constitutional articles on the press, the first of which prohibited the publication of material which encouraged "disobedience to the law, the debasement of the constituted powers, and the resistance to their acts. . . ."[59] Robespierre, the first to object to this article, insisted that only those who formally provoked disobedience to the law be prohibited from publishing their material. Furthermore, only private persons, not public officials, should be able to sue for slander. Pétion specifically objected to the prohibition against "the debasement of the constituted powers" which might be applied to any publication critical of the government. Even Barnave believed the article limited freedom of the press too severely. Roederer joined this chorus of opposition by calling for a prohibition on any prior censorship and the deletion of the phrase concerning the debasement of the constituted powers, which would prevent all criticism of the government by the press. Despite these arguments the article was carried basically as written by the committees.[60]

On the following day Thouret presented a second article on this topic which called for the prosecution of individuals who willfully slandered a public official or questioned his integrity in the performance of his duty.[61] Pétion and La Rochefoucauld adopted Robespierre's suggestion that slander apply to private but not public actions. Thouret defended the necessity of protecting public officials from willful attacks on the motivation which lay behind their official conduct. At this point Roederer made a passionate attack on the motives of the committees:

This [article] is the last blow given to liberty; it reserves for the new ministers the right of oppressing the remainder of the liberty left to us. When Voltaire wrote against the abuses of the parlements, he would have been punished as a slanderer if he had been judged by the law that you propose. This is a ministerial coalition that we have to foil.[62]

Murmurs punctuated Roederer's remarks, and D'André asked if all individuals should have the right to slander public functionaries. Amid the tumult in the chamber Roederer shouted: "It is inconceivable. They are interested in shielding the Ministry from criticism when they occupy it. They demand an inviolable Ministry because they want to be there. Liberty is killed."[63] During Roederer's harangue the Assembly was in a great uproar with constant demands being made to bring the speaker to order. D'André charged that Roederer's conduct had become "insupportable."

Roederer also caused a disturbance in the Assembly on 1 September

---

[59] Ibid., pp. 631–35.
[60] Ibid., p. 639.
[61] Ibid., pp. 645, 646, 654.
[62] Ibid., p. 655.
[63] Ibid.

during the debate on the manner of presenting the Constitution to Louis XVI, who upon his acceptance of the document would be restored to monarchial power. Robespierre first took the floor to remind the deputies that the safety of the nation required that they watch the king very carefully as they had no "more certain guaranties of his personal dispositions [nor] of those of the men around him than before the previous 21 June."[64] He also emphasized the danger from the enemies assembled on the border who had found allies among the false friends of the Constitution. Roederer was also very much concerned with the fate of the Revolution once power was restored to Louis. The previous evening at the Jacobins he had urged the passage of a decree requiring the king to remain within twenty leagues of the legislative body.[65] Following Robespierre to the tribune, Roederer told his fellow deputies that the restoration of the king to his functions necessitated his revealing that the defenses in Thionville on the northeastern border were not in the state of readiness the Military Committee and the minister of war had claimed.[66]

After Robespierre's accusations that France's enemies at the border had found allies among false friends of the Constitution, Roederer's remarks seemed to charge the Military Committee and the minister of war with treason or at least serious negligence. Roederer's attack on the Constitution Committee prompted members of the Military Committee and the moderate deputies in general to quash immediately his almost certain assault on them. Le Chapelier, one of the committee members, said that Roederer had provided him with this information three weeks earlier, so the news was hardly recent. According to Le Chapelier Roederer had interrupted the order of business only "to throw alarm into the *esprit du peuple*" and "to trouble the public tranquility."[67] Again the Assembly was thrown into a turmoil with many members calling for the order of the day and charging Roederer with creating an incident within the chamber. Roederer was only able to manage the remark, "this is an injustice," before being silenced.[68] In a written apologia later presented to the Assembly, Roederer justified his attempt to present the report as germane to the discussion of the king's resumption of power.[69] Within the context of Robespierre's statement, it was certainly relevant to the issue at hand; namely, the trustworthiness of the king and his associates. The moderates, however, were in no mood to have Roederer again questioning their motives in the blunt language which had characterized his recent speeches. Hence, they rapidly moved to have him declared out of order.

Roederer's conduct in the Assembly after 1 August was not inconsistent

---

[64] Ibid., 30: 138–39.

[65] Aulard, *Jacobins*, 3: 109.

[66] AP, 30: 139.

[67] Ibid., pp. 139–140.

[68] Interceding on Roederer's behalf, La Rochefoucauld did convince the Assembly to listen to Roederer the next day. However, the matter was not revived in the chamber. Ibid., p. 140.

[69] "Détails relatifs à l'observation concernant l'état de la ville de Thionville par Roederer," in AP, 30: 141–43.

with that which had preceded the flight of the king. From late 1790 much of Roederer's activity had been an effort to limit the executive power. After the king's flight and the events of July, Roederer became more intense and less restrained in his efforts to achieve this goal. Circumstances no longer permitted the kind of compromises the Assembly had arranged before June 1791. In the August debates over the Constitution Roederer was often spokesman for his Jacobin colleagues pleading with the Assembly to maintain the Constitution. When these tactics met with little success, Roederer distinguished himself from the other radicals by charging that there was personal corruption within the ranks of the Committees on the Constitution and Revision and hinting at treason within the Military Committee. These histrionics brought no change in the outcome of events in the Assembly but did identify Roederer in the minds of the deputies as one of the most passionate and intemperate of the radicals. In the Jacobin Club his deportment in the Assembly led directly to his election as president of the society.[70] As one of the few deputies remaining in the Jacobins, and as one of only four (Pétion, Buzot, and Robespierre being the other three) who took a major part in the defense of the Constitution in August, his election as president was quite natural.[71] The passionate manner in which he attacked the Feuillants made him the logical choice to follow Pétion and precede Brissot in that post. His conduct in the Assembly also brought him a measure of popularity in Paris. If the Marquis de Ferrières is to be believed, Robespierre, Pétion, and Roederer were the only leaders from the Assembly who still enjoyed the confidence of the Parisian populace at the close of the Constituent Assembly.[72]

Interestingly, Roederer's popularity was indicative of the peculiar political situation which existed in France in the late summer of 1791, namely that patriotism was measured more in negative than positive terms. For the Jacobins patriotism was equated with distrust of the king and the Feuillants. As noted, the radicals were at first unsure how to respond to both the king's flight and the threat this presented to the Revolution. They had been unwilling to adopt the tactics of the Parisian crowd and fell back on the defense of the Jacobin Club and the Constitution as the only means of demonstrating their hostility to the policy of the Triumvirate. Actually, the true radicals were not to be found in the Assembly at all but rather among the crowds who had demanded the dethronement of the king and threatened the destruction of the Constitution. The determination of the left in the Assembly to maintain the Constitution was almost bound to put them onto a collision course with the radicals in the street. Those, like Roederer, who were resolved to support this Constitution long after it became unpopular to do so, would find themselves quickly abandoned by the Revolution.

---

[70] His election on 31 August preceded the incident with the Military Committee. Aulard, *Jacobins*, 3: 107.

[71] Michon, *Duport*, pp. 286–343 chronicles the Jacobin defense of the Constitution.

[72] Charles-Elie, Marquis de Ferrières, *Mémoires*, ed. Berville and Barrière, 2nd. ed. (Paris, 1822), 2: 413.

V. THE ADMINISTRATION OF THE DEPARTMENT OF PARIS

By the end of 1791 Roederer had reaped great profit from the Revolution, but this reward was not financial. He satisfied himself with merely recovering the purchase price of his office in the Parlement of Metz and investing in some small vineyards in the nationalized church lands in the Trois Evêchés.[1] Politically, however, he had made a name for himself as a leader of the patriots, and he was eager to continue his public career. Barred from serving in the Legislative Assembly because of the self-denying ordinance passed by the Constituent Assembly, he chose to stand for election to the post of *procureur-général-syndic* of the department of Paris, an office which would continue to give him some influence in affairs and allow him to remain close to events in the capital. As procureur-général-syndic Roederer had the misfortune of presiding over the enforcement of constitutional law in the capital when the crowds were appealing to the higher law of the Revolution. This experience as an administrator during the revolutionary turbulence of 1792 eventually destroyed Roederer's faith in the ability of the Revolution, as it was developing, to provide rational government for France.

When Roederer had made himself available for election in late 1791, however, both he and the other patriots were very excited about the prospect of his serving as procureur-général-syndic. In the contest for this position Roederer's work in the Constituent Assembly had earned him the support of the Jacobin Club and the progressive departmental electors who met at the Club de l'Evêché.[2] The conservative electors who met at the club of the Sainte Chapelle supported the candidacy of D'André. The election, like that for the mayor of Paris which was to follow, was thought to be a significant indication of the political strength of the Jacobins and, therefore, generated much enthusiasm. On 11 November 1791, the day of the election, Brissot's *Le Patriote français* announced that even some

---

[1] AN 29AP9 Memorandum on the liquidation of Roederer's office of conseiller in the Parlement of Metz. This document shows that he received 33,413 livres in compensation for the office for which he had originally paid 32,000 livres in 1779. Roederer bought vineyards with a total selling price of 21,525 livres from the lands of Saint Clement and Saint Symphorien, the latter lands were where his father had served as bailli and juge. René Paquet, *Bibliographie analytique de l'histoire de Metz pendant la Révolution* (Paris, 1926), 2: 1268, 1274.

[2] P.-L. Roederer, *Notice de ma vie pour mes enfants*, in OR, 3: 282; Alphonse Aulard, ed., *La Société des Jacobins: recueil de documents pour l'histoire du Club des Jacobins de Paris* (Paris, 1889–97), 3: 242; Frédéric Braesch, *La Commune du dix août 1792: étude sur l'histoire de Paris du 20 juin au 2 décembre 1792* (Paris, 1911), p. 34.

members of the Sainte Chapelle club were scandalized by D'André's candidacy and would vote along with the patriots for Roederer.[3] After the announcement of the results of the election in which Roederer triumphed 285 to 202 votes, there was general jubilation in the Jacobins.[4] When Roederer appeared before the applauding membership, he characterized his election as a victory for the society and promised to continue in his new office to seek the advice of the club.[5] Condorcet's *Chronique de Paris* happily proclaimed that Roederer's election gave great satisfaction to patriots while *Le Patriote français* declared that the "cabal" which had backed D'André had been foiled.[6]

Roederer's election stimulated further interest in the contest for the mayoralty of Paris. Manuel, himself elected as procureur of the municipality, urged that the members of the Jacobins work hard to secure the election of Pétion to the position of mayor because "you know that M. Roederer has always been attached to M. Pétion," and it would not be wise to separate "these two men who have always served us so well."[7] *Le Patriote français* believed Roederer's selection "gave hope to the friends of liberty" that the mayor of Paris would be distinguished by "his virtues and his patriotism," a clear reference to Pétion.[8] When Pétion was victorious, the significance of the event was felt as far away as Edinburgh. A certain James Hall wrote Roederer from Scotland that "your elevation [to office] and that of your friend Pétion is a great triumph in the cause of freedom."[9]

In actuality offices in the departmental administrations seemed ill-suited as platforms for the display of revolutionary zeal.[10] The administrative structure of the departments set up by the Constituent Assembly called for a departmental Council of 36 members, a departmental Directory composed of 8 members chosen from the Council, and a procureur-général-syndic. All the members of the departmental administration were elected for four-year terms of office. The departmental Council was to meet once a year to establish the work and expenses for the coming year, and the Directory was to carry out the prescribed activity during the course of the year. In practice the main duties of the department concerned the assessment and collection of taxes. The procureur-général-syndic's duties were limited strictly by the Constitution. He was responsible for the ex-

---

[3] *Le Patriote français*, 11 November 1791.

[4] Aulard, *Jacobins*, 3: 242; Sigismund LaCroix, *Le Département de Paris et de la Seine pendant la Révolution* (Paris, 1904), p. 36. There seems to be no evidence to support Mathiez's contention that Roederer secured this position through the efforts of Lafayette. Albert Mathiez, *The French Revolution*, Catherine Phillips, trans. (New York, 1964), p. 134.

[5] Aulard, *Jacobins*, 3: 245.

[6] *Chronique de Paris*, 11 November 1791; *Le Patriote français*, 14 November 1791.

[7] Aulard, *Jacobins*, 3: 244.

[8] *Le Patriote français*, 14 November 1791.

[9] AN 29AP11 James Hall to Roederer, 27 November 1791.

[10] See John Hall Stewart (ed.), *A Documentary Survey of the French Revolution* (New York, 1951), pp. 132–35; and Jacques Godechot, *Les Institutions de la France sous la Révolution et l'Empire* (Paris, 1951), p. 98.

ecution of all laws and provided the only legal contact between the department and the central authority represented by the Ministry. Allowed only a consultative voice on the Council and Directory, he was permitted to speak regarding the department's legal obligations before any decisions were made by those bodies.

Once installed in office, however, Roederer was determined to make the most of his limited powers. He envisioned his position as one which would shape the policies of the Directory. As La Rochefoucauld had been chosen president of the Directory, Roederer could be expected to continue to influence the duc's thinking as he had on the Tax Committee. Furthermore, Roederer's knowledge and interest in the new tax structure established by the Constituent Assembly would provide added weight to his authority in both the Council and the Directory. The policies that he intended the Directory to implement were simply a continuation of those he had advocated on the Tax Committee; namely, the destruction of the ancien régime through the establishment and administration of equal taxation.

He made his position on taxation clear in his first report to the Directory on 5 January 1792.[11] He told the directors that they were legally obligated to collect not only the "contributions" of 1791 but also all direct taxes in arrears before that date. In Paris those arrears from 1786 to 1790 had amounted to 7,634,447 livres in direct taxes. In 1791 collections were even further behind with only a little over 1 million livres collected out of a total of nearly 21 million livres due. The examination of the registers of many tax receivers indicated that those who were not paying were largely former nobles and members of the privileged classes, "the declared enemies of the Revolution." Their failure to pay hurt the poor most severely since they relied on the salaries or public assistance provided for by taxes. Since "the public contributions are the patrimony of the poor," the rich had even more obligation to pay them, and their failure to do so only revealed "the secret of their hatred of the Constitution and equality." The departmental Directory's responsibility was not actually to collect the taxes, but rather to oversee the tax collection procedures of the municipality of Paris and the districts within the department. Since the arrears were so large, Roederer concluded that the tax receivers in Paris were remiss in their duties and urged the Directory, which quickly voted the required decree, to threaten with dismissal those receivers who failed to prepare their rolls properly or to issue writs to those in arrears.

An additional problem with taxation was a result of the Constituent Assembly's decision not to provide a district administration between the department and the municipality of Paris. This situation resulted in a certain amount of confusion regarding the execution of the district administration's functions in the collection of taxes. Both the department and the municipality claimed that they should assume the obligations of

---

[11] AN 29AP84 Département de Paris, "Extrait des registres", 5 January 1792.

the district. In his message to the Directory on 5 January Roederer had suggested that the responsibilities of the district administration, namely oversight of the collection of taxes in Paris, should be undertaken by the five member *comité contentieux*, a body whose principal function was to hear appeals of tax assessments.[12] This comité would have the same power of dismissing the municipal receivers and examining the tax rolls as would the district if one had existed. Only through such a procedure would the intended constitutional restraint be placed on the tax collecting operations of the municipality. The problem with Roederer's suggestion was that nowhere was such power for the comité contentieux specifically granted. However, by interpreting broadly the law of 5 October 1790 which allowed the departments to use the comité contentieux in a manner "useful to the service of the general administration," Roederer convinced the Directory that his proposal was legal and on 23 February the comité assumed the responsibilities of the district administration.[13]

The actual collection of direct taxes was to be undertaken by the sixteen arrondissements consisting of three sections each which had been established by the municipality in December 1791. Commissioners in charge of receiving the property declarations of the inhabitants of the arrondissement were to be named by the municipality as well as by the sections comprising the district. On 31 January the department established the regulations which were to be followed in the taking of these declarations, and it also provided printed instructions for the populace outlining the method for declaring their taxes.[14]

In early February Roederer took his case on taxation to the public in a letter placed in the *Moniteur* warning the readers that he planned to publish the names of the richest citizens whose taxes were yet in arrears.[15] In fact most of those who would appear on the list were members of the former privileged classes: dukes, barons, parlementaires, and financiers. These were to be made examples before the public since it was worse for the rich not to pay their taxes than for the poor. When the first list appeared on 21 February, it contained the names of the comte de Provence, the king's brother, and other members of the nobility.[16] The list proved to Roederer that there was still "power attached to titles" which was incompatible with "the political rights of simple citizens." On 7 March he defended in the *Moniteur* the publication of the names of delinquent taxpayers despite the criticism that it was a "list of proscription" or a "list of slanders."[17] Denying that he was only concerned with attacking the nobility, he made the promise, which he never kept, of publishing a similar

---

[12] Ibid.

[13] AN 29AP84 Département de Paris, "Extrait des registres," 23 February 1792.

[14] AN 29AP84 Département de Paris, "Extrait des registres," 31 January 1792; AN 29AP84 *Avis aux citoyens sur les contributions.*

[15] MU, 9 February 1792, 11: 330–31.

[16] MU, 21 February 1792, 11: 424–27.

[17] MU, 7 March 1792, 11: 557. This letter also corrected some errors in the 21 February list which Roederer said had been the fault of the tax receivers.

list of delinquents from the Jacobin Club. Instead he returned to his attack on the wealthy by threatening to publish a list of physicians, bankers, and négociants who had failed to obtain their *patentes*.[18]

Concerned not only that the wealthy pay their taxes but also that the poor not be burdened with a tax load beyond their means, Roederer reported to the Directory of the department on 15 March that artisans were paying too much tax on their workshops.[19] The *contribution mobilière*, a tax on non-landed property, generally was levied on the basis of the entire amount of rent paid for a dwelling, but in the case of such workshops it was assessed on the basis of one-third of the rent. Because the poorer artisans like wheelwrights needed very large workshops with high rents, he argued that their tax load was out of proportion to their incomes even though it was assessed on the basis of only one-third of the rent paid. As a result some artisans were ruined. By way of contrast he pointed out that some of the more well-to-do artisans such as jewelers required only small shops but still had their taxes assessed on the basis of one-third of the rent of their entire dwellings. His arguments persuaded the Directory to decree that those with special circumstances, such as the nature of their work or the number of their children, should make this situation known on their tax declarations.

These attempts of the Directory to control the tax collection procedures within the department of Paris were quickly challenged by the municipality. On 6 February it put into force only part of the Directory's decree of 31 January establishing the methods by which direct taxes were to be collected and specifically omitted the provisions allowing inspection of the tax rolls in each arrondissement by the comité contentieux.[20] On 27 February two tax commissioners for the municipality, Dacier and Tiron, instructed the commissioners in the arrondissements not to allow inspection of their tax rolls. In response Roederer denounced Dacier, Tiron, and the municipality before the Directory on 3 March. Having asked for but not having received an explanation of this matter from the Mayor Pétion, Roederer advised the Directory to overrule Dacier's and Tiron's directive.

Determined to bring the municipality into line with the law and the will of the department, Roederer charged the communal government with further improprieties on 15 March.[21] Each municipal government was permitted by law to add a surtax to the *contribution foncière*, the tax on real property, to meet local expenses if this surtax were first approved by the department. For 1791 the department had authorized the municipality to collect 1,800,000 livres from the surtax, but the municipality had actually collected 3,935,237 livres. Furthermore, the municipality had failed to place the names of many rich taxpayers on its rolls or to assess properly the value of royal buildings or the king's revenue including the civil list.

---

[18] MU 9 April 1792, 12: 74–75.
[19] AN 29AP84 Département de Paris, "Extrait des registres," 15 March 1792.
[20] AN 29AP84 Département de Paris, "Extrait des registres," 3 March 1792.
[21] AN 29AP84 Département de Paris, "Extrait des registres," 15 March 1792.

The fundamental problem, however, was the secretive and arbitrary procedures that prevailed in the tax bureau of Paris, still staffed by officials of the ancien régime. Instead of allowing citizens to make their declarations freely as provided by law, the tax officials of the municipality undertook a "clandestine census" of property and then refused to make the results public.[22] In addition they failed to inform the citizenry that they could deduct their payments for the contribution foncière from the amount due for the contribution mobilière. At Roederer's suggestion the Directory ordered the municipality to clean up its tax rolls for 1791 and 1792 and to conform to the procedures established by the department in January.

The municipality remained intransigent, however, and its Tax Commission instructed the committees in the arrondisements not to receive declarations from citizens for taxes due in 1791.[23] The quarrel was finally brought before the Legislative Assembly on 29 March by Pétion who charged that the department was trying to "destroy the municipal authority."[24] Pétion told the Assembly that the department had given undue power to the comité contentieux to carry out the responsibilities of the district administration regarding the collection of taxes. Specifically he cited as illegal the directives of the comité contentieux which ordered tax inspectors to examine the tax rolls in Paris. According to the laws of 20 and 29 September 1791 only the directories of the departments and not the comité contentieux could order inspectors into communes and then only if they were invited by the communal authorities or if the rolls were not up to date. Pétion said the municipality had not invited the inspectors and that delays in preparing the tax rolls were "inevitable" and did not warrant an inspection. In Pétion's view it was the municipality which should carry out the duties of the directory of the district regarding overseeing the inspectors. The mayor also complained that the department was intervening in the municipality's administration of public works, hospitals, colleges, houses of charity, and police. A further irritant in regard to the relationship of the two governmental bodies was the department's practice of publishing and circulating its decrees before informing the municipality of them.

When La Rochefoucauld and Roederer appeared in the name of the department before the Assembly on 3 April, the procureur-général-syndic read a report which attempted to justify the actions of the Directory. He maintained that the law of January 1790 required the department not only to administer the collection of taxes but also to supervise public works, hospitals, colleges, houses of charity, and police.[25] In regard to the comité contentieux, the department had assigned it the duties usually undertaken

---

[22] Roederer did soften this attack with the qualification that the municipality was undertaking a reform of its procedures. Nonetheless, the thrust of his message was that tax collection in Paris was not fulfilling the intent of the revolutionary legislation. Ibid.

[23] AN 29AP84 Département de Paris, "Extrait des registres," 31 March 1792.

[24] AP, 40: 681–82.

[25] AP, 41: 165–70. In referring to the law of January 1790, Roederer almost certainly meant that of 22 December 1789. See Stewart, *Documentary Survey*, pp. 135–36.

by the district administrations because Paris did not have such an administration. Specifically the comité was responsible for verifying and issuing writs of execution for the tax rolls of the contributions foncière and mobilière. Roederer did not believe that the municipality should handle this function since it had been responsible for preparing the rolls; and the comité, acting in the place of the district, was responsible for checking the municipality's work. An agency separate from the municipality was also necessary for collecting the patente as the Constituent Assembly had required that those applying for the patente make their requests to both the commune and the district. To allow the municipality of Paris to receive these requests by itself would defeat the purpose of the law, which was to double check the receipts from the tax. Roederer thought that the department had to take an active role in establishing the new taxes. He defended the visits of the members of the Directory and himself to the arrondissement committees to check their progress and encourage their efforts in assessing the taxes, and he argued that to have tried to work through the municipality in this instance would have been very inefficient.

Despite his vehement defense of the policies of the department and his attack on the position taken by the municipality, Roederer was careful not to charge his old political ally, Pétion, with misconduct. Instead he laid most of the blame for the obstinacy encountered by the Directory on the Tax Commission of the municipality. For instance he blamed the Tax Commission, which had opposed the Directory's reforms, with willful delay in passing on to the municipality the communications which it had received from the Directory.[26] To prove this charge he recounted an incident where the municipality had complained that they had not been informed of departmental decrees which were posted on the city wall on 3 April, despite the fact that he had sent Pétion notice of them on 26 March. The mayor had written Roederer on 28 March informing him that the notice of decrees had been turned over to the Tax Commission, where it then was obviously lost. Roederer blamed the entire misunderstanding between the municipality and the department on the Tax Commission. Its personnel, having remained unchanged by the Revolution, was trying to prevent the department from administering the tax reforms of the Constituent Assembly.

The Assembly voted to send the dispute to the Committees on Division, Finance, and Legislation which made a joint report on 16 June supporting the department's position. The Assembly did not vote on the issue at that time, and then the events of the summer prevented the matter from coming to any conclusion. Nevertheless, with the perspective of time Roederer's position appears quite sound. He understood his duty to be the establishment of the constitutional regime in the department of Paris. This was necessary not only to fulfill the law but also to consolidate the Revolution. By jealously guarding what it considered to be its prerogatives, the municipality was in a very real sense undermining the Constitution and the

---

[26] AP, 41: 168.

revolutionary settlement of 1791. Roederer, on the other hand, believed that the reforms of the Revolution could only be assured through adherence to the Constitution.

Somewhat ironically the more deeply Roederer became immersed in administering the revolutionary reforms in the department of Paris, the less revolutionary he appeared to the members of the Jacobin Club. There were a number of factors involved in Roederer's declining popularity within the extreme left. In the autumn of 1791 he became associated with the Girondin deputies who were at the time the most radical but who were soon to lose favor in the Jacobins. He developed an intense interest in the problems of administering the department of Paris, a subtle form of revolutionary activity that was little understood by the orators on the Rue Saint Honoré who preferred invective and vituperation to quiet accomplishment. Finally Roederer had a clear sense of strict obedience to the constitutional authority which rested on the revolutionary tradition. By the summer of 1792 faith in constitutional authority and the officials who supported it was replaced by the more powerful force of revolutionary authority which could override all legality including that established by the Revolution itself. Those who clung to constitutionalism, no matter what their record or accomplishments, could claim no place among the true revolutionaries.

In the autumn of 1791, however, Roederer was still considered a good revolutionary and his association with the Girondins could only strengthen this reputation. The most notable of the Girondins was J.-P. Brissot who was responsible for the popularity of the concept of a revolutionary war against Germany in order to deal a death blow to the counter-revolution. Roederer, attracted to Brissot's ideas, was soon echoing these sentiments for a foreign war. On 30 November he told the Jacobins that the "disguised enemies" of the Revolution within France, whom he identified as Feuillants, had joined forces with the émigrés to restore the nobility and end equality.[27] These enemies were trying to turn Frenchmen away from the Revolution by accusing the Jacobin Club and the administrative officers, such as the mayor of Paris and the procureur-général-syndic of the department, of leading the nation toward republicanism and anarchy. On 18 December Roederer, following Brissot's lead of a few days earlier, called for outright war against the émigrés.[28] In the existing state of affairs it was impossible to distinguish patriots from traitors, but open war would end this ambiguity as the internal enemies of the Revolution would hesitate to support the war fully. Furthermore, ending their petty quarrels, the patriots would join more closely together in order to defend the Revolution and even spread it to Germany.

Roederer's alliance with Brissot, so revolutionary in appearance in 1791, had made him a suspect patriot by the spring of 1792. Robespierre had

---

[27] P.-L. Roederer, Speech read at the Jacobins, 30 November 1791, in OR, 6: 616–18.
[28] P.-L. Roederer, Speech read at the Jacobins, 18 December, in OR, 6: 619–22.

distrusted the war policy of the Girondins since the end of 1791 and by early 1792 had created a split in the Jacobins between his supporters and those of Brissot.[29] Neither faction had complete control of the society, but debates were often heated with Robespierre's supporters attacking the Girondins. Roederer was drawn into these debates after being denounced by an unidentified member on 17 April for such a serious infraction of revolutionary demeanor as dining at the home of the Feuillant Jaucourt.[30] Collot d'Herbois joined the assault on Roederer's character charging that he did not have the required "uniform character" of a Jacobin. Specifically, Collot faulted Roederer for not preventing the department from sending Pétion instructions to keep order on the Sunday of 15 April and the following Monday when a fête was scheduled honoring the Swiss soldiers who had mutinied at Nancy in 1790. Interpreting such a directive as a "censure" of Pétion whom the department did not trust to do his duty, Collot argued that a true patriot and friend would have interceded on the mayor's behalf. This "crime" clearly indicated to Collot that Roederer "espoused the principles that you [the Jacobins] have condemned" and thus must have "chosen to be converted or has let himself be corrupted" with the clear result that now "he is corrupt."[31] Robespierre made the issue clearer to the society by criticizing the department for implying that assembly by the people was a criminal act which needed to be carefully watched by the magistrates.

When Roederer appeared to defend himself on 22 April, he denied having any political connection with Jaucourt, whom he rarely visited.[32] Regarding the fête of 15 April, Roederer said it was the Directory of the department, not he, who feared disturbances would accompany the celebration. In fact he had offered to assist in the ceremonies of the day, but affairs had kept him at home where he had to content himself with watching the proceedings from his balcony. Anxious to retain his revolutionary credentials, he reminded his listeners of his work with Robespierre and Pétion in preserving the society after the creation of the Feuillants. He also justified his recent absences from the club as necessary in order to fulfill his duties in the department, which were important to the course of the Revolution. After all, he argued, "what would you say of a soldier who would abandon his war in a perilous instant in order to go make some pretty phrases on the dangers facing *la patrie.*"[33]

This speech was well received and temporarily revived Roederer's standing in the Jacobins. The next day, however, Collot returned to the rostrum to reiterate the necessity of uncompromising actions on the part of true patriots and to imply clearly that Roederer did not act as a true

---

[29] M. J. Sydenham, *The Girondins* (London, 1961), pp. 107–09.

[30] *Journal des debats et de la correspondance de la Société des Amis de la Constitution séante aux Jacobins à Paris.* 19 April 1792.

[31] Ibid.

[32] *Journal des debats,* 24 April 1792.

[33] Ibid.

patriot should.[34] Roederer continued to be attacked before the membership on 25 April when Rabby charged that many were afraid to criticize Roederer "by their fear of having for an enemy M. procureur-général-syndic" while Collot announced that Roederer was "the figure-head of the entire coalition that I despise."[35] Responding to Collot's denunciation Roederer wrote open letters in the *Moniteur* and *Le Postillon de la guerre* announcing his intention of bringing suit against Collot for slander.[36] Robespierre in turn attacked Roederer in the Jacobins and in the *Defenseur de la Constitution* for his threat to prosecute Collot.[37] Thus by the end of April Roederer's revolutionary credentials were severely tarnished. What remained of his reputation was soon destroyed by the events of the summer of 1792.

The summer of 1792 was a turbulent one in France. The worsening economic crisis, the fear of invasion by the foreign powers, and the widely held conviction of the king's opposition to the Revolution led to unrest among much of the population of Paris and to the eventual overthrow of the Monarchy. During this period Roederer continued to carry out what he considered to be his duties as procureur-général-syndic, namely to enforce the laws and to support the Constitution. This brought him into conflict with the developing concept of revolutionary authority which could supersede the forms of constitutional government in defense of the Revolution. Roederer had faced this problem after the king's flight to Varennes and along with his colleagues in the Jacobin Club had taken refuge in a vehement defense of the Constitution itself. In regard to the crowds, which most graphically represented the revolutionary authority, Roederer had been unwilling to sanction their activity but had not actually called for their repression. As a magistrate responsible for maintaining order, Roederer was still unwilling to use actual force against the crowds, but he did urge the authorities not to encourage and actively to discourage all popular disturbances.

For instance, Roederer had never accepted the idea that the economic crisis could or should be solved by crowd agitation. On 22 January he helped the Directory draw up a condemnation of any attempts to remedy the high cost of sugar by *taxation populaire*.[38] He was responsible also for a departmental decree on 22 March which attempted to halt the practice in rural districts of armed bands searching for and forcing the sale of grain.[39]

He reacted to threats of political agitation in a similar fashion. Roederer requested the Directory of the department on 19 June to order the mayor,

---

[34] *Journal des debats*, 25 April 1792.

[35] *Journal des debats*, 27 April 1792.

[36] MU 26 April 1792, 12: 218. A copy of Roederer's letter in the first number of *Le Postillon de la guerre* can be found in AN 29AP6.

[37] Maximilien Robespierre, *Oeuvres complètes*, Gustave Laurent, ed., (Nancy, 1939), 4: 30.

[38] An 29AP62 Département de Paris, "Arrête," 22 January 1792.

[39] "Instruction des administrateurs du directoire et procureur-général-syndic . . .," in OR, 5: 555.

municipality, and the National Guard to prevent any illegal assemblies in connection with attempts by citizens to present a petition to the king and the Assembly on 20 June.[40] When it appeared that a demonstration was going to take place whether the municipality or the Directory sanctioned it or not, Roederer supported Pétion's suggestion, later refused by the Directory, that the crowd be accompanied by the National Guard to help keep order.[41] Having failed to prevent citizens from gathering, Roederer took it upon himself on 20 June to inform the Assembly of its duty.[42] He told the deputies that an armed group of citizens had gathered in defiance of the law in order to use force to present a petition to the king. Laws prohibiting such assemblages were designed for the "security of the legislative body" as well as the preservation of "general tranquility." Even if well-intentioned citizens were permitted to gather in such fashion, it would only set a precedent which could be utilized by the "secret enemies of the Revolution." Such crowds could not be dealt with in the future if the power of the law was weakened "by the National Assembly's condescending to receive armed multitudes into its midst."[43] In addition the Assembly should remember its obligation to do nothing that would diminish the "respect due to the powers which form the base of the Constitution."

Roederer's advice was not well received by the left, and the Girondins even encouraged the crowds to enter the Assembly on 20 June before moving on to the Tuileries.[44] Roederer's standing among the deputies fell even further the following day after sending a message to the Assembly that another crowd was threatening the king. Roederer had been told this by Terrier, Minister of the Interior, who had called Roederer to the Tuileries on the evening of 21 June to deal with this crisis. It was, however, not true.[45] When Roederer's message was read at the Assembly, it was greeted with widespread disbelief.[46] Kersaint, a Girondin, claimed that Roederer had been deceived by rumors of insurrection which had been spread by those who hoped to foment one. Delacroix, less charitable in his appraisal, asked the municipality to render a true account of the situation in order that the deputies might learn if "the procureur-syndic of the department was deceived or has deceived you." The Dantonist Thuriot hinted that

---

[40] Département de Paris, "Extrait des registres," 19 June 1792, in *Révue retrospective ou bibliothèque historique . . .*, seconde serie, (Paris, 1835–37), 1: 164–65; P.-L. Roederer, *Chronique de cinquante jours*, in OR, 3: 79.

[41] AP, 46: 447; Roederer, *Chronique*, in OR, 3: 80; Laura B. Pfeiffer, "The Uprising of June 20, 1792," *The University Studies of the University of Nebraska*, 12(1912): 50–52. Roederer did not really approve of this idea but could think of no reasonable alternative.

[42] AP, 45: 411.

[43] Ibid.

[44] Ibid., p. 412; M. J. Sydenham, *The French Revolution* (New York, 1965), p. 102.

[45] Terrier to the Directory of the department of Paris, 21 June 1792, in *Révue retrospective*, 1: 179; Roederer, *Chronique*, in OR, 3: 101. Actually the only "crowd" in evidence on that day was a group of citizens from the Halle aux Blès attempting to plant a liberty tree. AP, 45: 462.

[46] AP, 45: 456–62.

Roederer had sounded a false alarm purposely in an effort to attract a crowd at the Tuileries with the ultimate objective of producing another massacre like that of the Champs de Mars. Guadet, who was closely associated with Vergniaud and Brissot, agreed that the enemies of the people had planned another Champ de Mars but defended Roederer as one deceived by these enemies.

Roederer did not allow criticism in the Assembly to affect his performance in the department where he continued to work for the prevention of further popular disturbances. In a personal note on 21 June he urged Pétion to use his considerable influence with the Parisians to allow the king a certain amount of freedom of action to forestall another attempted flight from the city.[47] The following day Roederer wrote Pétion both in his official capacity as procureur-général-syndic and in a personal letter requesting the dismissal of Ramainvilliers, Commandant of the National Guard, for his ineffectiveness on 20 June.[48] Responding to a warning from the Minister of the Interior Terrier on 23 June, Roederer ordered that precautions be taken in the Faubourg Saint-Antoine to prevent the inhabitants from seizing the contents of the arsenal.[49] That same day Roederer again came under attack in the Assembly for his obsessive concern with public order.[50]

A vivid contrast to Roederer's attempt to maintain order in Paris was his defense of Pétion's conduct on 20 June. The Council of the department on 6 July had suspended Pétion and Manuel, the procureur of the municipality, for their failure to act more decisively on 20 June.[51] Roederer, however, had tried to prevent this suspension. He argued before the Council that Pétion had attempted to abide by the law but that events on that day were beyond his control.[52] The crowd could only be contained by the National Guard which proved to be ineffective. Furthermore, a severe repression would have been out of order as too many innocent people would have been hurt. When the crowd finally gained access to the Tuileries, Pétion exerted his influence to prevent harm coming to the king. Roederer clearly explained to the department that he was not condoning the events of 20 June which could only lead to divisiveness at a time when France needed unity to deal with its foreign enemy. All attacks, whether from the cannons of the Faubourg Saint-Antoine seeking to control the executive power or from the swords of generals (a reference to Lafayette) trying to influence the Assembly, could only hasten the creation of these

[47] Louis Mortimer-Ternaux, *Histoire de la Terreur 1792–1794* (Paris, 1863–1881), 1: 242.

[48] Roederer to Pétion, 22 June 1792, in *Révue retrospective*, 1: 188–89; Mortimer-Ternaux, *Terreur*, 1: 252–53.

[49] Terrier to the Directory and the procureur-général-syndic of the department of Paris, 23 June 1792, and Roederer to Terrier, 23 June 1792, in *Révue retrospective*, 1: 191–92.

[50] AP, 45: 508–09.

[51] AN 29AP103 Départment de Paris, "Extrait des registres," 6 July 1792; Mortimer-Ternaux, *Terreur*, 2: 42.

[52] AN 29AP103 "Rapport et conclusion de procureur-général-syndic du département de Paris relativement aux événements du 20 juin lu au conseil de departement 6 juillet 1792;" Roederer, *Chronique*, in OR, 3: 120–21, 126–27.

divisions. With so many threats to unity already present, a schism between the constituted authority of the municipality and the department would not be in the public interest.[53]

After the department's decision to suspend Pétion, Roederer, at the risk of losing his own position to the wrath of the department, published his defense of the mayor's conduct.[54] This defense was subsequently part of the case made for Pétion in the Assembly which overruled the department and reinstated the mayor.[55] The department Directory resigned in protest, but Roederer, quite satisfied with the final outcome of the affair, remained in office.

Roederer's support of Pétion can in part be explained by the friendship between the two which had developed in the last days of the Constituent Assembly. Carried through the departmental and municipal elections in the autumn of 1791, it continued into 1792. Roederer supported Pétion's efforts before the Legislative Assembly on 30 March 1792 to get immediate relief for those affected by the failure of the *Caisse patriotique de la Maison de secours* whose *billets de confiance*, private notes issued in exchange for larger denominations of assignats, were no longer negotiable.[56] Roederer publicly defended the mayor against charges made by Louis XVI that Pétion had acted unconstitutionally on 22 May in alerting the National Guard to possible public disturbances without informing the king of his actions.[57] More important as an indication of the nature of the relationship between the two men are Roederer's personal notes of 21–22 June which indicate that Roederer thought Pétion more susceptible to the advice of his friend than the directives of the procureur-général-syndic.[58]

Pétion, who was always primarily concerned with maintaining his own popularity, in actuality had done little to deserve this friendship.[59] He had failed to cooperate with Roederer in the proper administration of tax collection in Paris and had even gone so far as to take his case against the department to the Assembly. While Roederer was being attacked in the Assembly on 21 June for announcing that another insurrection was imminent, Pétion arrived at the Manége to report on events for the municipality, but said nothing in his friend's behalf.[60] The speech he made in Paris on 22 June to fulfill Roederer's request that he use his influence to increase the king's freedom of action was indecisive and trite.[61]

Why had Roederer remained so loyal to the mayor in the face of Pétion's self-centered conduct? By the summer of 1792 Pétion's "friendship" was

---

[53] AN 29AP103 "Rapport et conclusion."

[54] Ibid.; Mortimer-Ternaux, *Terreur*, 2: 43.

[55] AP, 46: 445: Roederer, *Chronique*, in OR, 3: 186.

[56] AP, 41: 8–9.

[57] MU, 25, 26, 31 May 1792, 12: 476, 484, 521.

[58] Mortimer-Ternaux, *Terreur*, 1: 242–43, 252–53.

[59] For an assessment of Pétion see Sydenham, *The French Revolution*, p. 102; Albert Mathiez, *The French Revolution*, p. 153; Pfeiffer, "The Uprising of June 20, 1792," pp. 236–49.

[60] Mortimer-Ternaux, *Terreur*, 1: 242.

[61] Ibid., p. 243.

the most visible remnant of Roederer's revolutionary reputation and connection with the Girondins. Though neither Pétion nor the Girondins were willing to offend the populace of Paris by preventing the popular demonstrations he so feared, Roederer was reluctant to discard the mantle of patriotism he had worn for so long. In reality, however, Roederer and the Girondins were moving along different paths. The Girondins were willing to use the unrest in Paris for their own political purposes whereas Roederer wanted an end to the popular disturbances which he saw as a threat to constitutional authority.

The *journée* of 20 June, of course, turned out to be only a prelude to the more decisive events of 10 August. Once again Roederer tried to prepare the departmental and municipal authorities to limit the effects of any popular disturbance. As early as 25 July he had warned the new Minister of the Interior, Champion, and Pétion that rumors of arms being collected at the Tuileries might be used as a pretext for disorders.[62] During the two weeks preceding the insurrection, Roederer made daily reports to the Council of the department about the steadily deteriorating situation in Paris, and he continually prodded Pétion to take the necessary precautions to prevent trouble.[63]

On the evening of 9 August Roederer was called to the Tuileries by the Minister of Justice Dejoly.[64] Here Roederer had the unenviable task of representing authority while lacking the means to enforce it. For most of the night of 9–10 August though he could hear the sounds of the toscin and the activity of the crowd through the windows of the chateau, Roederer could do little more than receive messages from Department Secretary, Blondel, as to the state of affairs in the city.[65] Even when word arrived that Manuel had ordered the removal of the cannon from the Pont Neuf, thus allowing the forces from Saint-Antoine and Saint-Marcel to unite, Roederer could only seek clarification of the report.[66] In response to the court's demand that he declare martial law, Roederer, ever the legalist, insisted such declarations were the responsibility of the municipality but retreated to the law books to check this point.[67]

Early in the morning Roederer suggested for the first time that the royal family seek refuge in the National Assembly—a proposal roundly condemned by the court.[68] He had to content himself with sending Dejoly and Champion to the Assembly to inform them of the situation at the chateau. When news came of the overthrow of the municipality by an

---

[62] Roederer to Champion and Roederer to Pétion, 25 July 1792, in *Révue retrospective*, 1: 324–25.

[63] AN 29AP105 Départment de Paris, "Extrait du registre du conseil général," 26 July–8 August 1792; Roederer to Pétion 8 and 9 August 1792, in *Révue retrospective*, 1: 337, 340.

[64] Roederer, *Chronique*, in OR, 3: 219. Roederer said he wrote his account of the events that followed his arrival at the Tuileries on the evening of 9 August the day after the insurrection "without adding or subtracting anything."

[65] Blondel's notes to Roederer are found in *Révue retrospective*, 1: 354–59.

[66] Roederer, *Chronique*, in OR, 3: 221–22.

[67] Ibid., pp. 220–21.

[68] Ibid., pp. 222–24.

armed uprising, Roederer again suggested taking the king to the Assembly, but was refused, and finally decided to report personally to the Assembly. On the way to the Manège he met Dejoly and Champion who informed him that no quorum was yet present. When the party returned to the Tuileries, Roederer told the National Guards on duty to fire upon the crowds which were beginning to arrive but only if they were fired upon first.[69] Upon re-entering the chateau, Roederer insisted that the royal family go to the Assembly. After meeting further protests from the king and queen, Roederer finally led the small procession in to the Manège.[70]

Meanwhile a quorum had been formed in the Assembly where a debate took place regarding the fate of the king.[71] When news arrived that the king was on his way to the Manège, the deputies voted to invite him to the session and Vergniaud, the president, met Louis in the garden and offered him asylum.[72] Once in the Assembly Roederer informed the deputies that the department had no other recourse than to bring the king into their midst, and he asked them to protect Louis in the name of his children, the law, and France.[73]

With the possible exception of his assistance in the coup d'état of 18–19 brumaire, Roederer is best remembered for his decision to conduct Louis XVI to the Assembly. Royalists condemned him for delivering the king to his enemies and thus hastening the collapse of the Monarchy.[74] Republicans, on the other hand, believed he betrayed the Revolution by interfering with the desires the people manifested on 10 August. When the insurrection came, Roederer was already suspect in the minds of the radicals in the Jacobin Club for his association with Brissot and his activities on and immediately following the journée of 20 June.[75] The suspicions of the radicals appeared to be confirmed on 15 August when officers of the king's Swiss Guard testified that Roederer told them to use force against the crowds at the Tuileries.[76] This was a particularly grave charge since nearly 400 citizens had died at the hands of the Swiss.

The issue of Roederer's alleged orders to the Swiss was raised on 15 August at the Jacobins where he was denounced by Tascherau and Faure and read out of the club two days later.[77] He also came under fire from the Jacobin press where Robespierre attacked him in *Le Defenseur de la Constitution* for conducting Louis to the Assembly and praised the cannoneers who had refused to follow Roederer's orders to fire on the peo-

---

[69] Ibid., pp. 224–25.
[70] The department also supported the king's seeking refuge at the Manège. AN 29AP105 Département de Paris, "Extrait du registre du conseil général," 10 August 1792.
[71] AP 43: 634–35.
[72] Ibid.; Roederer, *Chronique*, in OR, 3: 227.
[73] AP, 18: 639.
[74] See for instance J.-P.-L. Cléry, "Journal," in *Mémoires de Cléry, de M. le duc de Montpensier, de Riouffe*, F. Barrière ed. (Paris 1856), p. 20.
[75] After 20 June he had again come under attack in the Jacobins. Aulard, *Jacobins*, 4: 31, 53.
[76] MU, 19 August 1792, 13: 448.
[77] Aulard, *Jacobins*, 4: 206–07, 210.

ple.[78] Likewise Marat condemned Roederer in *L'Ami du peuple* for his orders to the Swiss.[79] Roederer, however, was not without his defenders. The *Moniteur* argued that it was inconceivable that the "incorruptible Roederer" had been a party to a royalist conspiracy while in the Girondin press Brissot's *Le Patriote français* and Condorcet's *Chronique de Paris* supported Roederer in a manner that Robespierre described as "scandalous."[80] Pétion, intent on guarding his popularity, was notable for his silence.

The statements by the Swiss officers resulted in the Revolutionary Commune's seizure of Roederer's papers and the order for his arrest.[81] Having been suspended from the office of procureur-général-syndic since 11 August when the insurrectionary Commune had dissolved the old administration of the department, Roederer now went into hiding.[82] He made a final attempt to salvage his revolutionary reputation with the publication of a pamphlet vindicating his activity on 10 August.[83] Here he denied having given the Swiss any orders whatsoever, pointing out that he had spoken only to the National Guards and cannoneers. The attack of the Swiss on the crowd could only be explained as a "conspiracy against the National Assembly" in which he had had no part. Escorting the king to the Assembly had been an act of partiotism which not only saved Louis's life but also gave the Assembly a hostage who might prove to be a valuable weapon in the war against the foreign powers.[84] In conclusion Roederer begged his readers to recall his past conduct which always had been honorable. Reminding them of his distrust of the Monarchy after Louis's flight in June 1791, he wrote: "one will see, I hope, that equality, liberty, . . . the non-hereditary monarchy, the *republic* itself are not such strangers, nor so unrespectable in my eyes that I would lower myself to conspire against them."[85]

What precisely was Roederer trying to accomplish on 9–10 August? He definitely was not guilty of wishing the immediate downfall of the Monarchy nor plotting a massacre of the Parisian crowd. A more sophisticated theory of Roederer's conduct during the insurrection is that of Albert Mathiez who argued that Roederer merely wanted to insure the political

---

[78] Robespierre, *Oeuvres,* 4: 355–56, 363–64.

[79] *L'Ami du peuple,* 13 August 1792.

[80] MU, 19 August 1792, 13: 448; Robespierre, *Oeuvres,* Marc Bouloiseau et al., ed. (Paris, 1953), 8: 452; *Le Patriote français,* 27 August 1792.

[81] Roederer, *Chronique,* in OR, 3: 240; Roederer, *Notice* in OR, 3: 285; MU, 19 August 1792, 13: 448.

[82] Braesch, *Commune,* p. 146.

[83] P.-L. Roederer, *Observations de P.-L. Roederer sur les réponses faites par les officiers Suisses dans leurs interrogations,* in OR, 3: 256–59. This pamphlet was published privately by a friend and distributed to the Commune and to the public before finally being published in the *Moniteur.* MU, 24 August 1792, 13: 474–507. There is no truth to the statement by François de la Rochefoucauld that Roederer fled to London to publish his defense. François de la Rochefoucauld, *Souvenirs du 10 août 1792 et de l'armée de Bourbon* (Paris, 1929), p. 74.

[84] He actually contradicted himself on this point by also arguing that the king was not a hostage. Roederer, *Observations de P.-L. Roederer,* in OR, 3: 259.

[85] Ibid.

supremacy of the Girondins in the Assembly over the king.[86] If the insurrection of 10 August succeeded in dethroning Louis, this domination
and the Girondin power that it insured would be impossible. Roederer's
solution was to conduct the king to the Assembly which would bring an
end to the insurrection and retain the power of the Girondins.

In Mathiez's theory the key to understanding Roederer is his connection
with the Girondins, of which there is ample evidence. In addition to the
visible support he received after 10 August from Brissot's and Condorcet's
papers and later praise in the Girondin Barbaroux's memoirs, there is
strong evidence that Roederer had been actively involved in Girondin
politics during the entire summer of 1792.[87] In June he had been sent to
Lafayette by the Minister of War Servan, a Girondin, in an effort to convince the general to stop interfering in politics and concentrate on winning
the war.[88] He had also acted as a go-between for Vergniaud and the
Minister of Justice Dejoly in their attempt to have a patriot ministry appointed by Louis.[89] Vergniaud had even hoped that Roederer and Pétion
could be brought into the Royal Council.[90] As to his motives Roederer
himself admitted that "I had hoped that the terror [of the summer of
1792] would throw the court into their [the Girondins'] arms and that it
would look for asylum in their talent and popularity."[91]

Despite this evidence Mathiez's theory does not fully explain Roederer's
conduct. Roederer was anxious for the king to make some accommodation
with the Assembly and had expressed himself openly on this subject in
his defense of Pétion in July. Constitutional government could never succeed until the king and Assembly agreed to cooperate, an arrangement
Roederer hoped to foster. For this reason he had joined Vergniaud and
Dejoly in trying to convince Louis to appoint a patriot ministry. Yet Roederer had distinguished himself from the Girondins in a number of ways
after assuming the office of procureur-général-syndic. For instance in the
matter of tax collection Roederer demonstrated an interest in the economic
plight of the lower classes that was not characteristic of his Girondin
associates. Furthermore, Roederer, unlike many Girondins, had never been
comfortable in using the popular disturbances as a means of acquiring
political advantage. Roederer clearly thought that forceful action should
be taken to prevent the populace from threatening constitutional authority.
On 20 June he advocated barring demonstrators from the Assembly and
on 10 August he hoped that a show of strength at the Tuileries might

---

[86] Albert Mathiez, *Le Dix août* (Paris, 1931) p. 107.

[87] C. Barbaroux, *Mémoires*, Alfred Chabaud, ed. (Paris, 1936), p. 149.

[88] AN 29AP10 Achille Duchatelet to Roederer 16 June and 20 June 1792; Roederer, *Chronique*, OR, 3: 75, 190; MU 2 September 1792, 13: 582–83.

[89] Albert Mathiez, "Les Girondins et la cour à la veille du 10 août," *Annales historiques
de la Révolution française*, 8 (1931): pp. 193–212; Roederer, *Chronique*, in OR, 3: 188;
E.-L.-H. Dejoly, "Mémoires de Etienne-Louis-Hector Dejoly," Jacques Godechot, ed., *Annales
historiques de la Révolution française*, October-December 1946, pp. 353–57.

[90] Dejoly, "Mémoires," pp. 344, 347, 356–57; Mathiez, *Dix août*, pp. 56–57.

[91] Roederer, *Chronique*, in OR, 3: 190.

prevent harm coming to the king. As events were to prove, however, Roederer was unwilling to go so far as to rely on the use of force in controlling the crowds. Here he, like the other revolutionary leaders, remembered all too well the events on the Champ de Mars. If the crowds were not intimidated by a mere show of force, no other action could be taken which would not destroy the fragile bond between the Parisian populace and the revolutionary leadership. Faced with the dilemma of saving the king and preserving the Constitution without openly confronting the crowds, Roederer decided to escort Louis to the Assembly, the repository of the national will.

This decision was no mere act of Girondin politics but rather a last ditch attempt to preserve the Constitution. Roederer can be faulted with remaining a constitutionalist long after the king had made the Constitution unworkable, but his resolution to take the king to the Manège was undertaken as an act of patriotism at some considerable personal risk to himself. His conduct contrasted dramatically with that of Pétion, who had slipped away from the Tuileries early on the morning of 10 August to avoid having to take any responsibility for what might occur there.[92]

Despite his motives, Roederer was seen in Paris as a traitor to the Revolution, and for two years after the insurrection his position was precarious. When the Commune issued a warrant for his arrest after the testimony of the Swiss officers, Roederer went into hiding, first with the agent for Saint-Quirin glass in Paris, Combe, in the rue de Dechargeurs and later in his "compatriot" Lebrun's lodgings at the Palais Royal.[93] In order for Roederer to escape arrest after the Commune had ordered a search of the city for suspects on 28 August, Lebrun devised a scheme in which his friend would pose as a National Guard during the search of Lebrun's rooms. As Lebrun was himself the commandant of a battalion of National Guards, his men refused to search his apartment, and Roederer was not discovered.

The events of 10 August caused Roederer to lose all confidence in the revolutionary movement. The hope of the nation to destroy privilege and create a government based on natural rights and the will of the majority had degenerated into a situation where the nation's representatives were at the mercy of the crowds of Paris, and the administrative officers were powerless to maintain constitutional authority. Roederer, who had so confidently entered the revolutionary era as a patriot, now found himself rethinking his whole concept of the basis of government. Up until August 1792 Roederer operated on the assumption he laid down in his *Députation aux Etats Généraux*, namely that the people should be fairly represented

---

[92] Sydenham, *The French Revolution*, p. 111.

[93] Roederer, *Notice*, in OR, 3: 285. Roederer was probably referring to P. Lebrun, the Girondin Minister of Foreign Affairs. It could not have been C.-F. Lebrun, who was to become one of the Consuls after 18 brumaire, as Roederer did not see him after the Constituent Assembly dispersed. Roederer, *Notice*, in OR, 3: 304.

in the National Assembly and the majority of that body, in the name of the people, should rule. He now began to think along the lines set out by Condorcet, that government, if it was to be enlightened, must be based on the knowledge of social science and not merely the so-called will of the majority exercised by a representative body. It was to this end that he began giving a series of lectures entitled *Cours d'organisation sociale* at the Lycée of Paris in 1793. His lectures were cut short because of the proscription of the Girondin deputies in the Convention in June 1793. Once again Roederer dropped from public view, remaining for the duration of the Terror at Pecq near Saint-Germain at the home of Madame Bernard, the mother-in-law of the banker Rousseau de Telonne.[94] Roederer's political disgrace was completed when he was named before the Convention in Amar's indictment of 3 October 1793 against the Girondins.[95] Nevertheless, Roederer survived the Terror and emerged afterward convinced that, if a new foundation for government, such as he had described at the Lycée, could be established, the early promise of the Revolution might yet be fulfilled.

---

[94] AN 29AP10 Note of A.-M. Roederer; A.-M. Roederer, *La famille Roederer* (Paris, 1849), p. 202; Bertrand Barère, *Mémoires*, H. Carnot and D. d'Angers, eds. (Paris, 1842–1844), 4: 404.

[95] MU, 25 October 1793, 18: 200.

VI. SOCIAL SCIENCE AND POLITICAL ORDER

Even before the development of the political turmoil in the late 1780s there was a strain of thought which argued that politics could be brought into conformity with the principles of social science. This development was essential in the minds of its proponents if society was to achieve the highest possible level of happiness. Condorcet, the leading advocate of this theory, believed that social science, the empirical study of all human activities and relationships, could be made as precise as the physical sciences through systematic observation.[1] In Condorcet's view an important aspect of social science was the development of a theory of social organization from first principles (natural law) and the creation of a practical "social art" in order to implement this organization. This aspect of social science, according to Condorcet, would be most precise if it could be subjected to mathematical evaluation, a project with which he concerned himself during the 1780s.

With the outbreak of the Revolution Condorcet and others believed that the opportunity had arrived for putting the principles of social science into practice. For instance Condorcet's *Essai sur la constitution et les fonctions des assemblées provinciales* outlined in 1788 a scheme for representative assemblies which would bring the theories of mathematical probability to bear on political decision making.[2] During the early years of the Revolution Condorcet, along with Sieyès, was instrumental in organizing the Society of 1789 in order to create and publicize this social science upon which revolutionary politics should be based. Begun in reaction to the disorders of the October Days, the very nature of the Society of 1789 placed its membership among the moderate revolutionaries. In the Society's view reason and science, not revolutionary crowds and inflammatory rhetoric, should be the basis for all political decisions.

Roederer came to share Condorcet's belief in the efficacy of social science only after his experience in August 1792. His own pre-revolutionary writings had concentrated almost entirely on economic problems and their political consequences. While he certainly believed political institutions should rest on natural law, he had no real concept of a social science which was essential for correct political decision making. During the early years of the Revolution, Roederer was confident of his own ability to shape legislation in the Assembly, particularly that relating to taxation and government finance. In constitutional matters he was hardly adverse to relying

---

[1] For Condorcet's conception of social science see Keith Michael Baker, *Condorcet: From Natural Philosophy to Social Mathematics* (Chicago, 1975), pp. 197–201.

[2] Ibid., pp. 253–59; 272–74.

on inflammatory rhetoric or revolutionary political associations like the Jacobin Club to achieve his goals. He had been a member of the Society of 1789, but there is no evidence that he was attracted to it by Condorcet's advocacy of social science. He seems to have joined the club largely for the political alliances he thought he would make there. In short Roederer, until August 1792, was content to play the role of the revolutionary politician who used the methods available to him to achieve his program. With his ultimate political failure after 10 August, however, Roederer became very disenchanted with the course of revolutionary politics and quite pessimistic about reversing that course through the type of political activity that had characterized his conduct during the first years of the Revolution. Roederer came to view the legislative process that he had worked so hard to master and influence between 1789 and 1791 as primarily responsible for the unacceptable political situation which existed after August 1792. At that point he began to formulate his ideas along the lines that Condorcet had advocated in the Society of 1789. Roederer had come to the conclusion that only by defining the true bases of society, which was the task of social science, could proper government be established.

With this end in mind Roederer made his principal contribution to the concept of social science in a series of lectures, the *Cours d'organisation sociale*, read during the winter and spring of 1793 at the Lycée. Having been established by Pilâtre de Rossier in 1781 and surviving into the Revolution, the Lycée provided a forum for lectures on the sciences, history, literature, and philosophy by such well-known individuals as La Harpe, Garat, and Condorcet; it was an ideal setting for Roederer's presentation of his social theories.[3] The lectures were an attempt to lay before the revolutionary public a scientific description of natural social organization and some suggestions concerning Condorcet's "social art." As Sergio Moravia has pointed out, the concept of the *Cours d'organisation sociale* owed much to Condorcet, but the component parts were made up of Roederer's own economic theories, the sensationalist pyschology of Condillac, the political ideas of the Enlightenment, as well as the social mathematics of Condorcet himself.[4] In the lectures Roederer presented the argument that social harmony could only result from the creation of a government which recognized and supported the natural laws of society. The revolutionary government, like that of the ancien régime, had failed to recognize these laws and would face continued social disorder and political failure until it did so.

In his introductory lecture Roederer described to his audience at the Lycée the nature and purpose of his social science. While the ultimate goal was to determine the principles of social organization which will

---

[3] On the Lycée see Charles Dejob, *De L'Etablissment connu sous le nom de lycée et d'Athénée et de quelques établissements analogues* (Paris, 1889).

[4] Sergio Moravia, *Il pensiero degli Idéologues: Scienza e filosofia in Francia, 1780–1815* (Firenze, 1974), p. 718.

make men happy, it was first necessary to establish and analyze the true elements of society which it was the duty of social organization to guarantee. "Ignorance of the physical elements of society and their spontaneous combination," for instance, "has caused the most distressing errors by political writers and governments: it is time to dissipate them or to prevent new ones."[5] Politicians and political writers also neglected "the study of the morals and physiology of man," an understanding of which was absolutely necessary for the proper "construction of a government." Roederer argued that since government was made for men, "it must then know the needs, the rights, the duties, the virtues, the vices, the imperfections of these same men in order to give them a government which suits them."[6] Likewise since government "is a machine composed of men," it was necessary to understand men fully if the machine was to operate properly. In order to arrive at this understanding of society and the men who composed it, Roederer proposed to unite into "a single science the principal notions of three sciences," namely the moral, political, and economic sciences, which up to that time had been kept artificially separated.

The first of the social elements that Roederer proposed to scrutinize with his unified science was the physical which included for him the conservation of society through economic activity and reproduction of society through the union of the sexes. Roederer's conception of economics, which envisioned economic growth through the development of manufacturing, had been formed during the tariff controversy of the 1780s. Before his audience at the Lycée in 1793 he developed more fully these views, which have much in common with the liberal economic theories J.-B. Say developed in the early nineteenth century.[7]

Implicit in Roederer's economic thinking was the belief that wealth was the product of human labor or work, capital investment, and *industrie*. In contrast to the physiocrats Roederer could not accept the theory that land itself produced wealth. Obviously without human labor land would produce only enough food to feed "a small number of isolated men consuming little."[8] For this reason he was insistent, as we shall see below, that society should foster a work ethic among all classes of society. Work by itself, however, could not produce wealth; capital investment was necessary for even simple enterprises. On the land investment was needed for clearing, tilling, and planting before any crop was harvested.[9] In manufacturing capital was needed for equipment, raw materials, and wages.

---

[5] P.-L. Roederer, *Cours d'organisation sociale*, in OR, 8: 131.

[6] Ibid.

[7] This connection between Roederer and Say is made by Michael James in his article "Pierre-Louis Roederer, Jean-Baptiste Say, and the Concept of *industrie*," *History of Political Economy*, 9 (1977): 455–475. James bases his argument on another series of lectures, *Mémoires sur quelques points d'économie publique*, that Roederer read at the Lycée in 1800 and 1801. While these later lectures expanded Roederer's concept of industrie somewhat the germ of his ideas had its origins in the 1780's and was developed almost fully by 1793.

[8] Roederer, *Cours d'organisation sociale*, in OR, 8: 139.

[9] Ibid. pp. 140–142.

The last element in the production of wealth was industrie. For Roederer the term industrie implied ingenuity and skill, essential elements in his view for real prosperity, which could be found in both agricultural and manufacturing enterprises.[10] In Roederer's usage industrie was not interchangeable with manufacturing nor did it connote factories or machine labor. Industrie was essential in the creation of wealth because only by this ingenuity would new types of economic activity be created and old varieties be stimulated to greater productivity. Roederer uses the example of agricultural workers who "imagined and executed some *meubles de commodité*" which they sold to their proprietors creating a new enterprise in the process.[11]

Of the three elements of wealth capital investment was the most crucial. The work of agricultural industrie could only result from capital investment in the land. "Likewise," Roederer wrote, "determination and industrie no more suffice for the work of manufactures than for that of land."[12] Capital funds were required for the building of workshops, the purchasing of tools and raw materials, and the payment of wages to the employees. Capital, according to Roederer, was a savings which could be accumulated either by the refusal to consume all of one's goods or by the extra work required to produce a superabundance.[13] These savings would only be made if there was hope that an ultimate profit would accrue from the capital investment. This was a particular problem for the landed proprietor who would hardly be inclined to the accumulation of capital if he had no use for the ultimate profits it would create. This was why manufacturing was so important for a prosperous economy. Manufacturers would create goods desired by the proprietors who would then seek higher profits from their land in order to purchase these goods. The increased produce which resulted from these investments in land would be used to provide means of subsistence for those who worked in the manufacturing enterprises. Thus a cycle of ever-expanding economic activity would be established where "*l'industrie manufacturière* will extend *l'industrie agricole* and add to the products of the land the value of its salaries."[14]

The manufacturing that Roederer discussed could include everything from a single artisan plying his craft to a truly industrialized factory of the nineteenth century variety. While Roederer did not deny the industrie or capital investment of the artisan, he had a more modern concept of manufacturing in mind as he developed his ideas. He argued that it was necessary to perfect the relationship between agriculture and manufacturing and to increase "the delights of industrie" as well as means of subsistence. For this to be done to the best advantage, a strict division of labor was necessary so that "each part of a single product is always able

---

[10] James, "Roederer and Say," pp. 458–59.
[11] Roederer, *Cours d'organisation sociale*, in OR, 8: 141.
[12] Ibid., p. 142.
[13] Ibid., p. 141.
[14] Ibid.

to be done by a hand or by a machine which does nothing else."[15] Such minute division of labor must be based on substantial production and an extensive market. To facilitate distribution, commerce, a third type of economic activity also requiring capital investment, was needed.

Thus Roederer's conception of the economic basis of society rested on his conviction that the wealth of society was a product of work, industrie, and capital, with capital being the most essential element in the combination. Integral to this conception of economics was his belief that capital would spur the development of something like modern industrial manufacturing, the products of which would foster further investment in agriculture and commerce. In this way Roederer was arguing for an industrialized economy in which the natural but complex interplay between these various kinds of economic activities would lead to prosperity for society as a whole.

In Roederer's opinion there were two existing political groups which failed to understand properly the true economic basis of society: the economists who subscribed to the tenets of physiocracy and the egalitarians who had attached themselves to theorists like Mably.[16] Since the economists supported aristocracy and absolute monarchy, Roederer was mostly concerned with the influence of the egalitarians who espoused equality while attacking wealth, ideas more compatible with the revolutionary mentality. He outlined the demands of the egalitarians in five categories: the abolition of inherited property, the placing of limits on fortunes, the equal division of property, the suppression of private property and the common exploitation of the land, and the establishment of a public ethic promoting modesty, simplicity, and austerity. While these measures might appear to foster equality, they would destroy the formation of capital so necessary to the economy so that "the result of all equalizing projects is always a deterioration of agriculture, a diminution of products."[17] The result for the populace would be increased poverty in an effort to create absolute equality. Only the system Roederer had outlined, which adhered to the true nature of society and met society's real needs, would lead to prosperity for all.

Another aspect of society that Roederer discussed was human reproduction, an element which actually preceded the formation of society.[18] Nature dictated the organization of this society; the woman was to give birth to and nourish the infants while the man was to aid her and protect the family from danger. "The conjugal society," as Roederer put it, "is then [as much] protection for the woman as it obviously is for the children."[19] The difficulty of preserving the family caused men to come to-

---

[15] Ibid., p. 142.

[16] Ibid., pp. 144–152.

[17] Ibid., p. 151.

[18] Ibid., p. 159. Roederer's theory of society as a compact among families first appeared in De la Députation aux Etats Généraux. See OR, 7: 552.

[19] Roederer, Cours d'organisation sociale, in OR, 8: 159.

gether to form society which would offer more security to each family. This assumption led Roederer to conclude that

if civil society is only a guarantee of domestic society . . . it would be absurd to maintain that women are able to take an immediate part in these social arrangements; this would go against the object, this would sacrifice the end to the means; this would . . . dissolve domestic society. . . .[20]

If women were to take part in political affairs, innumerable practical difficulties would arise. Would they be represented by deputies of their own sex? Would they be represented in all affairs or just those involving the relationship of the sexes? If they were represented in all affairs, there would be many points in which they would have a common interest with their husbands. Thus the married men would in effect have twice the political power of those who remained unmarried. If women had equal power with men in the assemblies, how would the inevitable deadlocks of sexual politics between the two ever be broken? "In communal affairs," Roederer warned, "there would be the danger of distractions or of seduction, the necessary effect of the invincible charm which always carries one sex toward the other. . . ."[21] Obviously then any tampering with the socially defined relationships between men and women could only lead to political disasters.

Roederer next turned to a discussion of the moral elements of society which he defined as the motives of human action. These motives were based on human needs, interests, and passions. The study of human motivation was a practical necessity if social rights were to be preserved from the passion of men. Roederer's understanding of the relationship of man's passions and his actions was based largely on his reading of Condillac. Passions were a product of man's sensibility, that is, his faculty for receiving sense impressions; therefore, they were based entirely on man's response to sensations. Passions were thus biological in origin, and it followed that "a general system of the principles of human actions would be essentially the result of anatomical and physiological knowledge."[22] Roederer even claimed that, if the sciences of physiology, anatomy, and chemistry were properly applied to the study of human motivation, politics and morals could be reduced to "principles as certain and as evident as those of geometry."

Man's sensations were basically either pleasurable or painful, and they could be classified as either physical (that which was dictated by nature and consisted of the sensations of hunger, thirst, sexual desire, and fatigue) or moral (that which was derived from society and consisted of the sensations of deprivation or possession of glory, power, wealth, and moral love.)[23] All passions were a response to these sensations; thus, all pas-

---

[20] Ibid., p. 160.
[21] Ibid., p. 163.
[22] Ibid., p. 182.
[23] Ibid., p. 183.

sionate desires and aversions were either physical or moral in origin. Moral passions, of course, were not a direct product of physical sensation but were instead intellectual pleasures and pains which resulted from fulfilled or unfulfilled expectations. Moral passions represented the desire for the means of satisfying the physical passions.[24] The physical passions were immutable and fixed in number by their very nature. For instance man obviously desired food because he was hungry. Seeking means of satisfying physical passions, the moral passions were infinite in number and "directable, removable, and destructible at the pleasure of the social institutions."[25] Society could determine the acceptable means by which man went about seeking his food.

How could society through legislation go about directing man's moral passions? The answer to this question, according to Roederer, would come with an understanding of how ideas were formed. Here again he was dependent on Condillac, who had argued that ideas were the product of the impression of sensations on the intellect. Man's will was a reaction of the intellect to these ideas. Once there was a general understanding of the relationship of man's senses, ideas, and will, then Roederer believed that it would be possible to regulate through legislation man's sensual perceptions in order to control his actions. Such legislation would "introduce order in the will of men, justice and virtue in their actions [and] . . . . assure the happiness of society. . . ."[26]

Roederer argued that the process of controlling man's will should consist of preparing the appropriate association of ideas, insuring the proper recall of these associations, and encouraging pleasurable activity which conformed to the general good.[27] The appropriate association of ideas was the result of the education of both young and old. Once the associations had been formed, Roederer thought they could be recalled to the advantage of the public utility if the correct stimulant was provided for the people.

Roederer was persuaded by the belief, common during the Revolution, that fêtes, works of art, and music served the function of shaping the public mentality in directions useful to the nation.[28] Here music was perhaps the most useful stimulant since it had the power to recall ideas and sentiments buried in the memory.[29] This power was especially useful in political situations where certain songs evoked patriotism. The same was true, although to a lesser extent, of art which could provide patriotic

---

[24] Ibid., pp. 204–5.

[25] Ibid., p. 205.

[26] Ibid., p. 208.

[27] Ibid., p. 227.

[28] Accounts of the revolutionary attitudes toward the use of art and festivals in shaping the mind of the citizens are found in James Leith, *The Idea of Art as Propaganda in France, 1750–1799* (Toronto, 1965), pp. 96–128; and Mona Ozouf, *La Fete révolutionnaire, 1789–1799* (Paris, 1976), pp. 236–259.

[29] Roederer, *Cours d'organisation sociale*, in OR, 8: 213–14, 218–20.

inspiration to the people.[30] The artist, however, should reject the traditional practice of producing a single creation to be placed in a museum
and mass-produce his work instead so that the various copies could be
found providing inspiration in every department of France. Other appropriate stimuli consisted of newspapers, placards, patriotic dramas, and
public festivities on historic dates. Finally the passions could be controlled
by administering penalties or rewards. Roederer definitely preferred that
men be guided to proper conduct by the desire for rewards rather than
by the fear of punishment. He envisioned an enlightened, virtuous, unanimous, and moralized public opinion which would "be present during the
entire life of the citizens, which would follow them in their public conduct
and into the interior of their families, which would . . . assist even all
their thoughts and discern the reward or punishment which each is due."[31]
How could such a public opinion be formed? According to Roederer, the
principles of human action that he had described produced the physical
laws upon which institutions could be created to bring about such public
opinion. Roederer was convinced that his analysis proved that a system
of rewards could be instituted to replace much of the existing penal code,
end much corporal punishment, and allow the construction of "altars of
Hope" and the destruction of "the temples of Fear."[32]

Roederer's program for moral improvement seems to have something
in common with the mind control systems of twentieth-century totalitar-
ianism. The concept of controlling man's sensations in order to introduce
order into his will and creating a public opinion that will follow him into
the bosom of his family and even into his innermost thoughts does not
strike the modern reader as a theory of political liberalism. Nevertheless
Roederer was convinced that only in this way could public conduct acceptable to the Revolution be established without resorting to the tactics
of the September massacres or to the direction of the Mountain in the
National Convention. Since Helvétius and others had proven that man
always acted in his own self-interest, only by controlling man's sensations
and hence his perceived self-interest could society expect men to conduct
themselves in a manner compatible with the general good. This in conjunction with a system that rewarded proper behavior as well as punished
that which was improper would lead to a society not governed by fear.
What Roederer advocated in the spring of 1793 foreshadowed Destutt de
Tracy's concept of idéologie presented to the National Institute in 1796.
According to Tracy, idéologie was a science of ideas which had as its goal
the "regulating of society in such a way that man finds there the most
help and the least possible annoyance from his own kind."[33]

---

[30] Ibid., pp. 222–23.
[31] Ibid., p. 228.
[32] Ibid.
[33] Quoted in Emmet Kennedy, A Philosophe in the Age of Revolution: Destutt de Tracy and
the Origins of "Ideology" (Philadelphia, 1978), p. 47.

Having established the physical and moral elements of society, Roederer turned his attention to its political principles which had to conform to the established physical or moral laws. The basis for all political society was the concept of natural rights, which preceded any political organization. Following Locke's argument in the *Second Treatise of Civil Government*, Roederer insisted the two most important rights were those of liberty and property, both of which were outgrowths of man's natural requirements of subsistence.[34] Man needed liberty in order to procure his food and other consumable items; and once he had obtained these goods through his work, they became his property. "To contest this," Roederer argued, "would be to contest that he has the right to live, because one is only able to consume the items over which he has acquired ownership."[35] Likewise if one tilled land in order to meet his needs and those of his family, he acquired the right to the land he worked. Roederer believed equality to be part of the rights of liberty and property, which were incompatible with honorific or real privileges. Perhaps the most formidable voice against the right of property would have been Rousseau, and Roederer went to some pains to prove that Rousseau was not the critic of private property that some might believe him to be. He argued that in the *Discourse on Inequality* Rousseau was attacking civilization not private property when he said crimes, war, death, misery, and horrors followed the enclosure of land into private domains.[36] Furthermore, Roederer was able to cite passages from some of Rousseau's other works in which he seemed to favor the right of property. With an authority of Rousseau's stature behind him, Roederer was confident of the strength of his case for including property among the natural rights of man.

While Roederer understood these concepts clearly, he was convinced that the deputies in the National Convention did not. He said that the deputies argued that man's rights were found only in society and had suppressed the word "natural" from their proposed declaration of rights.[37] He was especially critical of Robespierre's suggested declaration of rights because it called for limiting the right of property so that it did not violate the security, liberty, existence, or property of others.[38] Roederer argued that the right of property should not be limited and therefore subject to civil law, the magistrates, or popular prejudice because this right could not infringe on the rights of others in any way. Property might need limitation if landed proprietors refused to cultivate their land or destroyed their harvests in an attempt to starve out the population, but such was manifestly not the case. In fact the absolute right of property would pre-

---

[34] John Locke, *Treatise of Civil Government*, ed. Charles L. Sherman (New York, 1937), pp. 19–33.

[35] Roederer, *Cours d'organisation sociale*, in OR, 8: 235.

[36] Ibid., p. 239.

[37] Ibid., p. 232.

[38] Ibid., pp. 245–46. For the proposed Declaration of Rights and Robespierre's Declaration of Rights see AP, 62: 267; AP, 63: 198–99.

vent such occurrences because proprietors wanted to produce an abundance of goods in order to provide themselves with an income to purchase manufactured goods and other enjoyments. Those without property actually benefited most from a social system which guaranteed property because the opportunities for satisfying the desires of the rich proprietors would lead to their own employment and subsequent well-being.

In addition to natural rights, Roederer thought a proper understanding of the relationship of sovereignty to the separation of powers essential to political society. The concept of separation of powers had fallen into disrepute under the constitutional monarchy because it was so closely associated with the maintenance of royal prerogative.[39] In fact Roederer had been one of those in the Constituent Assembly who had favored the blurring of the distinction of powers especially on the issue of the Treasury. The constitutional project that Condorcet presented to the Convention in 1793 was notable in that it claimed to have no separation of powers. [40] To provide a philosophical basis for the necessity of separation of powers, Roederer utilized a somewhat unlikely source, Rousseau. Rousseau's concept of the general will, Roederer argued, was to be utilized to provide benefits for the entire society and must, therefore, be concerned with the common interest.[41] The problem for society was not only to develop laws in accord with the general will, but also to guarantee that these laws were justly administered. To insure that decisions were made according to the general will, they must be based on pre-existing laws, and these laws must be administered and judged by those other than the individuals who made the laws. Since Condorcet's constitutional project did call for an executive council of ministers, Roederer was not totally displeased with it, but he did think that the concept of the separation of powers should have been more clearly stated.

Having raised the question of the general will, Roederer was anxious to set out the means by which it could best be expressed. The general will should, as Rousseau had argued, be more than just the will of the majority; it should provide for the common interest of a society. The general will, therefore, had to be based on a true understanding of what the common interests of society were. How could this goal be accomplished? Condorcet had developed his social mathematics in answer to this question.[42] In his view politics had as its principal obligation the discovery of truth, while public debate, which was an important component of this discovery, was not to be a contest of wills but a rational investigation of the facts. In 1788 Condorcet wrote in his *Essai sur la constitution et les fonctions des assemblées provinciales* that correct political decisions could be reached in a representative body if, after a preliminary debate, a committee put all of the propositions in a yes or no form. The procedure for voting on the prop-

[39] Roederer, *Cours d'organisation sociale*, in OR, 8: 249.
[40] See Baker, *Condorcet*, pp. 323–24 for Condorcet's constitutional scheme.
[41] Roederer, *Cours d'organisation sociale*, in OR, 8: 251–52.
[42] See Baker, *Condorcet*, pp. 229, 240, 259.

ositions was to be based on Condorcet's mathematical theories of probability to insure that the results conformed to the truth.

In the *Cours d'organisation sociale* Roederer adopted parts of Condorcet's scheme, added some features suggested by Rousseau, and produced a plan for lawmaking that he claimed would truly lead to a realization of the general will. Roederer argued that Rousseau preferred that the people ratify all laws after they had been drafted by a single individual, the legislator. Roederer believed there were advantages (especially the give and take of debate) to having an assembly rather than Rousseau's legislator formulate the laws and put them to the public. Nevertheless, the recent history of France had made it all too evident to Roederer that reason was not necessarily the product of legislative debate. In order to reconcile Rousseau's idea of the wise legislator with the principle of elected assemblies, he combined Condorcet's idea of legislation (minus the mathematical formulas, however) with that of Rousseau. Roederer suggested that in the assembly a reporter be named who would become "the depository of all ideas" presented in the debates.[43] The reporter would reflect on these ideas and present to the assembly all their advantages and disadvantages. On this dispassionate summary the assembly could reach a rational decision. When the assembly had decided an issue, it would go to the people for ratification as Rousseau had suggested. He believed that representatives could not exercise sovereignty.

In advocating Rousseau's concept of sovereignty, Roederer did not mean that the populace should ratify every governmental decision. Law was to concern itself only with general principles. In Roederer's view, "Legislation ought to limit itself to two things: the point of departure and the point of arrival. Reason ought to trace the route between the two extremes."[44] Through their regulations, the duty of administrators was to provide the means of executing the general principles of the law. Roederer believed that a clear understanding of the differences between laws and administrative regulations was essential for the proper working of government, and he implied that in the past the revolutionary assemblies had concerned themselves too much with the latter at the expense of the former for fear that administrators would become independent of the assemblies. Roederer argued it was now necessary to lay down another principle: "The means of execution of most of the administrative laws demand the regulations that the administrators make and their faculty for making them ought not be contested."[45]

Roederer argued that a number of benefits not found under the present government would result from the popular ratification of laws. There would be more respect for laws because they would be fewer in number and would truly reflect the popular will. Good laws would be less vulnerable to alteration by succeeding assemblies since they had been sanc-

---

[43] Roederer, *Cours d'organisation sociale*, in OR, 8: 255–56.
[44] Ibid., p. 261.
[45] Ibid.

tioned by the voters. Given more freedom of action, the executive power would be more effective. In the assemblies he predicted that "the forms of deliberation in which imperfection is so manifest and so dangerous [and] in which perfection demands so much knowledge and experience and [which] seem still so far from us would be of less importance and their irregularity of less inconvenience."[46]

Another important aspect of political organization was the establishment of civil law which helped create society's morals and provided the link between the social pact and the constitution. Specifically Roederer believed civil law should foster the institution of work which was all important in the maintenance of society.[47] The law should encourage work both among rich and poor. The rich should fear losing their status through laziness, and the poor should hope to improve theirs through hard work. "In order to institute really, durably the work of the poor man, it is necessary to make him love the rich," because, Roederer argued, only when the rich tried to increase their capital through investment were they going to employ the laboring poor. Furthermore, "when the rich will work, the power of the example will act also on the poor. The emulation of work will animate all ages and all *états*; the ideas of affluence, esteem, and work will unite them tightly together."[48] The institution of work "develops the talents, multiplies the riches, and increases the common patrimony" of society while "ennobling all the relations of man with his fellow creatures . . ., creating a fraternity of talents, and making the diverse gifts that nature has given to individuals contribute to the common good." Finally the institution of work is "the great manager of order, the great agent of all police," the protector of all property, and "the founder of good morals."[49]

How could the principle of work be inculcated in society? Roederer believed this could be accomplished through the implementation of proper civil laws. Most importantly property must be established as an absolute right and the right of inheritance guaranteed.[50] Without this foundation no one would be willing to work because there would be no rewards. Equal division of inheritance was also important if property was not to be denied to a large number of a man's children. To subdivide property further, Roederer recommended that children be declared legally adult at an earlier age and a divorce law be passed to encourage more marriages and presumably more children. To insure that all men who married would work, they would have to prove that they had *"un métier"* before their marriage was approved. To encourage the development of skilled crafts, each department would have statues erected to all the métiers of society with a fête for each on particular Sundays during the year. In Roederer's

[46] Ibid., p. 262.
[47] Ibid., p. 265.
[48] Ibid., p. 266.
[49] Ibid.
[50] Ibid., pp. 266–67.

view it was not sufficient that each citizen learn a skill but that he also learn "to live in a manner contenting himself with the profit of his métier."[51]

Roederer believed it necessary to instill the habit of work in both males and females. He was convinced that women had deep-seated tendencies toward indolence and frivolity which would adversely affect their husbands and destroy the work ethic in society. This was especially true of women with dowries who had a propensity toward luxury and who were the most likely to captivate men.[52] The obvious solution to this problem was to end the practice of providing marriageable young women with dowries. Roederer argued that he was not trying to disinherit women from their fathers' estates, but rather to postpone the inheritance until the women were older and presumably more mature:

We do not want them to be at the same time rich and young, rich and beautiful, rich and frivolous; we do not want them to be able to dissipate [their fortunes] when it is necessary to amass [them] in order to establish a family, to abuse their goods while their husbands are able to make them productive; we do not want them to have separate and, at least morally [based on social custom], independent fortunes from their spouses. . . .[53]

Roederer even argued that modest sumptuary laws might further aid the establishment of the habit of work.[54] Once the proper attitude toward work was established in society, property, economic prosperity, and civil tranquility would be assured.

Roederer was convinced that his unified social science had demonstrated the complex interrelationship of natural rights, free economic activity, and morality in the organization of society. Government had the obligation to defend natural rights (liberty and property), to encourage unfettered economic development and the accumulation of capital, and to create a civil law to promote morality.[55] All political activity should be devoted primarily to these ends. Of course the governments of the Revolution had not fulfilled these goals and often had worked to subvert them. Could a government be formed which did not run counter to society's true needs? In his search for such a government Roederer surveyed the political systems of democracy, aristocracy, and monarchy as analyzed in the works of Rousseau, Montesquieu, and Hobbes and came to the conclusion that no existing government or theory of government was satisfactory. Of course Roederer had made certain suggestions of his own concerning legislative organization which would produce decisions more compatible with society's needs. His scheme, however, only dealt with legislative decisions, and thus he urged that "the sincere friends of humanity, especially the enlightened ones, ought to occupy themselves with the formation of a

---

[51] Ibid., p. 267.
[52] Ibid., p. 269.
[53] Ibid., p. 271.
[54] Ibid., p. 273.
[55] Ibid., pp. 295–99.

new system of government."[56] Only with the creation of a new type of government which did not threaten the social pact upon which society rested would progress, prosperity, and social harmony prevail.

Roederer's *Cours d'organisation sociale* raises some interesting questions regarding the nature of his liberalism. Roederer's economic ideas which supported the freedom to engage in capital investment and profit-making as the means of creating industrialized manufacturing and general prosperity were certainly liberal in tenor. However, Thomas Kaiser in a stimulating article argues that the economic thought of the *idéologues*, prominently including Roederer and J. B. Say, fostered the idea of industrialism, a term used rather loosely here, and economic liberalism in an effort to bring an end to the Revolution and the social discord associated with it.[57] According to the idéologues it was most important to discover the essential elements of social organization which they found to be primarily economic. The goal of society was to be high economic production, and industry was the means to assure that goal. Industrialization would promote general prosperity while creating a generally accepted social stratification based on the division of labor and promoting the work ethic throughout a society striving for wealth. Political institutions would play a supportive but clearly secondary role in this process. Political organization would now be understood as relatively unimportant, and men would cease to tamper with political institutions in the vain hope of perfecting them. Decisions would be made not on a political basis, but by entrepreneurs and scientists in order to maximize production. Democracy and political liberalism would give way to a highly elitist concept of government. The result would presumably be a prosperous and contented, if highly stratified, society with no political disagreement since all would be united in the continuance of the industrial order.

There is much truth in Kaiser's argument as it pertains to Roederer. The latter did believe that industrialized manufacturing could help bring social harmony and was the first of the idéologues to make this contention when he articulated the theory in the *Cours d'organisation sociale*. By placing so much emphasis on Roederer's economic theories to the exclusion of his social science, however, Kaiser somewhat distorts Roederer's concept of society and implies a unity of opinion among the idéologues that perhaps did not exist on this issue. As the *Cours d'organisation sociale* made clear, Roederer believed that only a total understanding of society could lead to improvement of its present condition. Thus relying solely on industrialization, using the term either in the sense of promoting industrie or a manufacturing system, to bring social harmony was likely to fail. Furthermore, Kaiser's assertion that the idéologues faith in the powers of industrialism caused them to be indifferent to political reform does not

---

[56] Ibid., p. 305.
[57] Thomas E. Kaiser, "Politics and Political Economy in the Thought of the Ideologues," *History of Political Economy*, 12 (1980): 141–160.

apply in Roederer's case. Despite Roederer's statement, quoted by Kaiser, that government was "only a part of the social organization and not even an absolutely necessary part," Roederer remained interested in and committed to fundamental political reform in France.[58] In the *Cours d'organisation sociale* Roederer had argued that government must influence morals. Even in an industrialized society the work ethic would not develop unassisted. Furthermore, government must preserve the natural rights of liberty and property which were essential to proper social organization. Finally the emphasis on the development of social mathematics indicated that Roederer was very much interested in developing a procedure for correct political decision making.

Despite the problems with his emphasis, Kaiser's study is correct in asserting that the economic thought of Roederer, like that of the other idéologues he discusses, was counter-revolutionary, elitist, and potentially illiberal. Was Roederer's economic liberalism in particular and his social science in general just a facade behind which to erect an authoritarian government which could end the Revolution and its social disorder? Keith Baker argues that Condorcet's social science, while certainly not devoid of its elitist aspects, was fundamentally liberal in its intention and would have been ultimately democratic if enlightenment could be spread to the masses.[59] There seems to be no reason to assume that Condorcet was not sincere in his belief that scientific government was desirable, workable, and essentially liberal.

Likewise, Roederer seems to have been convinced by Condorcet's enthusiasm for social science that here indeed was a liberal answer to the political chaos of the Revolution. In the *Cours d'organisation sociale* Roederer hoped that social science could lead to the development of a society which would be naturally harmonious and beneficial to all of its members. Government would be somewhat elitist since administrators made the majority of the decisions, and it would smack of illiberalism with its determination to mandate society's morals. Yet Roederer did not stress the powers of government that would be necessary to implement his system because he almost certainly believed, no matter how naively in twentieth-century eyes, that extensive government power would not be required. The whole thrust of his argument in the *Cours d'organisation sociale* was that a properly organized society would need fewer repressive measures by government than were already in place in the France of early 1793. If Roederer's insistence that all major legislation must be ratified by the entire citizenry is added to his implicit liberalism, then his social science can be understood as neither a facade for authoritarianism nor a call for overt illiberalism. The fact that Roederer later in the decade became more elitist and less democratic, does not alter the essentially liberal message of his social science in 1793.

---

[58] Ibid., p. 146; Roederer, *Cours d'organisation sociale*, in OR, 8: 130.
[59] Keith Baker. "Scientism, Elitism and Liberalism: the Case of Condorcet," *Studies on Voltaire and the Eighteenth Century* 55 (1967): 164–165.

When Roederer emerged from hiding after the fall of Robespierre, he maintained his interest in the development of social science as the means of achieving a rational politics and political order. He retained a strong interest in formulating some variant of Condorcet's scheme for legislative reorganization and in 1797 published such a plan in his *Journal d'économie publique, de morale et de politique*, a new sheet, the very name of which implied a continuation of the *Cours d'organisation sociale*.[60] Here he argued that the legislative body, which had the same function for the nation that the intellect had for the individual, ought to provide *la raison publique* for France. Such an assembly had the obligation to render just and necessary decisions which could only be made if it were able to make its collective judgement through a *logique organisée*. Roederer pointed out to his readers that the revolutionary assemblies had failed to produce reasoned decisions largely because of the nature of parliamentary oratory where the speakers were more concerned with interesting, astonishing, and most importantly, pleasing their fellow deputies and the galleries than with searching for the truth. In such a situation to see "mediocrity take the place of genius by the favor of the hearers" was not uncommon.[61] In order to overcome the deficiencies of assemblies, Roederer argued that it was necessary to introduce into the deliberations a reasoned analysis of each proposed law. This analysis would be carried out by first determining which interests were to be affected by a proposed law; second, by distinguishing the advantages or prejudices that the proposal would present to each interest; and third, by deciding if the advantages outweighed the prejudices or vice-versa. Furthermore, in making these decisions it would be essential to distinguish clearly between primary and secondary interests, that is natural rights versus those pertaining to certain individuals or groups in society.

The analysis in the assembly would be carried out by three separate committees: the first to analyze the interests affected by the proposed law, the second to analyze the effects of the law on those interests, and the third to weigh the advantages and disadvantages and propose the final solution. The assembly as a whole would be required to pass on the report of each committee before the next committee could undertake its analysis. Final passage of the law would be based on the report of the third committee. This process, Roederer believed, would make legislation entirely rational since it would be based on the truths discovered by the committees. The deputies in the assembly required to sanction the reports of the committees at each stage and, therefore, forced to accept the logic of the committees' work, would have no choice but to vote for laws based on reason rather than on the political rhetoric of certain powerful orators. To make this logique organisée even more persuasive, Roederer informed his readers of the mathematician Laplace's theory that numerical values could be assigned to the advantages or disadvantages of legislation to particular

---

[60] JEP 10 Messidor V (28 June 1797), in OR, 7: 72–84.
[61] Ibid., p. 74.

interests. These values could then be calculated in order to provide the greatest certainty that each piece of legislation was the product of reason.[62]

Political order, however, could not be restored merely by reorganizing the methods of deliberation in the legislative body. What became apparent to many moderates who had survived the Terror was that France lacked the proper philosophic underpinning to achieve stable and rational government. This had basically been Roederer's argument in the *Cours d'organisation sociale* and his reason for providing a description of the true social laws upon which government had to be based. But how was this philosophic basis to be discovered and transmitted to the nation? Here the republican intellectuals looked to the newly created National Institute and especially its Class of Moral and Political Sciences. In proposing in 1792 the inclusion of the moral and political sciences in a new national academy, Condorcet had believed this would provide France with the development of a social science so necessary to proper government.[63] By 1796 many of the members of the Class of Moral and Political Sciences had come to believe that Condillac's theory of knowledge, which rested on the understanding of how ideas were formed, was the key to discovering the truths upon which society was founded. In defining the nature of this science of ideas before the Institute, Destutt de Tracy argued that idéologie, as he called this study, was essential for the establishment of the true moral and political sciences.

Roederer, who became a member of the section on political economy in the Class of Moral and Political Sciences, shared the enthusiasm for the program of idéologie and became one of the idéologues who spread the new gospel.[64] He had already stressed the value of Condillac's concept of the relationship between sensations and ideas in the formation of morals in the *Cours d'organisation sociale*. In his summary of Condillac's Logique in 1795, Roederer explained the value of Condillac's emphasis on the importance of the proper analysis of man's observations in order to arrive at truth. While observation was an activity open to all, proper analysis required education. Without education "we are condemned to errors."[65] In Roederer's view improper analysis was all too common: "In place of observing things we want to imagine them." The result of such behavior was the accumulation of errors for generations with men holding "false,

---

[62] Ibid., p. 84. Roederer also edited a work on mathematical politics in 1796. P.-L. Roederer, ed. *Collection de divers ouvrages d'arithmétique politique par Lavoisier, de Lagrange et autres* (Paris, An IV).

[63] Baker, *Condorcet*, pp. 302, 371.

[64] While Roederer has traditionally been classified as an idéologue, Martin Staum, using more rigid criteria for evaluation than other historians, has argued that Roederer was peripheral to the main group of idéologues. This view seems quite sound. Roederer's principal philosophical work, the *Cours d'organisation sociale*, preceded the creation of the National Institute, and his later work was minor in character. Consequently Roederer was sympathetic and supportive of the idéologues but never an intimate member of the group. See Martin Staum, "The Class of Moral and Political Sciences, 1795–1803." *French Historical Studies*, 11(1980): 371–72.

[65] P.-L. Roederer, *Extrait ou abrégé de la Logique de Condillac*, in OR, 5: 406.

contradictory, and absurd ideas which superstition had distributed every-where." Politically the situation was a disaster: "What laws! What insti-tutions! The Greeks, the Romans, ourselves, who follow such men of genius, what a spectacle we offer to a philosophic observer!"[66] The key to true knowledge then was not simple observation of phenomena but a proper education which would lead one to correct analysis of the ob-servations.

While Roederer made no outstanding contribution to the theory of idéologie as a component of social science, he was anxious to provide literate Frenchmen with an understanding of its principles and devoted much space in his journals to the work of the Institute.[67] For instance in the notice on the proceedings of the Institute (9 January 1797) in the *Journal d'économie publique* Roederer described in some detail Tracy's con-cept of idéologie which has been presented for the first time and also summarized Laromiguière's study on Condillac which had been read at the same session.[68] He gave Laromiguière's work an even more detailed treatment the following *décade.*[69] When the idéologue Saint-Lambert's famous work on morals, *Principes des moeurs,* was published, Roederer gave the event considerable space in the *Journal d' économie publique.*[70] He also provided readers with reviews of posthumous works by particular favorites of the idéologues including Adam Smith's *Theory of Moral Sen-timents* and a new edition of Helvétius' works.[71] In addition he analyzed works, such as Madame de Staël's *De l'Influence des passions* and Dupont de Nemours' *La Philosophie de l'univers,* which failed to live up to the standards of Condillac and the idéologues.[72]

The culmination of Roederer's work on behalf of idéologie was his analysis, unique among the idéologues, of the relationship between the Revolution and Enlightenment philosophy. This topic had much to rec-ommend it not only because of its subject matter but also because it in effect allowed him to use the techniques of idéologie, the proper analysis of observation, to arrive at his conclusion. For Roederer this analysis in-volved an understanding of the historical as well as the philosophical implications of the subject. Keenly interested in a clear understanding of the history of the Revolution, he had written long reviews of Necker's *De*

---

[66] Ibid.

[67] Roederer was very active in the Institute. On 26 and 30 April 1799 he defended Condillac from Domergue's grammatical propositions; and on 26 April and 9 May 1798 he read a paper on the government of China. See *Refutation de la théorie de la proposition grammaticale publiée par Urbain Domergue,* in OR, 8: 25–41; and *Mémoire sur le gouvernement de la Chine,* in OR, 8: 97–112.

[68] JEP 20 nivôse V (9 January 1797), in OR 5: 347ff.

[69] JEP 30 nivôse V (19 January 1797), in OR, 5: 382–85.

[70] JEP 20 brumaire VI (10 November 1797), in OR, 5: 117–122. For the reaction of the idéologues to this work see Van Duzer, *Contribution of the Idéologues to French Revolutionary Thought* (Baltimore, 1935), p. 64.

[71] JP 21 messidor VI (9 July 1798), in OR 4: 495–98; OR, 4: 470.

[72] JP 2 frimaire V (22 November 1796), JEP 10 frimaire-20 nivôse V (30 November–20 December 1796), and JEP 10 fructidor V (27 August 1796), in OR, 4: 467–94.

la Révolution française and Adrien Lezay's *Des Causes de la Révolution* in order to shed some light on this subject for his readers.[73] Neither of these works, however, had much to say regarding the relationship of philosophy to the Revolution. His attack on Rivarol's *De la Philosophie moderne* in the *Décade philosophique*, was another matter.[74] Rivarol's basic argument was that the Enlightenment had destroyed religion, morals, politics, and monarchy itself, thus laying the foundation for the destructive impulses of the Revolution. Roederer, on the other hand, argued that modern philosophy was not destructive but had replaced "arbitrary hypotheses and the mania of systems" with experience and observation which had led to a true understanding "of the origin of ideas."[75] Nevertheless, Roederer argued that while "philosophy would approve the grand and durable results of the Revolution . . . it is easy to prove that it is not precisely this [the Enlightenment] which made it [the Revolution]."[76] Philosophy had "prepared a financial, military, civil, moral, and religious reformation, not a political revolution." What made the Revolution was "the public fury excited by the odious resistance to the most justifiable reformation." The Enlightenment could hardly have paved the way for the destruction of the institution of monarchy when philosophes like Voltaire formulated their ideas with the aim of strengthening kings like Frederick of Prussia. The Constitution of 1791 itself was not the product of "philosophical discussions" but rather "the English and American constitutions which it took for models."[77] Likewise, the Enlightenment did not bring on the Terror which was not even a necessary consequence of the Revolution. The Terror was in fact the result of certain circumstances (the war, food shortages, and the weak *assignat*) which might never have developed. Certainly no philosophers had ever advocated anything approaching the "plunder, pillage, proscription, death, [and] massacre" of the Terror.[78] The chief apostle of the Terror, Robespierre, had even gone so far as to call the philosophes "ambitious charlatans" who were all "dishonored in the Revolution."[79]

Roederer's argument that the Enlightenment had laid the foundation for just reform and that the turmoil of the Revolution had destroyed the prospect of its realization was basically a restatement of his thesis in the *Cours d'organisation sociale*. Only when the proper philosophical foundation had been laid could just and lasting reform be established. Idéologie in particular and social science in general were essential if this proper foundation was to be put in place. The problem with the work of the Institute, however, was that though progress was being made toward

---

[73] JEP 10 nivôse–20 germinal V (30 December 1796–9 April 1797), in OR, 4: 561–603.
[74] P.-L. Roederer, *De la Philosophie moderne*, in OR, 4: 503–516. The essay appeared in the *Décade* on 30 fructidor VII (16 September 1799).
[75] Ibid., p. 504.
[76] Ibid., p. 509.
[77] Ibid., p. 511.
[78] Ibid., p. 512.
[79] Ibid., p. 513.

greater philosophical understanding of society, political disorder was not abating. This was because those who had had the proper understanding of society's needs were not in a position of power. Roederer, among others, became aware that Condorcet's program which called for the development of the first principles of social organization was of little value if there was no method available for the institution of his "social art" as well. To Roederer the manifold weaknesses of the government of the Directory would never produce political decisions based on the knowledge of social science. For this reason Roederer and other idéologues became involved in the conspiracy of brumaire which led to the advent of Bonaparte and the implementation of the Constitution of the Year VIII. In order to make the ultimate connection between social science and Roederer's political role in 1799, we must trace Roederer's political and journalistic activities through the years of the Thermidorian Reaction and the Directory.

VII. THERMIDORIAN JOURNALIST

During the Thermidorian Reaction Roederer, who had devoted himself to writing his lectures for the Lycée in early 1793 and to translating Hobbes's *De Cive* while hiding during the Terror, once again became concerned with political reality. Roederer had two immediate goals to accomplish after the fall of Robespierre. One was to clear his reputation so that he could move openly in society, and the second was to work in any way possible for the dissolution of all vestiges of the Terror and revolutionary government. Once the Terror was eradicated, then the possibility existed that a new government which better conformed to the laws of society as Roederer understood them might be created.

Since Roederer was hardly in a position to reenter public office, he marked his return to public life only timidly by writing anonymous and pseudonymous political tracts. Meeting with some success in the acceptance of his ideas, he gradually moved into full-time journalism by writing for and editing the *Journal de Paris*. Exhibiting a natural resentment for his treatment at the hands of the Revolution after August 1792, the tone of his writings was hostile to the dictatorship of the Committee of Public Safety. He urged the complete eradication of all aspects of the Terror, the restoration of rights to its victims, and a return to the true principles of the Revolution. Unable to play any direct political role himself, Roederer had to be satisfied with molding public opinion in support of the Thermidorian Reaction.

His first effort was an article condemning the Terror that he submitted to the journal *Le Republicain*.[1] Impressed with the piece, the editor Charles His brought it to the attention of the deputy Tallien, who believed it would be possible to use the material for a speech in the Convention. Roederer allowed Tallien to make some minor revisions and to present the material as his own to the Convention on 11 fructidor (28 August 1794).[2] Roederer wrote one other speech for Tallien on the necessity of returning the land confiscated from the families of those condemned by the Terror as well as an unflattering *Portrait de Robespierre* and a speech concerning the possibility of peace with the European powers for Merlin de Thionville.[3]

---

[1] P.-L. Roederer, *Notice de ma vie pour mes enfants*, in OR, 3: 217.

[2] Ibid.; P.-L. Roederer, *Discours prononcé par Tallien sur la Terreur*, in OR, 7: 3–10; MU, 21: 612–15.

[3] Roederer, *Notice*, in OR, 3: 288; P.-L. Roederer, *Un mot sur la necessité de rendre les biens des condamnés*, in OR, 7: 22–24. This speech for Tallien was never delivered. P.-L. Roederer, *Portrait de Robespierre*, in OR, 3: 267–71. Regarding Roederer's relationship with Merlin de Thionville, the royalist writer Richer-Sérizy, who was unfriendly to both men, believed that Roederer used Merlin for his mouthpiece, *L'Accusateur public*, 5: 23–32.

Madame Tallien and Madame Beauharnais had commissioned Roederer to write the second speech for Tallien, but none of his other writings seems to have been solicited in this fashion.[4] Roederer's other political tracts were simply written with pseudonyms or anonymously.

Roederer maintained this anonymity due to the uncertainty of his position among the Thermidorians. Because of his role on 10 August, much of the public considered him a royalist. If he did not write anonymously, he feared that "demagogues" would accuse him of promoting royalism.[5] In an effort to clear his reputation he appealed to Merlin de Thionville, who had entered the Committee of General Security after Robespierre's fall.[6] Writing Merlin on 25 fructidor II (11 September 1794), Roederer asserted his patriotism and asked Merlin to seek the aid of the committee in "delivering me from my captivity."[7] In another, undated letter to Merlin Roederer briefly defended his activity on 10 August and asked Merlin to look at a mémoire he had written to justify further his actions on that date.[8] Merlin replied that he saw no need to reopen a case which had already been judged in Roederer's favor by the Legislative Assembly, the Committee of General Security of the time, and even the Paris Commune.[9] (There seems to be be no evidence to support Merlin's contention that Roederer's name had indeed been cleared by these bodies.) Furthermore, he urged Roederer to "resume with a new zeal the occupations in which you can be useful to the Republic."[10]

Despite his failure to receive the complete exoneration that he requested from the Committee of General Security, Roederer did resume his public activity. After writing some anonymous articles in the *Journal de Paris* he finally gathered the courage to initial the article "Esprit public" published on 28 pluviôse III (16 February 1795).[11] In that same month he purchased half-interest in the *Journal de Paris* from Olivier de Corancez and undertook its editorship.[12]

The *Journal de Paris* had had a noteworthy past; when founded by Corancez and others in 1777, it had the distinction of being the first daily newspaper in France.[13] Its format consisted of information on the theater and literature as well as government announcements. After the outbreak

---

[4] P.-L. Roederer, "Tableau des articles de ma composition insérés au *Journal de Paris* dans l'année 1795," in OR, 6: 43.

[5] Roederer, *Notice*, in OR, 3: 289.

[6] Georges Lefebvre, *The Thermidorians*, trans. Robert Baldick (New York, 1964), p. 12.

[7] Roederer to Merlin, 25 fructidor II, in Jean Reynaud, *Vie et correspondance de Merlin de Thionville* (Paris, 1860), p. 26.

[8] Roederer to Merlin, no date, ibid., pp. 27–28.

[9] Merlin to Roederer, no date, ibid., p. 28. This letter was probably written some time in 1795 as it makes reference to Roederer's editing the *Journal de Paris*.

[10] Ibid.

[11] In this article Roederer signified his authorship with the initial R, the first time he had done so since 1793. JP 28 pluviôse III (16 February 1795). Roederer, "Tableau des articles," in OR, 6: 44.

[12] Note of Roederer, in OR, 6: 45.

[13] Charles Ledré, *Histoire de la presse* (Paris, 1958), p. 80.

of the Revolution, the increasingly popular journal began reporting the sessions of the Assembly from a generally conservative political point of view.[14] Roederer had used the paper to express his opinions in late 1792 and early 1793 after the journal had become closely associated with the Girondins. Given the nature of its format and its high subscription price in early 1795 of 42 livres per year, the *Journal de Paris* was obviously directed to the educated and affluent elite of Paris and France. Yet it did have a fairly large readership with almost 3,000 subscribers at the time Roederer purchased half-ownership.[15] In the agreement he made with Corancez, Roederer was to pay 30,000 livres for half-interest in the publication and the right of editorship. While this arrangement caused problems later, Roederer was able to use the *Journal de Paris* effectively during the Thermidorian period to express his political views.

Flexibility appears to have been the principal characteristic of this journal, which had survived the successive governments from Louis XVI through Robespierre. It again demonstrated its malleable nature in 1795 when Roederer announced that the editorial policy of the sheet was to be different in the future. To make the announcement, Roederer used the tactic of writing an anonymous letter on 1 ventôse III (19 February 1795) to the journal and then answering it himself.[16] The letter charged the newspaper with Jacobin extremism and called the writer of the articles on the Convention a "vassal of Robespierre." Other charges made against the sheet were that the current opinions of the populace of Paris were never reported, that foreign affairs were overlooked, and that literary news was not discussed because of the political points of view contained therein. On 3 ventôse (21 February) Roederer wrote a "Response of the Authors of the Journal" in which he announced that all of these criticisms were to be met.[17] First he announced that a new reporter, who would report only the truth, had been assigned to cover the sessions of the Convention. In addition an attempt would be made to discover the public opinion of Paris and to report foreign news. In regard to the reviews of books Roederer expressed the hope that the journal would be able to provide not only reports on French publications but also information on foreign works. He said that reestablishing a "republic of letters" was the best means of "pacification, even fraternization" with the people of Europe.[18]

For the remainder of the Convention Roederer was to devote almost all of this energy to editing and writing for the *Journal de Paris*. At first he directed most of his talents to writing a series of articles entitled "Esprit public" in which he attempted to determine current public attitudes in Paris. Since the science of public opinion polls had not yet been developed, Roederer had to rely on a less objective criterion for determining what

---

[14] Claude Bellanger et al., *Histoire générale de la presse française* (Paris, 1969), 1: 464, 504.

[15] AN 29AP91, Roederer to Corancez, 20 floréal III (9 May 1795).

[16] JP, 1 ventôse III (19 February 1795), in OR, 6: 45.

[17] JP, 3 ventôse III (21 February 1795), in OR, 6: 46–47.

[18] Ibid., p. 47.

was on people's minds. He gathered his information from the press and pamphlets of the day, from theatrical productions, and from conversations that he overheard in cafés, public places, and shops.[19] For instance on the basis of such sources he reported on 28 pluviôse (16 February) that the conservative journals *L'Orateur du peuple* and *L'Accusateur public* were outselling the Montagnard *Journal universel* and that the conversations in public places were antagonistic to "the tyranny" even though there was still some talk of the Jacobins.[20] By the late spring and early summer of 1795 Roederer, having lost all fear of writing openly, was producing commentaries on the political events of the day. Most notable among his articles were his suggestions for and criticisms of the new constitution. From Roederer's various writings of the Thermidorian period emerges a clear indication of how the events of the first years of the Revolution shaped his political ideas for the remainder of the decade.

The initial goal of the Thermidorians had been the overthrow of Robespierre, but with his death they directed their efforts toward dismantling the apparatus of the dictatorship of the Committee of Public Safety. Roederer, sharing completely the Thermidorian revulsion of the tyranny of the committee and the Terror which it had brought to France during the Year II, made an initial attack against the dictatorship in the article Tallien used as a speech before the Convention. Here he argued that liberty and justice were goals that the Revolution sought to achieve and that any form of government which did not seek those goals could not be truly revolutionary—in fact it would be "counter-revolutionary."[21] In his opinion not even a temporary reign of terror could be tolerated for "a momentary tyranny cannot be considered a means of establishing liberty."[22] A tyrannical government found it necessary constantly to threaten its citizens with punishment for their words and actions as well as their silence and inaction. The result of such policies necessarily led to a police state atmosphere where it was necessary to maintain "a trap under each step, a spy in each house, a traitor in each family, [and] assassins on the tribunal."[23] The government under the Terror rested upon arbitrary and absolute power which "necessarily tends toward royalty."[24] Even if such a government consisted of several men, it would be able to function effectively only if they gave blind obedience to one "whose will took the place of law" (an obvious reference to his conception of Robespierre's role on the Committee of Public Safety).[25] Instead of arbitrary power the true purpose of revolutionary government was "to terminate and guarantee [the achievements] of the Revolution."[26] Such a government could not

---

[19] JP, 28 pluviôse III (16 February 1795), in OR, 6: 44.
[20] Ibid.
[21] Roederer, *Discours prononcé par Tallien*, in OR, 7: 5–6.
[22] Ibid., p. 6.
[23] Ibid.
[24] Ibid., p. 7.
[25] Ibid.
[26] Ibid., p. 5.

exist if it were itself an agent of "counter-revolution," or terror.[27] In order for a revolutionary government to do its proper work, "to make the majority of people love a revolution, it suffices not to pervert, to alter the principles, nor to thwart its goals."[28]

If the Terror had been "counter-revolutionary," then the victims of Robespierre's tyranny had suffered unjustly; and Roederer maintained that some restitution would have to be made to these victims if justice was to prevail. For instance the seventy-one Girondin deputies proscribed by the Convention after the 31 May–2 June crisis must be restored to their places. Roederer made such a case for the proscribed deputies in a pamphlet written under the pseudonym Jacques.[29] According to Albert Mathiez the pamphlet had some considerable influence on the Convention's decision to readmit these deputies on 18 frimaire III (8 December 1794).[30]

The issue in question was the arrest of the Girondin deputies on 3 October 1793 for signing a protest on 6 June concerning the *journées* of 31 May–2 June.[31] The protest stated that the insurrection had violated the Convention and handed power to a minority, but the Girondins had made no effort to circulate this protest, which remained secret until it was found in the papers of its probable author, Lauze-Deperret, when he was arrested later in the year.

In defense of his former political allies Roederer argued that the protest could not possibly be considered an illegal act since the deputies had not made it public nor could it have affected the course of the federalist revolt which preceded its discovery.[32] Even if the document had been published, it contained no appeal for departmental revolt but only expressed an opinion, a right due to all deputies and citizens, that a faction had taken power in Paris. The seventy-one deputies, having committed no crime, should be readmitted to the Convention where they would bolster the ranks of the Thermidorians and insure the end of the Terror.[33] The failure to restore them to their positions would do irreparable damage to the concept of justice, the principle of which could never "be in opposition to the public safety."[34] Also at stake was the tenet of the inviolability of the elected representatives: "The nomination of a deputy is an immediate act of the sovereignty of the people; . . . the arbitrary rejection of a deputy would be an infringement of the sovereignty of the people."[35]

---

[27] Ibid., p. 6.

[28] Ibid.

[29] Jacques [P.-L. Roederer], *De L'Interêt des comités de la Convention nationale et de la Nation dans l'affair des soixante et onze députés détenus*, in OR, 7: 10–17.

[30] Albert Mathiez, *After Robespierre: The Thermidorian Reaction*, trans. Catherine A. Phillips (New York, 1965), pp. 100–01.

[31] There were actually seventy-five deputies not seventy-one as Roederer asserts. This error is understandable as there has been a great deal of confusion surrounding this event down to the present day. See M. J. Sydenham, *The Girondins* (London, 1961), pp. 41, 44–48.

[32] Roederer, *De L'Interêt des comités*, in OR, 7: 10.

[33] Ibid., pp. 13–14.

[34] Ibid., p. 13.

[35] Ibid., p. 16.

Roederer was not so firmly attached to these principles that he was unwilling to advocate their suspension in combating the remnants of the Terror. He was particularly interested in the aftermath of 12 germinal, a popular journée during which a crowd invaded the Convention demanding bread, the Constitution of 1793, and the release of imprisoned patriots. The crowd received support from the Montagnard faction in the Convention. After the journée of 12 germinal the Convention, in need of scapegoats on which to lay the blame for the insurrection, ordered the old leadership of the left, Barère, Billaud, Collot, and Vadier, deported to Guiana without benefit of a trial.[36] Roederer maintained that the Convention's action was fully justified, arguing that as depository of national sovereignty the Convention had the duty to handle cases, like those of Louis XVI and the "Four," involving treason.[37] Before the insurrection Roederer had argued that the Convention could demonstrate that tyranny had truly ended by pursuing a policy of clemency in the cases of the leaders of the Terror.[38] He had suggested either exiling them to an island or, better yet, granting an amnesty to all former terrorists which would remain in force as long as the "public peace" was not disturbed.[39] With the disruption of the "public peace" on 12 germinal Roederer came to believe it expedient to eliminate the troublesome element in the Convention.

The Convention was not content merely to order the deportation of the leadership of the left, but during the days immediately following the uprising it also ordered the arrest of seventeen other deputies who shared their views.[40] Roederer concurred with the Convention's decision, justifying the purge with the reasoning that it restored vigor to the Assembly and would prevent the further pillage, hunger, and torment that the Jacobins would have caused.[41] The action of the Convention resembled the arrest of the deputies after the insurrection of 31 May–2 June, which Roederer had pronounced earlier to be counter-revolutionary.[42] He was to reconcile his two apparently contradictory positions by claiming that the purposes of the two purges were entirely different: "The 31 May fell on upright men because they had declared themselves the defenders of liberty and property; the 12 germinal fell to the contrary on the preachers and the agents of death and pillage . . . the 31 May proscribed some victims; the 12 germinal only dispersed the agents of proscription."[43] These

---

[36] Lefebvre, *The Thermidorians*, p. 120.

[37] JP, 19 germinal III (8 April 1795), in OR, 6: 64.

[38] Roederer, *De L'Interêt des comités*, in OR, 7: 15; JP, 16 ventôse III (6 March 1795), in OR, 6: 51.

[39] JP, 16 ventôse III, in OR, 6: 52; JP, 22 ventôse III (12 March 1795), in OR, 6: 52–53.

[40] Lefebvre, *The Thermidorians*, p. 120.

[41] JP, 19 germinal III (8 April 1795), in OR, 6: 66.

[42] Roederer, *De L'Interêt des comités*, in OR, 6: 16.

[43] JP, 19 germinal III, in OR, 6: 67. During 1794–95 Roederer wavered between outright adoration of the Girondins and harsh criticism of their leadership of 1793. However, he was basically sympathetic with the Girondin point of view.

deputies were not arrested, he argued, because of what they had said on the floor of the Convention but for what they had advocated "in seditious assemblies" or in the Convention when it had been threatened by the crowd. Roederer insisted that in such instances the majority had the right to curb the actions of an unruly minority or that minority would in the end succeed in removing the majority from power. Obviously Roederer was more interested in supporting the elimination of terrorists than the fulfillment of the lofty principles of justice and inviolable representation.

To right the wrongs of the Terror further, Roederer advocated allowing most of those who had fled France to return.[44] These "fugitives," as he termed them, included such notables as Talleyrand and Montesquiou, who he believed had fled only because of the increasing disorders in France after 10 August 1792. Even if some of these individuals were nominally royalists, they would pose no threat to the Republic; they would actually support it if they could be assured that law and order would prevail.[45] The return of such persons, supporters of the Constitution of 1791 and "the old friends, the proven friends of liberty, of order, and of peace," would be a definite benefit to the Revolution.[46] The "fugitives" were not to be confused with the émigrés, whom Roederer classified as aristocrats (by which he apparently meant those who had fought with the Prussians and the Habsburgs) whose goal was nothing short of the restoration of the ancien régime. The "fugitives" had had no connection with the émigrés in exile or with the émigré attempt to invade France at Quiberon.[47] As these "fugitives" had not been disloyal to the Revolution, they should be readmitted to France in full possession of their property.[48] Similar motives prompted Roederer to urge that the confiscated land of those condemned by the Terror, most of whom were almost certainly innocent of any crime, should be returned to the victims' families.[49]

With the eradication of the last vestiges of the Terror Roederer was convinced that the economic situation in France would shortly improve. Because the land unjustly confiscated during the Terror was not selling well, it pulled down the price of the land which legitimately belonged to the nation and thus was destroying faith in the assignat.[50] Returning the confiscated lands to all who had been unjustly deprived of them during the Terror would result in higher selling prices for national land and restored faith in the assignat. He also believed that the policies of the maximum and forced requisitions carried out by the Committee of Public Safety had dissuaded individuals from investing in landed property.[51]

---

[44] Roederer, *Des Fugitifs françaises et des émigrés*, in OR, 7: 46–47.
[45] Ibid., p. 48.
[46] Ibid., p. 49.
[47] Ibid., pp. 49–50.
[48] Ibid., p. 54. He made no mention of what should be done with the property already sold by the government.
[49] Roederer, *Un Mot*, in OR, 7: 22–23.
[50] JP, 20 ventôse III (20 March 1795), in OR, 6: 22.
[51] JP, 10 ventôse III (28 February 1795), in OR, 6: 19–20.

People with money to spend had preferred to buy merchandise which could be transported readily or sold instead of purchasing land. The tremendous demand for goods led to a corresponding rise in prices. Only when the entire apparatus of the Terror was dismantled, a constitutional regime reestablished, and property rights guaranteed would investors once again purchase land thereby lessening the demand for consumer items. Once the demand for land increased, Roederer was convinced that the price of land would rise which in turn would lead to a more stable assignat.[52]

Roederer basically supported the decisions of the Thermidorian Convention except in the matter of freedom of the press. With the increasing threat of royalism during the Thermidorian period, the Convention at the insistence of Louvet and Chenier curtailed the freedom of the press, which had been renewed in the first days after the fall of Robespierre.[53] The law of 12 floréal III (1 May 1795) ordered the arrest of all who by seditious writings or speeches degraded the Convention or attempted to reestablish the monarchy. Criticism was immediately forthcoming from some deputies, such as Tallien and Fréron, as well as journalists, such as La Harpe and the Abbé Morellet.[54] Roederer had established his position on freedom of the press in the *Journal de Paris* as early as 9 pluviôse III (28 January 1795), when he argued that the royalist Lacroix could not be enjoined from publishing merely because he had monarchial sympathies.[55] After the passage of the law of 12 floréal he joined the chorus of protests with a series of articles in the *Journal de Paris*.

Roederer maintained that the law was a return to the principles of the Terror.[56] As the act of writing was itself harmless, only an overt crime could justify arrest and prosecution. The danger in curtailing the press lay in restricting it from free commentary on political matters especially the drafting of the new constitution. A censored press would be worse than inane because "as soon as it is oppressed it necessarily becomes oppressive; as soon as it no longer propagates truth . . . it necessarily corrupts." If the press could not instruct the citizenry it would deny to the people "the great privilege of the human species, the boundless perfectibility of its faculties and the unlimited enlargement of the means of happiness."[57]

As Roederer viewed the situation after 9 thermidor, dismantling the Terror was not the only duty that the Convention had to undertake. He was equally concerned that the popular disorders which had characterized

---

[52] Roederer also cited the continuation of the war and the demand it caused for printing of more assignats as well as the lack of interest in the Convention for stopping the decline in the price of assignats as factors in the grave financial situation in which France found herself. Ibid., p. 20; JP, 30 ventôse III, in OR, 4: 21; JP 30 germinal III (19 April 1795), in OR, 4: 23–24; JP, 28 floréal III (17 May 1795), in OR, 4: 30.

[53] Mathiez, *After Robespierre*, pp. 200–01.

[54] Bellanger, *Histoire générale*, 1: 520–21.

[55] JP, 9 pluviôse III (23 January 1795), in OR, 5: 77–78.

[56] JP, 18–21 floréal III (7-10 May 1795), in OR, 6: 76.

[57] Ibid.

France since 1792 be halted. There was no doubt in his mind that this unrest was the work of a small group of political activists on the left primarily centered in the Jacobin Club. These activists not only had interfered constantly in the political processes of the Republic but had repeatedly encouraged popular insurrections. The obvious solution to this problem was to reorganize the popular societies in a manner which would render them impotent politically and to suppress forcibly any popular disturbances. Roederer advocated such a policy to the Convention in the *Journal de Paris* and even joined the military forces of the Convention in suppressing the insurrection of prairial.

After the Convention had closed the Jacobin Club on 12 November 1794 Roederer wrote an anonymous pamphlet, *Sociétés populaires,* concerning the future organization of such associations.[58] He did not believe that the clubs should serve as the watchdogs of the Revolution by denouncing counter-revolutionaries or defending the interests of the people before the assemblies.[59] Rather they should have as their sole purpose the friendship among and instruction of the members. Political subjects should not be discussed because of the possibility that the society would act on its discussions, which could lead to the arrogation of power from the public authorities. In an effort to prevent "all opposition to the government, all factious or seditious maneuvers" Roederer said that the societies should be prohibited from affiliating or corresponding with one another.[60] All new members of the association would have to be approved by all of the old members in order to prevent any faction in the society from building a strong following which could be used for "perverse or suspicious schemes."[61] The membership in each society should be strictly limited to eighty in communes of fifty thousand or more inhabitants and fifteen in the smaller communes.[62] He thought limiting the number of members in the clubs would allow all members to express their opinions and encourage the formation of a larger number of organizations which he believed would permit more people to participate in the discussions. More importantly for Roederer, the small societies would be less dangerous to the government: "The limitation of the number [of members] is useful . . . because it avoids assemblies capable of subverting the constituted authorities. . . ."[63]

The Jacobins and other Parisian clubs had taken it upon themselves to be the guardians of the Revolution and to press the various legislative bodies into sustaining the revolutionary movement. Roederer, at least partially because of his own unhappy experience at the Jacobins, was anxious to see an end to this role of the societies.[64] Conceding that the

---

[58] Roederer, *Sociétés populaires,* in OR, 6: 17–22. The pamphlet was written on 20 November 1794.
[59] Ibid., pp. 17–18.
[60] Ibid., p. 21.
[61] Ibid., p. 19.
[62] Ibid., pp. 17, 19–20.
[63] Ibid., p. 20.
[64] Ibid.

clubs had been successful in holding the representatives of the nation accountable for their actions, he denied that this was a proper function for an organization that itself was responsible to no one but its own members. If the government was to act in a tyrannical fashion, the people always had the right to resort to insurrection, which he described as "a resource which could be used against the national representation . . . that . . . has no need of an intermediate association [i.e. the clubs] between it and the people."[65]

The popular uprisings which occurred in the spring of 1795 gave Roederer plenty of opportunities to comment on the *sans-culotte* activities in his series of articles, "Esprit public," in the *Journal de Paris*. The severe winter of 1794–95, the food shortage, and the abolition of the law of the maximum and its price controls made the life of the sans-culottes exceedingly hard. Mounting dissatisfaction had developed among them during the winter and reached the point of explosion by early spring.[66] Roederer, apparently aware of none of this unhappiness, wrote on 4 ventôse (22 February) that the quiet in Paris was an indication of the support the populace gave to the government.[67] On 29 ventôse (19 March) he reported that the disturbance by women at bakeries was the result of the fear of the lack of bread and not the result of an actual bread shortage; the women always became calm when they obtained their bread.[68] That Roederer should engage in such wishful thinking before the insurrection of 12 germinal (1 April) is perhaps understandable, but even after that journée he kept insisting that the situation in Paris was stable. In an article on 5 floréal (24 April) he complimented Paris for its patience with the bread shortage, which he had finally come to realize did exist, and praised the people for their sacrifices for the nation.[69] When the Montreuil section tried to get other sections to follow its example of 10 floréal (29 April) by going into permanent session to discuss the food problem and failed to obtain any support, Roederer enthusiastically proclaimed that Paris would remain calm.[70]

Despite the mounting evidence, including the insurrection of 12 germinal, that there existed considerable dissatisfaction among the sans-culottes, Roederer was able to maintain this confident attitude regarding public opinion in Paris because he believed that there was no *real* food crisis among the populace, but only the activity of some conniving instigators of anarchy. Responding to some minor disturbances at the Convention, Roederer wrote on 9 ventôse (24 February) that factions had used the rising prices of goods to stimulate agitation against the Convention, citing as proof a pamphlet which was distributed calling for reestablishment of the Terror.[71] He also insisted that there would have been no

---

[65] Ibid.
[66] George Rudé, *The Crowd in the French Revolution* (London, 1959), pp. 142–47.
[67] JP, 4 ventôse III (22 February 1795), in OR, 6: 48.
[68] JP, 29 ventôse III (19 March 1795), in OR, 6: 55–56.
[69] JP, 5 floréal III (24 April 1795), in OR, 6: 70.
[70] JP, 12 floréal III (1 May 1795), in OR, 6: 71.
[71] JP, 9 ventôse III (27 February 1795), in OR, 6: 49–50.

uprising in germinal despite the shortage of bread if it had not been for "the factional spirit" exciting the people to violence.[72]

According to Kare Tønnesson the uprisings were often interpreted by the Thermidorians as the work of scheming agitators manipulating the crowds to their own selfish advantage.[73] Tønnesson, specifically referring to Roederer's article of 15 germinal (4 April), finds it hard to believe that the Thermidorians sincerely held this interpretation of events. Indeed Roederer was only able to arrive at such a conclusion by including in the category of "the faction" both the members of the clubs and the sans-culottes who had been clamoring for bread. According to him these were not just poor, hungry people trying to obtain food, but "men without property who are joined to those who do not own one-fiftieth of the nation," "a handful of outcasts" who have "robbed, pillaged, enchained, imprisoned, massacred" the rest of the nation.[74] Among them the women were distinguished for their love "of pillage and blood" and their ability to stir up passions against the government while standing in queues at the bakeries.[75] Convinced that the food shortages were being exploited by propertyless, bloodthirsty terrorists, Roederer believed the important task was not to solve the food crisis but to curb the activities of the group trying to disrupt the Republic.

Roederer anxiously sought methods to reduce the interference of the Jacobins and sans-culottes in political affairs. Before the journées of germinal and prairial Roederer had suggested that the time of the section meetings which were held on the last day of each décade be changed from the evening hours to the afternoon hours between midday and three-o'clock.[76] The "friends of order" would be more likely to attend the afternoon assemblies than those of the evening when they preferred remaining home with their families. Also no particular day should be set aside for rest, days of rest being taken only when an individual was weary because the Jacobins used the *décadi* for formulating intrigue.[77] Not opposing violent measures to quell the terrorists if such efforts would lead to the strengthening of the government, Roederer praised the work of the bands of youth, the *jeunesse dorée*, whose activities consisted mainly of breaking up Jacobin gatherings and destroying the presses of their journals. On at least one occasion, he claimed that their interference in Jacobin intrigue had saved France from a "disastrous commotion."[78] The jeunesse dorée never acted on their personal whim but only at the insistence of what he regarded as "public opinion."[79] Denying that they had any roy-

---

[72] JP, 15 germinal III (4 April 1795), in OR, 6: 62.

[73] Kare D. Tønnesson, *La Défaite des sans-culottes: movement populaire et reaction bourgeoise en l'an III* (Oslo, 1959), pp. 346–47.

[74] JP, 18 germinal III (7 April 1795), in OR, 6: 65.

[75] Ibid.

[76] JP, 9 ventôse III (27 February 1795), in OR, 6: 65.

[77] JP, 4 germinal III (24 March 1795), in OR, 6: 57.

[78] Ibid.

[79] JP, 8 ventôse III (26 February 1795), in OR, 6: 48–49; JP, 29 ventôse III (19 March 1795), in OR, 6: 56.

alist affiliation, Roederer insisted that the youth were strongly republican and acted only as an auxiliary to the regular armed force.[80]

With the actual journées of germinal and prairial the hit-and-miss technique of the youth was not adequate to calm the crowd, and the National Guard and the regular army (during the prairial uprising) had to be called out. Roederer praised the decision to summon the National Guard to restore order in germinal and marched himself in the front line of the forces of the Convention when they moved into the Faubourg Saint-Antoine on the 4th of prairial.[81] Ecstatically Roederer described the events of prairial as a turning point in the Revolution, the end of the popular disturbances:

We have just escaped one of the most dreadful disasters that has ever menaced a great people. But we have more than escaped it, we have surmounted the cause of it, and we have learned the means of always surmounting it. The 4th of prairial has been the 10th of August for anarchy.[82]

The method of "surmounting the cause" of disturbances was the deployment of armed force into the faubourgs, and his prediction that 4 prairial would be the end of popular disturbances proved to be remarkably accurate. With the Terror dismantled and the crowds under control, Roederer was convinced that the forces which he believed would destroy the Republic had themselves been destroyed.

Roederer's hopes for the French Republic rested heavily on the new constitution that the Convention's commission of eleven was to draft.[83] As Roederer had made clear in the Cours d'organisation sociale, government had to rest on the natural rights which guaranteed the maintenance of society. To create such a government Roederer had described a number of practical approaches which included among other things some suggestions along the lines of Condorcet's social mathematics. Before the commission of eleven made its report to the Convention, Roederer revived a few of these suggestions and added others designed to limit democracy, which he had come to see as a threat to stable and rational government.

Perhaps because he believed it would have no chance of acceptance, he did not suggest his earlier idea that the Assembly make its decisions only after a reporter had made a dispassionate summary of all the advantages and disadvantages of a proposed law. He did argue that the new legislative body should be divided into two houses or sections so that "the interest of a faction will not be able to dominate all."[84] However, he was emphatic that there should be no upper house of notables. He did

---

[80] JP, 8 ventôse III, in OR, 6: 48–49; 5 germinal III (25 March 1795), in OR, 6: 59.

[81] JP, 15 germinal III (4 April 1795), in OR, 6: 63; JP, 8 prairial III (27 May 1795), in OR, 6: 88.

[82] JP, 7 prairial III (26 May 1795), in OR, 6: 86.

[83] Lefebvre, The Thermidorians, p. 176.

[84] JP, 9, 11, 13, 15, 16 prairial, 1, 2, 3, 19, messidor III (28, 30 May, 1, 3, 19, 21 June, 7 July, 1795) in OR, 6: 91–93.

reproduce in its entirety the concept of the popular ratification of laws.[85] He argued that if the legislature proposed irresponsible laws, the electorate, guided by a free press, would be able to reject them. Once a law was ratified, the populace would be more likely to obey a law it had approved. Suffrage should of course be limited only to persons possessing landed or non-landed property, those who were literate, and those with a métier or profession, as these were the attributes which tie "the interest of the individual to the social order."[86] In order that there be no misunderstanding about the value of manufacturing or commercial wealth to the political order, Roederer vigorously opposed Dupont and others who wanted to limit the suffrage to landowners.[87] Since merchants and manufacturers had larger investments than landowners and since they stood to lose more from riots and pillage, Roederer argued that they actually had an even greater stake in the social order than the landowners. The final reform necessary to improve the electoral system was the abolition of the primary assemblies, including the troublesome sections of Paris, which only provided a platform for schemers who wished to disrupt the political process.[88]

After the report of the commission of eleven to the Convention on 5 messidor III (23 June 1795) Roederer wrote a series of articles critical of the proposed Constitution in the *Journal de Paris* which was later published as the pamphlet *Du Gouvernement* on 3 thermidor (21 July). Here he argued that proposals of the commission of eleven had a number of inherent weaknesses that would almost certainly lead to future problems. The alternatives that he suggested were the product of his own revolutionary political experience and his theory of social science.

The purpose of government, as Roederer had outlined it in the *Cours d'organisation sociale* was to provide rational political decisions that would support man's social organization. This rational, political decision-making could only take place if government was properly instituted and could conduct itself in an atmosphere of calm. In the 1793 lectures Roederer had also argued that effective legislation should only set out general concepts and that more responsibility should be given to the executive to provide the necessary details to laws in the process of administration. In Roederer's view the recommendations of the commission of eleven provided neither the proper institutions, the requisite atmosphere for calm deliberation, nor the necessary power for the executive.

The proposed Constitution was to have a collective executive in the form of a five-man Directory, a concept Roederer was willing to accept.[89] Despite his admiration for the United States, he did not think that France

---

[85] Ibid., p. 90.

[86] Ibid., p. 95.

[87] Ibid., pp. 96–100.

[88] Ibid., pp. 94–95.

[89] For the Constitution of the Year III see John Hall Stewart, *A Documentary Survey of the French Revolution* (New York, 1951), pp. 571–612; P.-L. Roederer, *Du Gouvernement*, in OR, 7: 29.

could elect a chief executive like a president without "a terrible commotion" since the royalists would try to use the office to restore the Monarchy.[90] Even if a republican was elected, one man could only represent a faction and never the entire population. A collective executive was not without its drawbacks, of course. Factions could form within the executive as had "all of the councils of government that we have seen in France for the last three years. . . ."[91] There was also the very real possibility of graft and corruption with deputies trying to bribe members of the executive, factions trying to place their men in the Directory, and the directors operating only from selfish motives. If such a situation developed, chaos would necessarily follow:

When those of different interests and passions oppose each other in a governing body, its will is weak, vacillating, contradictory, its commandments without energy. . . . When anarchy is at the center of a state, it is shortly at its borders.[92]

How could such a situation be avoided? Roederer believed allowing the legislature to remove directors at will in order to insure harmony would only lead to dissension within the ranks of the deputies.[93] Instead he had two novel suggestions for executive organization. One was the creation of a *grand électeur* in the Directory whose sole function would be to insure unity by removing its uncooperative members. Roederer admitted that with such a limited function, the grand électeur might never command enough influence to bring about the removal of directors. The other and probably preferable solution was the election of a *grand procureur national* who was to be chosen by a majority of the directors and who would serve as a professional administrator much as the procureur-général-syndics were to have functioned in the departmental directories of 1791. This official would deliberate with the directors and would have sole responsibility for communicating with the departments. He was not merely to follow the orders of the directors but to "elicit the necessary decisions" from them.[94] Roederer did not explain the role of this office in great detail, but he obviously envisioned such an official as the moving force behind the executive.

The commission of eleven proposed that the Directory have very limited powers to prevent a recurrence of the executive tyranny of the Terror. Roederer certainly shared their abhorrence of dictatorship but believed that it had been largely the product of an irresponsible legislature. The proper method of preventing tyranny or chaos was to strengthen the executive by allowing it to examine all proposed legislation, to refer legislation it considered unconstitutional to the courts, and to control the Treasury.[95] To prevent anarchy the Directory, not the Council of Elders

---

[90] Roederer, *Du Gouvernement*, in OR, 7: 42–43.
[91] Ibid., pp. 35–36.
[92] Ibid., p. 37.
[93] Ibid., p. 44.
[94] Ibid.
[95] Ibid., p. 40.

as stipulated in the constitutional draft, should control the police powers in the city where the government sat. Otherwise popular pressure might force the Elders to support the disturbances and would "obviously put the executive council under the hand of some member of a committee."[96] Perhaps the greatest weakness would be the inability of the Directory to control local administrators who were to be elected by their local communities as had been the case under the Constitution of 1791. Such administrators would be likely to resist any orders which conflicted with the wishes of their constituents. He argued that it "is necessary that orders and powers emanate from the same source."[97] As an example he recalled his own experience in the department of Paris where the elected officials had found it nearly impossible to collect taxes.[98] Agreeing that local administrators should be residents of the area that they were to administer, he insisted that the government could have the best of both worlds by choosing their officials from lists presented by the primary assemblies. This procedure would insure that the government could control its agents while inhabitants would be governed by men who knew the local conditions and problems.

The greatest danger to the Republic would be the inability of the legislature and the executive to work together in the interests of order. The constitutional proposal before the Convention, however, did not provide an adequate framework for creating harmony between these two branches. Roederer feared that the balance of power lay on the side of the legislature which, given the recent history of the Revolution, had proven itself unable to withstand popular pressure. Therefore, if order was to return to France, a strong executive must be created. Under the system presented by the commission of eleven the directors were to be chosen by the legislature; but once selected, they were to have no influence on legislation. Roederer argued that such a provision would limit the Directory's ability to deal with popular insurrections since the legislature could outlaw any punitive actions undertaken to restore order.[99] Furthermore, on a vote of both houses the directors could be indicted for treason or criminal actions. While in normal circumstances such a procedure would be unlikely, under popular pressure the legislature might carry out such indictments. If the upper house of the legislature were less subject to popular pressure, as it was in Britain or the United States, then there would be less to fear on this score. The mere difference of ten years in the minimum ages (30 and 40) between the Councils of Five Hundred and Elders would not be sufficient to induce restraint on the part of the upper house.

Roederer suggested certain changes in the Constitution that he thought would provide the necessary harmony between the two houses of the legislature and the executive. The Council of Elders should be chosen from

---

[96] Ibid., p. 32.
[97] Ibid., p. 29.
[98] Ibid., p. 30.
[99] Ibid., pp. 31–34.

among the Council of Five Hundred to prevent jealousy from developing between the two houses.[100] The Council of Elders sitting as an electoral assembly should then choose the directors from among their number with those chosen remaining members of the upper house.[101] One of the members of the Directory could function as spokesman in the Council of Elders in order to inform them which legislation passed by the Five Hundred was opposed by the executive and to defend the executive from attacks made against it in the lower house. With such an arrangement the executive and the legislature would have a natural link between them, the Directory would have some influence on legislation and the means of defending its conduct, and the Elders would be removed from the popular pressure which so often had swayed past assemblies. Presumably such a constitutional scheme would inaugurate an era of law and end the era of chaos.

Roederer's commentary on the Constitution in the *Journal de Paris* did not go unnoticed. As a result of the suggestion of Isnard among others, Madame de Staël wrote Roederer concerning his articles and invited him to dine with her.[102] More significantly the commission of eleven requested that he, Sieyès, Vaublanc, and Dupont de Nemours be present at the commission's meeting on the evening of 3 thermidor III (21 July 1795) in order to "assist it with your wisdom."[103] The previous day, 2 thermidor, Sieyès, highly regarded by the Thermidorians as an astute political theorist, had presented his own constitutional project to the Convention.[104] The commission, not being able merely to dismiss the efforts of a man of Sieyès's stature, had to examine his proposals. They probably called this meeting in order to do so and asked Sieyès as well as other critics of the proposed Constitution to attend. There seems to be no record of the meeting, but when the Constitution was finally approved none of Roederer's proposals was to be found in it.[105]

Sieyès's proposal received considerable attention in the Convention before being defeated on 25 thermidor (12 August). Sieyès had called for an extreme separation of powers among four institutions: a *jurie de proposition* of seven individuals who represented the interests of the government and proposed laws; a tribunate of two hundred and fifty deputies which represented the interests of the people and examined the proposed laws of the jurie de proposition in that light; a legislative body which accepted or rejected the proposed laws without debate; and a *jurie con-*

---

[100] Ibid., p. 40.

[101] Ibid., pp. 44–45.

[102] Madame de Staël to Roederer, 21 prairial III (9 June 1795), in OR, 8: 645–646. This is the first letter of a correspondence which lasted until 1800.

[103] AN 29AP6 La Commission de onze to Roederer, 3 thermidor III (21 July 1795).

[104] Lefebvre, *The Thermidorians*, pp. 182–84.

[105] A perusal of the memoirs of Thibaudeau, La Revellière-Lépeaux, and Louvet de Couvray (all members of the commission of eleven) did not yield any information on the meeting of 3 thermidor. Whatever Roederer said in behalf of his own ideas, he also spoke in favor of Sieyès's project. AN 284AP9 dossier 5 Roederer to Sieyès, 10 fructidor III (27 August 1795).

stitutionnaire which served as a court of appeals, handled questions of constitutionality of laws, and every ten years initiated a revision of the Constitution.[106] In regard to the execution of laws the jurie de proposition (or more simply referred to as the "government") appointed ministers who were responsible for the administration of laws which were in their jurisdiction. By this complicated arrangement of power Sieyès hoped to restore to the "government" the right to initiate legislation which it believed to be vital to the interests of the nation as well as to continue to represent the interests of the people through the tribunate.[107] However, throughout the entire legislative process the legislature itself was to remain without any initiative or voice. According to Paul Bastid, Sieyès's biographer, Sieyès believed that such a system would still allow useful ideas to reach the legislature but would prevent the excesses and disorder which resulted from giving the lawmakers the right to initiate and debate legislation.[108] Sieyès hoped that his plan which restored an active executive branch of government, while reducing the power of the legislature, would end the turmoil which had characterized the Revolution.

Roederer's and Sieyès's concerns were thus very similar in 1795. Both believed that the disorders of the Revolution could be traced to legislative irresponsibility, and both thought that only by strengthening the executive branch of government could the legislature be controlled. Perhaps their principal affinity was the belief that politics must be made to conform more closely to the principles of social science if government was to produce happiness for France. Sieyès's proposal for executive control of legislative initiative and the removal of the right of debate from the legislative body was similar in intent to Roederer's suggestion of 1793 that the legislature vote only after hearing the reporter's summary of facts. Both men believed that uncontrolled legislative debate was unlikely to produce rational legislation. Thus Roederer had high praise for Sieyès's brilliance as well as his constitution in the *Journal de Paris* of 25 thermidor (12 August).[109] He was particularly impressed with Sieyès's suggestion that the "government" be able to propose laws and indicate to the legislature the means to carry them out. Nevertheless, Roederer was critical of Sieyès for being too imprecise in the language of the project and for favoring too much independence in the communes.

In order to retain power once the Constitution of the Year III became effective, the Thermidorians passed the infamous two-thirds decrees which stated that two-thirds of the new legislature would have to be chosen from the deputies of the Convention. Roederer strongly opposed this decree, arguing that free elections would bring men into power who were more favorable to the Constitution than the members of the Convention

---

[106] Lefebvre, *The Thermidorians*, pp. 183–84; J. H. Clapham, *The Abbé Sieyès: An Essay in the Politics of the French Revolution* (London, 1912), pp. 169–72.

[107] Paul Bastid, *Sieyès et sa pensée* (Paris, 1970), pp. 418–46.

[108] Ibid.

[109] JP, 25 thermidor III (12 August 1795), in OR, 6: 105–6.

because of the past association of the latter with the Terror: "I sincerely believe that they [the deputies] want the Republic, but I also believe that they have a propensity toward tyranny."[110] In a free election some of those elected might tend toward royalism, but Roederer believed that these "royalists" were essentially "friends of liberty and especially friends of peace and order."[111] Certainly forcing the electorate by the two-thirds decree to choose deputies in whom they had no confidence would result, in his opinion, in a serious loss of respect for the new Constitution itself.[112] If the Convention wanted to insure continuity under the new Constitution, it would be better to insist that the directors be chosen from those who served on the Committee of Public Safety after 9 thermidor or on the commission of eleven as these men would all have an interest in maintaining the Constitution.[113]

In the midst of the discussion about the proposed Constitution the old question of Roederer's loyalty to the Republic and, therefore, his political motivation in criticizing the Constitution arose once again. The first attack was at the hand of Louvet de Couvray, a Girondin who had returned to the Convention after 9 thermidor. In a review of Roederer's pamphlet *Des Fugitifs français et des émigrés* written for his journal *La Sentinelle* on 21 fructidor (7 September) Louvet opposed Roederer's suggestion that all those émigrés who had not actually borne arms against France should be allowed to return. While some of those who had fled France should be welcomed back, Louvet believed that such an open invitation to the *émigrés* would only "reinforce the royalism of a great number of its most criminal partisans."[114] Louvet also found that Roederer's remark that there was little to fear from returning royalists because the Republic was now firmly established was not consistent with his "very strange slander" against the founders of the Republic. In the review he quoted Roederer as saying: "the proscribed of 2 June [the Girondins] and all those who fought with them against anarchy [were] men *without wisdom and without prudence*," and "that Vergniaud *speaks only a shocking language, that Guadet, Ducos, Valady have separated themselves forever from the honest and peaceful citizens.*"[115] In a reference to Roederer's allegedly improper conduct on 10 August Louvet added that it was necessary to have a record of irreproachable conduct to speak of these men in such a manner.

Responding in the *Journal de Paris*, Roederer charged Louvet with an "odious falsification" of his ideas. In his pamphlet Roederer had merely tried to explain how the Girondins had been unable to withstand the Montagnard offensive of May-June 1793. Without using any proper names, he described some of those who had opposed the Mountain as "men

---

[110] JP, 22–24 fructidor III (8-10 September 1795), in OR, 6: 113–14.
[111] Ibid., p. 114.
[112] Ibid., p. 115.
[113] Ibid., p. 117.
[114] *La Sentinelle*, 21 fructidor III (7 September 1795).
[115] Ibid.

without wisdom and without prudence . . . [men] who fortified the enemy party, spoke its shocking language, and separated themselves forever from honest and peaceful citizens."[116] By pointing out the discrepancies between the two versions, Roederer made Louvet appear as the libeler. He added that the men he intended to criticize were not Vergniaud, Guadet, Ducos, or Valady but the more irresponsible members of the faction, especially Brissot and Louvet himself.[117] To deal with Louvet's reference to 10 August, he could only recount his activity and stress that he had merely done his duty in escorting the king to the Assembly.[118]

In the same series of articles in which he defended himself from Louvet's accusations, Roederer dealt with a rumor concerning his alleged attempts at preventing the ratification of the proposed Constitution. He reported that there had been a meeting of "Montagnards" at some unspecified date which had accused him of sending to the departments a proposal, presumably his critique of the Constitution in the *Journal de Paris*, for a constitution which would be an alternative to that adopted by the Convention.[119] Roederer's only defense was to reply that it was ridiculous to believe that he had distributed such a constitution.

Roederer's political position, despite the innuendo of men such as Louvet, was solidly republican. His comments on the Constitution indicate that any sort of restoration was the furthest thing from his mind. Rather he wanted to create a republic based on law which neither the tyranny of the masses nor the deputies in the assembly could threaten. If he encouraged the repatriation of the royalist supporters of the Constitution of 1791, it was only to strengthen liberty not to revitalize monarchy. He did not approve of all the measures passed by the Thermidorian Convention, but even in the matter of the two-thirds decree he argued that it was the Conventions' prerogative to set limits on those eligible to serve in office.[120] He had even opposed the selection of Richer-Sérizy as an elector because of his open hostility to the Republic.[121] In short Roederer made the pragmatic decision to support the Thermidorian Republic, even if it did not fulfill his requirements for government based on social science, because no better alternative had presented itself.

---

[116] Roederer, *Des Fugitifs françaises*, in OR, 7: 47.
[117] JP, 26–28 fructidor III, (12–14 September 1795), in OR, 6: 121, 123.
[118] Ibid., p. 124.
[119] Ibid.
[120] JP, 8 vendémiaire IV (30 September 1795) in OR, 6: 128.
[121] JP, 11 vendémiaire IV (3 October 1795), in OR, 6: 130.

VIII. THE SEARCH FOR STABILITY

R oederer had great hope that the new Constitution, flawed though it was, would provide France with the stable, orderly government he thought so essential. He envisioned his role in the new order to be that of a political journalist who would maintain a vigilant watch over the government to increase the likelihood that the goal of stability would be achieved. In addition as a member of the National Institute, he could continue to support the development of social science which would lead to an even more improved government in the future. Roederer maintained a reasonable confidence in the Directory until the coup d'état of fructidor convinced him that political and social order could never come from the Constitution of 1795. At that point he began to fall back on his previous belief that a new form of government based on the principles of social science was needed. In 1799 he collaborated with his friend Sieyès to establish a government which he thought met these criteria and to bring Napoleon Bonaparte to power.

During the era of the Directory the *Journal de Paris* remained the cornerstone of Roederer's influence despite his founding of the *Journal d'économie publique, de morale et de politique* in August 1796.[1] This new sheet, appearing only once every décade, was designed to allow the publication of longer essays than those possible in the *Journal de Paris* but could never equal the prestige of the older publication with its long history and international readership.[2] When Roederer lost interest in political commentary after the coup d'état of fructidor, the *Journal d'économie publique* ceased to appear. Certainly it was Roederer's connection with the *Journal de Paris* that first attracted Madame de Staël to him. She found his political ideas of great interest and was anxious to use the journal to secure favorable reviews of her work and that of her friends.[3] There can be little doubt that Bonaparte found Roederer to be a useful associate because of his editorship of the journal and the influence it presumably had over the more affluent levels of society.

More than just the influence he might exert on certain elements of society, Roederer believed that newspapers had a positive role to play in

---

[1] Corancez was not enthusiastic about the new journal but did not think it would compete against the daily *Journal de Paris*. AN 29AP10 Corancez to Roederer 13 thermidor IV (31 July 1796); P.-L. Roederer, *Notice de ma vie pour mes enfants*, in OR, 3: 290–92; JEP 10 fructidor IV (27 August 1796), in OR, 6: 158.

[2] The number of subscribers outside of France is not known but was substantial enough to warrant a notice of foreign subscription procedures. JP 9 frimaire IV (30 November 1795).

[3] De Staël to Roederer, 1 October 1796, 5 November 1796, and 15 April 1797, in OR, 8: 651, 653.

the development of government based on social science. As Jeremy Popkin has demonstrated, Roederer believed that government could gauge public opinion by evaluating the number of subscribers for particular journals.[4] Since each journal had a definite political point of view, determining the opinions of the readers would not be difficult. The government then had the obligation of acting on the opinions of those journals held in the highest public esteem since the readers were all among the economic and intellectual elite and had the truest sense of the needs of society. Roederer believed the prestige of the *Journal de Paris* to be high, despite the fact that it had fewer subscribers than some sheets, because it was published in the capital and more people read each copy. If the Directory had accepted this line of reasoning, which it did not, Roederer and the *Journal de Paris* would have had a major influence on the direction of government policy after 1795. In actuality the newspaper remained an opposition sheet.

In 1796 the *Journal de Paris* went through something of a crisis because of the strained relationship of Roederer and his partner Corancez over their financial arrangements. The dispute between them centered around the price Roederer was to pay for half-interest in the journal. The agreement in February 1795 had called for a payment of 30,000 livres in assignats, but by March of 1796 assignats had been replaced by mandats at a ratio of 30 for 1.[5] The adjustment of Roederer's remaining obligation to Corancez was made more difficult by the fact that the assignat was worth a good deal more in early 1795 than later. A graphic example of this is the price of a subscription to the *Journal de Paris* itself which had stood at the relatively low price of 42 livres per year in February 1795 but had climbed dramatically to 1600 livres by the end of the year.[6] The basic question between Corancez and Roederer, then, was what the value of 30,000 livres in assignats in February 1795 would be in the spring of 1796. Corancez argued that it would be 6,000 livres while Roederer claimed it was only 3,000. To bolster his case, Roederer charged that Corancez had not compensated him for his editorial work and had misled him about the number of subscribers by implying there were 3,700 when in fact there were less than 3,000.[7] Corancez in turn argued that he had reduced the price of sale by 10,000 livres to compensate Roederer for his work on the journal. In the end Roederer refused to go beyond his offer of 3,000 livres.

The real cause for this bitterness is difficult to determine. The *Journal de Paris* was a lucrative venture earning profits of over 190,000 livres in 1795, over 680,000 livres in 1796 (due in large part to inflation), and over

---

[4] Jeremy D. Popkin, "The Newspaper Press in French Political Thought," *Eighteenth-Century Culture*, 10 (1981): 120–123.

[5] AN 29AP91 Corancez to Roederer, 11 floréal IV (30 April 1796), Roederer to Corancez 20 floréal IV (9 May 1796): M. J. Sydenham, *The First French Republic, 1792–1804* (Berkeley, 1974), p. 97.

[6] JP 17 pluviôse III (5 February 1795) and JP 25 frimaire IV (16 December 1795).

[7] AN 29AP91 Corancez to Roederer, 11 floréal IV; Roederer to Corancez 20 floréal IV.

41,000 in 1798.[8] With such profits, it is difficult to believe that this bitter dispute arose over a mere 3,000 livres. The correspondence between the two men does suggest another possibility, but many of the letters are not clearly dated so that an accurate chronology cannot be established. One letter from Corancez dated simply 26 prairial but found among other letters from the year IV revealed a growing uneasiness with Roederer's criticism of the Directory.[9] If this letter was indeed written in the spring of 1796, it would indicate that Corancez's unhappiness with Roederer went deeper than the affair over payment for the partial sale of the journal. Another letter which seems to date from the year IV disclosed that Corancez had tried to buy back Roederer's share of the *Journal de Paris* and that Roederer had refused but offered to purchase Corancez's interest.[10] Corancez wrote that Roederer was not offering a large enough purchase price and declined the offer. Obviously neither man wanted to give up his share of the journal but each found it increasingly hard to work with the other due to their political disagreements.

What Corancez had come to dislike was Roederer's increasing hostility to the policies of the men in power. In Roederer's mind the individuals who sat in the Directory and in the Councils failed to understand the proper course necessary to consolidate the gains of the Revolution while at the same time ending the chaos associated with it. The Directory's policy of alternately attacking the Jacobin left and the conservative right could never result in stable government. To achieve order the government had to ally itself with those elements of society which favored stability and destroy those elements which threatened it. This could only mean allying with the right and attacking the left. The Directory could begin to achieve such an alliance by undertaking a reconcilation with the class of well-to-do proprietors, who had been alienated from the government by the Revolution.[11] He argued that "wisdom and wealth are always in proportion the one with the other, not in individuals but in the aggregate. . . ."[12] The lower classes certainly had legitimate grievances, but it was the duty of the men of the highest order, the men of wealth and talent, to reflect upon these sentiments and propose solutions to them.[13] According to Roederer this was the process that led to the formation of true public opinion upon which good government ought to operate. Besides their capacity for government service these individuals had the capability of financing the government as did the gentry in England.[14] Most importantly the men "in this class, more than any other, are the friends of order,

---

[8] AN 29AP91 Receipts for the annual profits of the *Journal de Paris*.

[9] AN 29AP10 Corancez to Roederer 26 prairial.

[10] AN 29AP10 Corancez to Roederer 6 ventôse.

[11] JEP 30 vendémiaire V (21 October 1796), in OR, 6: 200.

[12] P.-L. Roederer, *De la Majorité nationale, de la manière dont elle se forme, et des signes auxquelles on peut la reconnaître, ou théorie de l'opinion publique*, in OR, 6: 377.

[13] Ibid., p. 379.

[14] JP 22 vendémiaire V (13 October 1796), in OR, 6: 200.

tranquility . . . the men in whom the executive power will find the most sure, the most constant assistance."[15]

A successful alliance with the right also necessitated some accommodation with the royalists. Here Roederer was stepping on dangerous ground as the Directory was very much afraid of a restoration which would not only threaten the achievements of the Revolution but also the very lives of the regicides. Certainly the absolutist royalists personified by the Pretender Louis XVIII had every intention, upon restoration of monarchial power, of returning to the ancien régime and dealing harshly with the regicides.[16] The constitutional monarchists, who themselves participated in the early successes of the Revolution, wanted to restore a monarchy which would retain most of the features of the Constitution of 1791. However, Roederer believed that the latter group, without any clear-cut program of its own, would rally to the Republic if it were not characterized by the policies of the Jacobin left.

In order to win the moderate royalists' allegiance, the Directory had to adopt a conciliatory attitude toward them. For instance the vendémiarists, whom he considered constitutionalists, should be included in the amnesty of 4 brumaire IV.[17] He vigorously opposed the anti-royalist law of 3 brumaire IV which stipulated that no relatives of émigrés could hold public office, that those who had suggested or signed seditious motions in primary assemblies (i.e. the vendémiarists) could not hold public office, and that the revolutionary legislation against priests should be revived.[18] Not only was the law unconstitutional, but it also strengthened the left by denying well-to-do proprietors public office.[19] When it proved unlikely that the Councils would repeal the law, Roederer supported an amendment later accepted by the Council of Five Hundred which also barred from office those who had been given amnesty on 4 brumaire IV, that is, the Jacobin left. He conceded that the law would still be unconstitutional but added: "It is obviously advantageous to keep dangerous men from positions of power when those who are able to restrain them are excluded from it."[20] Likewise he was highly critical of the Directory's vigorous response to the royalist conspiracy of pluviôse V in which the Abbé Brottier tried to lay the groundwork for a coup.[21] Betrayed by informers, Brottier and his accomplices were arrested on 11 pluviôse (30 January 1797) and brought before a court martial. Roederer maintained that the Directory had acted unconstitutionally in bringing the defendants before a military commission instead of a justice of the peace and in trying to influence the commission

---

[15] JEP 20 vendémiaire V (11 October 1796), in OR, 6: 197.

[16] For a discussion of royalist attitudes during the Directory see Jacques Godechot, *La Contre-révolution: doctrine et action, 1789-1804* (Paris, 1961), pp. 298–314.

[17] JP 20 fructidor IV (6 September 1796), in OR, 6: 167.

[18] Georges Lefebvre, *The Directory*, trans. Robert Baldick, (New York, 1964), p. 31.

[19] JEP 20 vendémiaire V (11 October 1796) and JP 22 vendémiaire V (13 October 1796), in OR, 6: 192–93, 200.

[20] JP 19 brumaire V (10 November 1796), in OR, 6: 213.

[21] Sydenham, *The First French Republic*, pp. 122–23.

to return a verdict of guilty.[22] The royalists posed no danger to the Republic as demonstrated by the weakness of the conspiracy. The Pretender could never raise a substantial army to invade France, and the royalists in the Councils would be unable to convince their colleagues to support a restoration.[23]

For Roederer the real danger to the Republic was not from the right but rather from the left which sought a restoration of anarchy and terror. As proof of this contention he published numerous incidents of disorders which were inspired by the left. For instance, in reporting on disturbances in Lyons between some of the inhabitants and soldiers, he denied the Directory's assertion that those citizens involved were royalists and blamed the unrest on the "terrorist soldiers" who should have been arrested by the government.[24] Likewise, the events of 13 messidor IV (2 July 1796), when a band of men and women descended on Parisian markets to regulate prices and the value of the mandat and assignat, were clearly the work of "anarchists" whose goal was "a violent sedition."[25] On 12 fructidor IV (29 August 1796) there was a disturbance which involved people assembling in various parts of Paris and shouting royalist slogans. Roederer interpreted this to be a demonstration staged by the "terrorists" to encourage the Directory to move against the royalists.[26] He cited notices in the Jacobin sheet, *Journal des hommes libres*, that a royalist uprising was going to be staged on that date as proof of a "conspiracy" by the left. On the night of 23-24 fructidor IV (9–10 September 1796) certain Jacobins arrived at the Grenelle camp and tried to fraternize with the troops.[27] They had hoped that such direct action would bring about the release of Babeuf, who was then imprisoned at Vendôme, but their efforts were foiled by the Directory, which had them arrested at the camp. Reporting on this event, Roederer said the journalists and orators of the left had hired men at four livres per day for "the legions of the Terror" which went to the Grenelle camp.[28] In this case he applauded the Directory's handing the prisoners over to a military commission for the trial despite the fact that the majority of them were civilians. The left was able to continue this kind of activity, he speculated, because it had access to sources of money (he did not pretend to know what these sources were) even though they had no chance of arousing the masses as long as "there is bread in Paris and no society of Jacobins in France."[29]

Roederer was convinced that the disorders which were occurring were not merely spontaneous eruptions but events planned by "terrorists," that

[22] JEP 10 germinal V (30 March 1797), in OR, 6: 266–68.

[23] JP 13 pluviôse V (1 February 1797), in OR, 5: 63–64; JP 30 pluviôse V (18 February 1797), in OR, 6: 247–48.

[24] JP 14 prairial IV (2 June 1796), in OR, 6: 141–42.

[25] JP 14 messidor IV (2 July 1796), in OR, 6: 147.

[26] JP 13 fructidor IV (30 August 1796), in OR, 6: 165–66. This interpretation of events is also found in the *Moniteur*. MU 13 fructidor IV, 18: 410.

[27] Lefebvre, *The Directory*, pp. 40–41.

[28] JP 26 fructidor IV (12 September 1796), in OR, 6: 176–77.

[29] JP 28 fructidor IV (14 September 1796), in OR, 6: 177–78.

is, the Jacobins of the Directorial period. After the Jacobin Club was closed in November 1794, the supporters of democratic policies were forced to seek alternative means of influencing the course of politics. The clubs that they established before the coup d'état of 18 fructidor did not meet with much success; therefore, Jacobin activity before that *journée* was centered on the press, particularly René Vatar's *Journal des hommes libres*.[30] According to Isser Woloch these Jacobins were not interested in creating disorders but in encouraging a more democratic Republic through their newspapers, clubs, and petitions. Roederer, however, was convinced that the Jacobin sheets, especially Vatar's, were fomenting popular disturbances. As noted above he reported that the *Journal des hommes libres* was linked with the "royalist" demonstration of 13 fructidor.[31] In reporting the Jacobin demonstration at the Grenelle camp, Roederer accused the journalists and orators of the left of organizing it. He wrote that two of those arrested, Fion of *La Sentinelle* and Saunier of *L'Ami du peuple*, were connected with the Jacobin press.[32] (In actuality only *L'Ami du peuple* could be considered pro-Jacobin.[33])

Roederer, also fearful of the revival of strong political clubs similar to the old Jacobins, supported the deputy Mailhe's proposal to place severe restriction on these clubs.[34] By the summer of 1797 Roederer was convinced that the recently formed Clichy Club and Constitutional Club, which met at the Hôtel de Salm, posed a threat to the Republic even though neither was pro-Jacobin.[35] Some of the members of each were deputies, and Roederer feared the possibility that legislation would emerge from the clubs rather than the Assembly. He also feared the creation of factions such as the Jacobins and Feuillants. He called on the Clichy Club, the more conservative of the two, to dissolve in order to set an "example of holy respect for public tranquility."[36]

Since the Directory did not establish a secure political base for itself by an alliance with the major elements of society, it tried to strengthen its own powers through limitations on the press in order to consolidate its position. On 9 brumaire V (30 October 1796) the Directory sent to the Five Hundred a message critical of the attitude that certain journals, both Jacobin and royalist, had taken toward the government and suggested that some laws prohibiting complete liberty of the press were in order.[37] Roederer, whose views on the liberty of the press had been published first

---

[30] Isser Woloch, *Jacobin Legacy: The Democratic Movement Under the Directory* (Princeton, 1970), p. 28 and passim.

[31] JP 13 fructidor IV (30 August 1796), in OR, 6: 166.

[32] JP 26 fructidor IV (12 September 1796), in OR, 6: 177.

[33] Woloch, *Jacobin Legacy*, pp. 423–25.

[34] JP 13 germinal IV (2 April 1796) and JP 15 germinal IV (4 April 1796), in OR, 6: 137. In brief Mailhe's proposed legislation would have limited the size of the clubs to no more than sixty members in the largest communes and twenty in the smallest. Their activities would be confined purely to discussion. MU 11 germinal IV (31 March 1796), 28: 88–92.

[35] JP 1 messidor V (19 June 1797), in OR, 6: 309.

[36] Ibid.

[37] MU 14 brumaire V (4 November 1796), 28: 469–71.

in 1795, as indicated above, opposed any limitations on the journals. He characterized as "extravagant exaggerations" the Directory's assertion that the journalists were delivering the nation into anarchy, attacking the social order, paralyzing measures of legislation, and giving aid to the enemy by disorganizing the army.[38] Only when journals had been read in the clubs had they affected political events. Furthermore, the Directory had acted illegally by proposing legislation to the Five Hundred and was threatening France with despotism with such a law. In addition to his criticism of this proposal, Roederer on two separate occasions denounced the Directory for arresting the staffs of journals which the government had found offensive.[39] He also argued that the tax of two sous levied on every sheet of newspaper sent through the mails in effect suppressed many journals, especially those favoring order.[40]

Roederer was no more sympathetic to the Directory's attempt to solidify its authority through military victory. As long as victories were forthcoming, domestic politics might remain on an even keel; but defeats were certain to bring a return of disorder to France.[41] Faced with chronic financial problems, the Directory had resorted to the policy of levying heavy exactions from defeated territories, a practice which Roederer said would only induce the government to continue the fighting in order to maintain "its arbitrary disposition of the spoils of war."[42] The great dependence on these war indemnities also gave greater power to the generals who often had the audacity to act independently of the central authority. Roederer was particularly critical of Bonaparte's activities in Italy which he called an "abuse of power" that "could only delay the peace and inspire new wars."[43] He urged the Directory to make peace with England during its discussions with the British representative Malmesbury at Lille in October 1796. He thought the Directory should demand only territory of direct interest to France (almost certainly a reference to Belgium) and conclude peace on that basis. He was bitter with the lack of interest the Directory demonstrated in trying to bring a cessation of hostilities and blamed the directors, not the enemy, for the failure to end the war.[44]

Roederer did not believe that the men who served the Republic under the new Constitution were laying the foundation for the orderly and stable society for which France longed. Disorders inspired by "terrorists" continued, the war was not ended, the Directory tended toward despotism

---

[38] JEP 20 brumaire V (10 November 1796), in OR, 6: 217.

[39] In one case the owner of the *Messager du soir* had printed a false report concerning the defeat of the army of Italy, and in the other the staff of the *Postillon des armées* had written an anecdote making fun of the deputies in the Councils. JP 13 messidor IV (23 June 1796) and JP 30 fructidor IV (16 September 1796), in OR, 5: 45–46.

[40] JP 1 thermidor IV (19 July 1796), in OR, 6: 150.

[41] JEP 20 fructidor IV (6 September 1796) and JEP 10 pluviôse V (29 January 1797), in OR, 6: 174, 236.

[42] JP 16 thermidor IV (3 August 1796), in OR, 6: 155.

[43] JEP 10 messidor V (28 June 1797), in OR, 6: 315.

[44] JEP 10 brumaire V (31 October 1796), JEP 20 brumaire V (10 November 1796), and JEP 20 pluviôse V (8 February 1797), in OR, 6: 210, 215, 242.

in its attitude toward the press, and many of the most useful and upright men were political outcasts because of their monarchist sympathies, real or imagined. Yet Roederer did not despair as the elections of 1797 offered the prospect that men of moderation who opposed tyranny and disorder would come to power. The citizenry of France was anxious for "calm, liberty, and general security" which could be obtained only by the deputies of the "reasonable party" and *"les citoyens honnêtes et éclairés."*[45] These men were the enemies of both old and new abuses "who have not taken the pretext of old disorders in order to contribute to new ones and of new ones to restore old ones."[46] They were men who rejected the extremism of the left and the right and "who marched under the banner of Voltaire and Montesquieu. . . ."[47]

Those that Roederer termed men of the "reasonable party" the Directory classified as monarchists bent on the destruction of the Republic. The Director Barras even suggested that Roederer was supporting the election of these deputies in an effort to bring the downfall of the Republic and in the process revive his own political fortunes.[48] There was also considerable speculation in the press concerning Roederer's candidacy in the elections.[49] Roederer, however, denied any interest in office and maintained that the right, far from desiring the collapse of the Republic, only sought a return of stability to France.[50] For instance the Parisian electors, suspected of royalism by the Directory, were in Roederer's opinion only opposing "the incendiary fanatics" while favoring "order, peace, pleasure."[51] Likewise the fervor present in the Parisian primary assemblies was not an opposition to the Republic as thought by the Directory but "a proof of zeal for public affairs." Conceding that many of those chosen to be electors had been vendémiairists, Roederer argued that they had been selected because they were the enemies of the Terror and not enemies of the Constitution. Even if the new deputies were secretly counter-revolutionary, the Directory could always intervene to prevent an alteration of the Constitution or a restoration.[52]

---

[45] JEP 20 pluviôse V and JP 3 ventôse V (21 February 1797), in OR, 6: 241, 252.

[46] JP 3 ventôse V, in OR, 6: 252.

[47] Ibid.

[48] P. Barras, *Mémoires* (Paris, 1895), 2: 207. According to the police agent Bréon some of the patrons of one of the cafés at the Palais-Egalité believed that the purpose of Roederer's newspaper articles was to win favor with the "haut public" so that he would be named to "some important place." Alphonse Aulard, *Paris pendant la reaction thermidoriene et sous le directoire: recueil de documents pour l'histoire de l'esprit public à Paris* (Paris, 1898–1902), 3: 741–42.

[49] I am indebted to Jeremy Popkin for providing me with the following references in the press to Roederer's personal political goals in the election of 1797: *Courrier républicain*, 19 nivôse V; *La Sentinelle*, 21 vendémiaire V; *Messager du Soir*, 23 pluviôse V; *Journal de Perlet*, 7 ventose V, *Tableau de la France*, 8 germinal V.

[50] JEP 30 nivôse V (19 January 1797), in OR, 6: 235.

[51] JP 13 germinal V (2 April 1797), in OR, 6: 270.

[52] JEP, 30 germinal V (19 April 1797), in OR, 6: 275–76.

The results of the elections of 1797 which unseated most of the old *conventionnels* have been widely interpreted as a royalist victory.[53] Most historians concede that the division between constitutional and absolute monarchists prevented any immediate danger to the Republic, but efforts after the elections on the part of the Councils to weaken revolutionary legislation and hence the Republic are understood as preludes to a revived monarchy. Furthermore, the intense activity of the royalist d'André, who had tried to organize an electoral victory which would favor a restoration, seemed to imply that future elections held grave dangers for the Republic. Therefore, the majority of newly elected deputies and their supporters have been considered opponents of the Republic. In a notable departure from this traditional interpretation M. J. Sydenham argues that those elected did not seriously believe a restoration to be possible and sought instead to create an alliance with the Directory that could lead to a stable and moderate Republic.[54] He lists those most outspoken in this view to be Carnot, Benjamin Constant, Madame de Staël, Mathieu Dumas, and Thibaudeau; and he summarized the objectives of the moderates before the elections as the removal of objectionable ministers, the repeal of the law of 3 brumaire IV, and the conclusion of peace. If this informal group had a publicist, it was certainly Roederer who had advocated virtually their entire program since the beginning of the Directory.

There seems to be no evidence that there was any concerted action by these individuals, but Madame de Staël had close associations with Constant and Roederer. Her correspondence with the latter adds weight to Sydenham's argument. As early as August 1796 she was lamenting the poor quality of Republican officials. Praising the nature of the Constitution itself, she told Roederer if it were placed "between the hands of the *honnêtes gens*" that it "would be recognized for what it is, the most reasonable in the universe."[55] In October she wrote: "I hope, as you, that the 1st of germinal will bring *les honnêtes hommes* to power, but I am far from being sure of it. . . ."[56] As she analyzed the situation "the scoundrels have only conserved their advantage because *les honnêtes gens* dragged themselves along after the Republic instead of marching in advance of it." She believed Roederer, a perfect example of this phenomenon, to be

---

[53] For instance see J. Suratteau, "Les élections de l'an V aux Conseils du Directoire," *Annales historiques de la Révolution française*, 154 (1958); 43–56; Lefebvre, *The Directory*, pp. 61–74; Martin Lyons, *France Under the Directory* (Cambridge, 1975), pp. 47–49; Harvey Mitchell, *The Underground War against Revolutionary France: The Missions of William Wickham, 1794–1800* (Oxford, 1965) pp. 140–161.

[54] Sydenham, *The First French Republic*, pp. 107–08, 125–27. See also G. E. Gwynne, *Madame de Staël et la Révolution française* (Paris, 1969), p. 60. Interestingly Harvey Mitchell lends credence to this view with the revelation that Wickham was glad that moderates like Talleyrand, Garat, Desmeuniers, and Roederer were not chosen as deputies and that he interpreted the results of the elections as a "repudiation of the framers of the Constitution of 1791. . . ." Mitchell, *The Underground War*, p. 159.

[55] De Staël to Roederer, 20 August 1796, in OR, 8: 647.

[56] De Staël to Roederer, 1 October 1796, in OR, 8: 650.

notable for his *"veritable opinion republicaine."* As the elections approached, she urged him to continue his work which would "influence the destiny of the Republic."[57] The election results rather frightened her, however, because of the extreme royalism of some of the deputies. She chastised Roederer, who possessed "enlightenment, success, and virtue," for not seeking office and providing the leadership needed to maintain a republican course.[58] Without men such as himself France would return to a monarchy more despotic than that of the ancien régime.

As Madame de Staël feared, the extreme royalists became a highly vocal minority seemingly bent on the emasculation of the Republic.[59] They were only effective, however, in alliance with the more numerous and moderate elements in the Councils, whom they joined in repealing the widely despised repressive laws against the clergy as well as the law of 3 brumaire. Roederer, in basic agreement with the Councils on these measures, advocated requiring no more of priests than an oath of submission to the laws and welcomed the repeal of the law of 3 brumaire.[60] He even urged the Councils to go further by replacing the death penalty for returned émigrés with a year's imprisonment and eventual deportation.[61] Specifically advocating the removal of Merlin de Douai from the Ministry of Justice, he backed the Councils' efforts to obtain some control over the Directory's ministers.[62] However, Roederer refused to sanction the efforts of the extremists to weaken the Republic and was particularly critical of Gibert-Desmolières' proposal to deprive the Directory of any control over its own finances.[63]

The right had enjoyed some success in the Councils but really failed to establish the monarchist majority many had feared. For instance, the most extreme measure, Gibert Desmolières' financial reform, had failed to pass the Elders. The Directory, nevertheless, decided cooperation with the Councils was impossible and chose to rid itself of the opposition.[64] General Hoche began to move troops near Paris on 13 messidor V (1 July 1797) while the directors dismissed the ministers favored by the right and maintained those, particularly Merlin de Douai, disliked by it. When the Councils learned of the actions of the Directory, they immediately began to fear a coup d'état. Roederer, also disturbed by the news, believed that the Directory had destroyed any possibility of cooperation with the Coun-

---

[57] De Staël to Roederer, 10 pluviôse V (29 January 1797), in OR, 8: 653.

[58] De Staël to Roederer, 15 April 1797, in OR, 8: 654.

[59] Sydenham, *The First French Republic*, pp. 130–37; W. R. Fryer, *Republic or Restoration in France, 1794–97: The Politics of French Royalism with Particular Reference to the Activities of A. B. J. D'André* (Manchester, 1965) pp. 225–68.

[60] P.-L. Roederer, *De l'Usage à faire de l'autorité publique dans les circonstances presentes,* in OR, 6: 284; JEP 30 prairial V (18 June 1797), in OR, 6: 304.

[61] Roederer, *Usage,* in OR, 6: 286–87.

[62] Ibid., pp. 290–91.

[63] For Gibert-Desmolières's proposals see Marcel Marion, *Histoire financière de la France depuis 1715* (Paris, 1927), 6: 37–39. Roederer's position is found in JEP 10 messidor V (29 June 1797), in OR, 6: 314–15.

[64] Sydenham, *The First French Republic*, pp. 136–43.

cils.[65] While favoring the appointment of Talleyrand to the Ministry of Foreign Affairs, Roederer thought that the Directory should have appointed other ministers who held the public confidence in order to win the support of the Councils.[66] He viewed Bonaparte's speech of 14 July to the Army of Italy, implying that the army would intervene in political affairs if the Republic was in danger, as a threat to the Councils.[67]

Even though he did not agree with the action taken by the Directory, Roederer did not share the feeling prevalent in the Councils that a coup d'état was imminent.[68] He reasoned that Bénézech and Cochon had been removed from the Ministries of the Interior and Police because of their attachment to the Director Carnot whose influence the majority of the Directory was trying to reduce. Hoche was not in collusion with the government as evidenced by his refusal to take the War Ministry, for which in any case he was too young. Convinced that public opinion, fearing a restoration of the Terror by the directors, would support the Councils if the Directory made a show of force, Roederer wrote that even a successful coup would merely put the government under the control of a general. The danger was not in a coup d'état but in a confrontation between the Directory and the Councils which would lead to civil war and a return to the "anarchy" of 1793 with each side blaming the other for the disturbances. Both the executive and the legislature had to become less antagonistic each to the other in order to prevent a catastrophe.

Even after reporting on 20 thermidor (7 August) that Hoche was moving an army of 25,000 toward Paris, Roederer branded rumors of a conspiracy by the Directory "revolting absurdities invented by the enemies of public tranquility."[69] He did believe that some agreement would have to be reached between the Councils and the Directory before irreparable harm was done to the Republic. To protect the Republic from its enemies the Directory should ally with the Council of Elders which was intent on preserving the Constitution.[70] If the Directory acted illegally, however, the Councils should either attempt to arrest them or reconvene in a provincial town like Tours in order to maintain their independence.[71] Roederer advised the Councils not to use force in their struggle with the Directory which would only give "a plausible motive for assault to all the enemies of the public tranquility."[72]

As late as 10 fructidor Roederer publicly expressed the belief that the crisis had passed because neither side was willing to risk a confrontation.[73]

---

[65] JEP 10 thermidor V (29 July 1797), in OR, 6: 333–34.

[66] Ibid. Roederer was particularly opposed to the appointment of Sotin, a supporter of the Jacobins, to the position of Minister of Police and of Hoche to the post of Minister of War. See Woloch, *Jacobin Legacy*, pp. 218–33 on Sotin's relationship to the Jacobins.

[67] JEP 10 thermidor V, in OR, 6: 335; Felix Markham, *Napoleon* (New York, 1963), p. 53.

[68] JEP 10 thermidor V, in OR, 6: 335–39.

[69] JEP 20 thermidor V (7 August 1797), in OR, 6: 343–44.

[70] JEP 30 thermidor V (17 August 1797), in OR, 6: 351–52.

[71] JP 24 thermidor V (11 August 1797), in OR, 6: 346–47.

[72] JEP 30 thermidor V, in OR, 6: 350.

[73] JEP 10 fructidor V (27 August 1797), in OR, 6: 354.

Privately, however, he was much less optimistic. On 13 fructidor he wrote to General Hoche his view that eventually "the quarrel will be between the generals, because . . . they are not unanimously behind the government although all are for the Republic and liberty."[74] The principal blame for affairs lay with the Directory which prompted the revival of royalism "by its lack of skill in domestic affairs." In turn royalism would prompt the return of terror "by its foolish and vain discourse, by its insolent platitudes, rather than by its enterprises." Despondent over the turn of events, Roederer concluded:

Now, I can only hope that if there is a civil war the general who secures the advantage will be strong enough against his enemies, his friends, and himself, so that his victory will only be used to favor liberty.[75]

Civil war did not erupt, but on 18 fructidor the Directory announced the discovery of a royalist plot, ordered a military occupation of Paris, nullified the election of 177 deputies, and arrested and sentenced to deportation about 65 deputies along with the Directors Carnot and Barthélemy.[76] About 42 newspapers had been suppressed and the owners and staffs ordered deported to Guiana. Perhaps exaggerating the danger to himself, Roederer claimed to have been one of the journalists marked for deportation until Talleyrand, the Minister of Foreign Affairs and his former associate on the Tax Committee and in the department of Paris, intervened on his behalf with the directors.[77] Whatever the truth of this claim, the *Journal de Paris* ceased its hostility to the Directory after the coup d'état.[78]

Before 18 fructidor Roederer, arguing that only if the Councils and Directory were dominated by the proper individuals could a stable republic evolve, had sought the selection of such men to office. After the elections Roederer had quickly come to doubt whether this electoral success would by itself bring the desired changes in government, and he began to revive and modify his proposals for a government based on social science from the *Cours d'organisation sociale*. In June 1797 he made suggestions for a legislature organized so all decisions were a result of the preliminary work of three committees, a plan he claimed would result in a logique organisée. After the coup d'état he resurrected the Constitutional theories he had developed in 1795 and sought a constitutional revision despite the nine year prohibition on amendments in the Constitution of the Year III.[79] To restore harmony between the executive and the legislature, Roederer ad-

---

[74] AN 29AP11 Roederer to Hoche, 13 fructidor V (30 August 1797).

[75] Ibid.

[76] Lefebvre, *The Directory*, pp. 99–101.

[77] Roederer, *Notice*, in OR, 3: 293.

[78] Most right-wing journals curtailed considerably their attacks on the Directory after fructidor. See Jeremy D. Popkin, *The Right-Wing Press in France, 1792–1800* (Chapel Hill, 1980), pp. 6, 8, 98.

[79] Roederer's proposed constitutional reforms are found in *Mémoires d'économie publique, de morale et de politique*, the journal with which he replaced the JEP after the coup d'etat, for 10 vendémiaire V (1 October 1797), in OR, 6: 367–73.

vocated that the directors be chosen from the Elders but remain deputies while serving in the executive. Once again he urged the creation of two additional officials, the grand électeur who would nominate and dismiss directors and ministers and the procureur-général-national who would serve as the director's professional administrator. To provide the Directory more control over local officials, Roederer proposed that the Directory appoint the members of the departmental and municipal councils from lists supplied by local electors. These local councils would then be expected to execute the orders of the Directory without debate except in the area of local tax matters.

Events had proven, however, that these proposals of 1795 were not in themselves sufficient to bring harmony and stability to government. A great problem for the Directory was the existence of a number of irresponsible deputies who were "the natural confidants of the complaints of malcontents."[80] There could be no assurance that such deputies would be loyal to the Constitution or willing to cooperate with the executive. To remedy this situation Roederer proposed giving the Directory a veto power and the right to recess the Councils for a maximum of three months per year. Also the implementation of "gradual promotions," whereby every office holder in France would have to serve in the lowest elected offices before moving on to higher ones, would end the likelihood that irresponsible deputies would be chosen to sit in the Councils. Under this system the first office in which a man could serve would be municipal after which he could move up to a departmental position and eventually secure a national post. All of those serving in the Elders would first have to sit in the Five Hundred, and, of course, the directors would be chosen from among the Elders. Since all municipal and departmental offices were to be filled by the directors, loyal republicans should control every official post in France. Harmony would thus be imposed on France by a government which would be virtually self-perpetuating and immune from popular pressure.

After presenting his suggestion on constitutional revision, Roederer discontinued his political commentary, which in any case was no longer possible after fructidor.[81] Roederer's disappointment in the direction of events led to a renewed interest in the study of social science. Just as he had responded to the events of 10 August 1792 by writing his *Cours d'organisation sociale*, Roederer now devoted his energies to the work of the Institute which culminated with his attack on Rivarol in 1799.

Roederer returned to writing political commentary on 22 prairial VII (10 June 1799) only after his interest in public affairs was rekindled by the revival of the political fortunes of the Jacobins in 1798–1799 and the entrance of Sieyès into the Directory.[82] In the elections of 1798 the Jacobins

---

[80] Ibid. pp. 367–68.
[81] Roederer, *Notice*, in OR, 3: 294.
[82] JP 22 prairial VII (10 June 1799), in OR, 6: 384–85.

picked up a great many seats in the legislature.[83] On 22 floréal VI the Directory, fearing a revival of terrorism, quashed 106 of the elections. In the elections of 1799 the left picked up fifty seats in the Councils where they thenceforth constituted a vocal minority. The Councils then engaged in a reorganization of the executive known as the coup d'état of prairial VII. Of the directors only Reubell was scheduled to retire; he was replaced by Sieyès. The Councils, however, also annulled the election of Treilhard on a technicality and forced Merlin de Douai and La Revellière to resign. Roger-Ducos, Gohier, and Moulins were subsequently elected directors. After entering the Councils, the Jacobins were able to enact legislation reminiscent of the Year II. Democratic clubs sprang up with one in particular, the Manège Club, composed of deputies and citizens alike. Needless to say, Roederer was disturbed by the course of events; but apparently heartened by the election of Sieyès to the Directory in May 1799, he returned to writing political commentary less than one month after Sieyès's election.

In many ways Roederer and Sieyès were kindred spirits. Both had written pamphlets criticizing the traditional organization of the Estates General, and they had had similar ideas regarding the revision of the Constitution in 1795. In his memoirs Roederer stated that he had "always been attached by admiration and friendship" to Sieyès.[84] An indication of Roederer's respect for Sieyès's ability can be found in an article from the *Journal d'économie publique* where Sieyès (engaged in a conversation with Locke, Bayle, Hobbes, Voltaire, Helvétius, Montesquieu, and Rousseau) tells the great men, who cannot agree among themselves, the necessary steps for determining the proper form of government which will succeed in making men happy.[85] Before Roederer had purchased his interest in the *Journal de Paris*, he had even tentatively agreed to work for Sieyès on a new journal, which apparently never appeared.[86] The two were linked together in the public mind when certain journalists claimed in 1795 that they had formed "a faction of recluses" or a "society of unsociables."[87] However there seems to have been no contact between the men during the three years which preceded the conspiracy of 18 brumaire.[88]

In 1799 both men were anxious to arrest the leftward drift in France. In August Roederer, disturbed by the revival of political clubs, had reprinted his 1794 pamphlet attacking such organizations under the new title *Des Sociétés particulières*.[89] Sieyès, as director, was responsible for

---

[83] Woloch, *Jacobin Legacy*, pp. 364–65, 369, 379–82; R. R. Palmer, *The Age of the Democratic Revolution: The Struggle* (Princeton, 1964), pp. 258–59, 563.

[84] Roederer, *Notice*, in OR, 3: 294. Certainly their correspondence indicated a certain amount of intimacy. AN 284AP9 dossier 5.

[85] P.-L. Roederer, "Entretien de plusieurs philosophes célèbres sur les gouvernements républicain ou monarchique," JEP 20 prairial V (8 June 1797), in OR, 7: 61–71.

[86] AN 284AP9 dossier 5 Roederer to Sieyès 23 pluviôse III (11 February 1795).

[87] JP 21 ventôse III (11 March 1795), in OR, 6: 54.

[88] J.-B. Couteulx de Canteleu, "Souvenirs," in *Mémoires sur les journées révolutionnaires et les coups d'état*, ed. A. Lescure, (Paris, 1875), 2: 220.

[89] P.-L. Roederer, *Des Sociétés particulières telles que clubs, reunions, etc.*, in OR, 7: 87–94.

closing the Manège Club and reversing the leftward trend in the Councils.[90] Likewise Roederer and Sieyès were of the opinion that a constitutional revision strengthening the executive was necessary. Roederer had suggested such a revision as early as 1797 and by 1799 was more convinced of its necessity than ever.[91]

His views were well enough known that his return to political writing touched off speculation that he was involved in some sort of covert activity. In the Five Hundred the deputy Garrau asserted that Roederer and Talleyrand were to be named to positions in the department of Paris, a move which signaled "a new reaction."[92] Corancez, also suspicious of Roederer's newly rediscovered political interest, began criticizing and even censoring Roederer's articles in the *Journal de Paris*.[93] On 20 fructidor VII (6 September 1799) Corancez accused Roederer of writing only in the interest of "the mission of Syeies [sic] and Fouché" and warned him that "I do not want my journal to become a *journal de parti*."[94] Denying any political motives, Roederer argued that his articles were merely designed to rebuild the list of subscribers which had declined dramatically after his partial retirement in 1797.[95] If a political position was being taken by either, Roederer charged it was Corancez, who had placed "revolting letters" against Barthélemy in the journal and allowed Talleyrand to be slandered.

Despite his denials to Corancez Roederer was drawn into the plans being made for the coup d'état of 18 brumaire. Sieyès, in need of a general with strong republican credentials to effect his coup, entered into negotiations with Napoleon Bonaparte. However, with plans of his own Bonaparte did not intend to let Sieyès remain in control of the affair; and in making the arrangements for the coup d'état, it was Bonaparte who invited Roederer to join the conspirators. That such should be the case was ironic given Roederer's harsh criticism of Bonaparte's unauthorized political activity in the Italian campaign.[96] Similarly Bonaparte had not always been favorably disposed toward Roederer. According to Miot de Melito, Bonaparte had expressed in August 1797 "an extreme repugnance" for Roederer because "of the duplicity and treason" he had demonstrated in conducting Louis XVI to the Assembly on August 10.[97] Nevertheless, Bonaparte had a certain admiration for Roederer's political thought and asked the Di-

---

[90] Lefebvre, *The Directory*, pp. 204–06.

[91] As evidence of his continuing interest in constitutional revision, Roederer had demanded in June 1799 that the Constitution be amended to maintain freedom of the press. JP 27 prairial VII (15 June 1799), in OR, 6: 385–86.

[92] MU 3 jour complémentaire (19 September 1799), 39: 813.

[93] This activity is revealed in a number of letters in 1799 between Roederer and Corancez found in AN 29AP10.

[94] AN 29AP10 Corancez to Roederer 20 fructidor VII (6 September 1799).

[95] AN 29AP10 Roederer to Corancez 20 fructidor VII. Specifically Roederer said that he wanted to regain 1000 subscribers in six months. In part he had tried to do this with his lengthy articles on literature, grammar, and morals which Corancez had rejected as too long.

[96] JP 7 thermidor IV (25 July 1796) and JEP 10 messidor V (28 June 1797), in OR, 6: 35–36, 315.

[97] A. F. Miot de Melito, *Mémoires* (Paris, 1873), 1: 174.

rectory to send him along with Sieyès and Benjamin Constant to Italy to write a constitution for the Cisalpine Republic.[98] In March 1798 Bonaparte met Roederer at Talleyrand's home and after the general's return from Egypt in 1799 invited Roederer through Regnaud de Saint-Jean d'Angély to discuss joining the enterprise.[99] Talleyrand, who had introduced the two men, probably was responsible for convincing Bonaparte to bring Roederer into the conspiracy. Roederer certainly had assets which would be beneficial to the general: he was a known supporter of constitutional revision, he admired and respected Sieyès with whom Bonaparte had to work, and he had the *Journal de Paris* which might prove useful as events unfolded.

Roederer's role in the conspiracy was limited to acting, along with Talleyrand, as an intermediary between Sieyès and Bonaparte, who preferred not to meet face to face.[100] During the secret nightly visits they made to the leaders, Talleyrand handled negotiations for the mechanics of the coup d'état while Roederer dealt with the role the two men were to play in the future government. Roederer also was responsible for producing the placards that were to be placed around Paris on 18 brumaire explaining that Bonaparte's actions were necessary to preserve liberty and the constitution.[101]

Roederer's real contribution to events came during the drafting of the new constitution which he believed would provide the government based on social science that he had so long desired. As is well known the constitution theoretically was to be drawn up by two commissions from the Councils, but in actual fact all were relying on Sieyès to provide the basic document. Since he refused to write a draft, Sieyès's constitutional program only emerged through conversations with Boulay de la Meurthe, Daunou, and Roederer. Boulay and Roederer were then responsible for transmitting this information to Bonaparte. Given the manner in which the constitutional project was formulated and then conveyed to Bonaparte, absolute certainty regarding Sieyès's intentions has never been possible.[102] Nor have historians been sure of what influence, if any, Sieyès's confidants had in the formulation of his plan. Jean Bourdon has argued, however, that Roederer had a better understanding of the proposals than Boulay, despite the latter's insistence that he was solely responsible for recording

---

[98] Raymond Guyot, "Du Directoire au consulat: les transitions," *Revue historique* 111 (1912): 14.

[99] AN 29AP8 Roederer's note of a conversation with Bonaparte, 23 ventôse VI (13 March 1798); Roederer, *Notice,* in OR, 3: 295–96. The date of the interview was probably 5 brumaire VIII (27 October 1799). Roederer, note of a conversation with Bonaparte, in OR, 3: 327.

[100] Roederer, note of a conversation with Bonaparte, in OR, 3: 327; Roederer, *Notice,* in OR, 3: 296.

[101] Roederer, *Notice,* in OR, 3: 298–99. Regnaud Saint-Jean d'Angély and Roederer's son Antoine handled the printing of the placards and Bonaparte himself did the final editing.

[102] Jean Bourdon. *La Constitution de l'an VIII* (Rodez, 1942), pp. 11–37; Sydenham, *The First French Republic*, p. 224.

Sieyès's ideas.[103] Roederer did indeed have a very clear conception of the scheme since some of its component parts originated with him.

During the discussions on the Constitution of 1795, both Roederer and Sieyès had argued in favor of strengthening the executive at the expense of the legislature. At the time of these discussions Roederer had praised Sieyès's plan which had called for the extreme separation of powers into a jurie de proposition, tribunate, legislative body, and jurie constitutionaire, but he had criticized the proposal for not giving the government enough influence on the local level. Roederer's own proposal, it will be remembered, had included among other features a plan for the selection of local officials by the executive from lists presented from the primary assemblies and the creation of a grand électeur who could remove uncooperative directors from office. After the coup d'état of fructidor Roederer had reiterated the value of the grand électeur, an official he now said should nominate as well as remove directors and ministers. To his original idea of the appointment of all local officials, he added the suggestion of "gradual promotions," a requirement that all officials serve on the local level before assuming national office.

The constitutional project resulting from his conversations with Sieyès that Roederer took to Bonaparte was a combination of the ideas of both men.[104] It called for Sieyès's separation of the legislative power into a corps of 30 individuals to propose laws in the name of the government, a corps of 500 to propose and debate laws, and a corps of 400 to vote yes or no on the passage of laws. The executive would consist of two consuls, one for the interior and the other for foreign affairs. In addition to the judicial branch there was also to be a conservative power, the Senate, of 100 magistrates "who were to judge the incompetence of the superior powers."[105] All of this differed only in detail from Sieyès's proposals in 1795. Regarding the elections, their proposal called for all individuals who paid three days wages in taxes to elect one-tenth of their number to form a local list of notables who would then meet by department to select one-tenth of their number to serve as departmental notables. These in turn

---

[103] F.-J. Boulay de la Meurthe, *Théorie constitutionnelle de Sieyès* (Paris, 1836), p. 8; Bourdon, *La Constitution,* p. 22. Not only did Roederer have rapport with Sieyès, but he also had the confidence of Bonaparte. According to Boulay if Sieyès and Bonaparte could not agree on the provisions of the new constitution, Bonaparte wanted Roederer quickly to draw up a constitution which could be presented to the primary assemblies. *Théorie constitutionnelle,* p. 50.

[104] AN 29AP79 P.-L. Roederer, "Organisation d'un gouvernement répresentatif." Boulay and Roederer both acted as intermediaries between Sieyès and Bonaparte in the initial stages of the drafting of the constitution. Here Roederer was certainly the dominant party due to his familiarity, understanding, and sympathy with the project and the force of his intellect. Daunou, the other great constitutional theorist among the Brumairians was more influential in the latter stages of the process when called upon by Bonaparte to come up with a draft document for the constitutional commissions from the Councils. See Bourdon, *La Constitution,* pp. 26–27.

[105] AN 29AP79 Roederer, "Organisation."

would elect one-tenth to serve as national notables. All communal administrators would be chosen from and by the local notables while civil judges would be chosen by departmental notables. Commissioners for each department would be named by the ministers presumably from the departmental list. Ministers would be named by the consuls and the consuls chosen by the grand électeur. All legislators would be chosen from the national list in an unspecified manner. If the consuls performed poorly or improperly, they could be removed by the grand électeur. The grand électeur could be called to enter the Senate which then would choose a successor.

The entire electoral and administrative system outlined in the project smacks of Roederer's influence. The grand électeur was to serve precisely the functions Roederer had outlined when he developed this concept between 1795 and 1797.[106] Likewise Roederer's scheme for a communal list from which all local officials were chosen appeared in virtually the same form as his original suggestions.[107] Perhaps most importantly his concept for departmental administration by commissioners appointed by the ministers fulfilled his desire for executive control of local affairs. In this case Roederer's dictum of 1795 that it "is necessary that orders and powers emanate from the same source" seems to have directly inspired Sieyès's comment to Boulay in 1799 that "no one ought to be named *fonctionnaire* by those on whom his authority ought to weigh," a requirement which demanded that "authority always come from above."[108] Roederer's ideas had obviously been altered somewhat in the discussions with Sieyès. For instance the communal notables were to be allowed to elect their own administrators, and the concept of "gradual promotions" had been transformed into the idea of departmental and national lists of notables. Yet

---

[106] Sieyès's papers, containing the manuscript version of the constitutional project he presented on 2 thermidor to the Convention, mention the creation of an office, the grand électeur, who would promulgate legislative decisions. Sieyès made no mention of this official when he presented the project to the Convention, however. Whether Sieyès picked up the term of grand électeur at this time from Roederer is uncertain. Roederer wrote between 25 messidor and 3 thermidor the articles which composed the pamphlet *Du Gouvernement*, where he first proposed the creation of the grand électeur. Whatever the origin of the term, Sieyès must not have been overly taken with the concept since he omitted the office from the plan he presented to the Convention. Furthermore, Sieyès's grand électeur differed considerably in function from Roederer's. See Paul Bastid, *Sieyès et sa pensée*, 2nd ed. (Paris, 1970) p. 457; and Roederer, *Du Gouvernement*, in OR, 7: 24–46.

[107] Sieyès had proposed in his pamphlet *Quelques idées de constitutution applicables à la ville de Paris en juillet en 1789* something similar to the communal and national lists with administrative personnel being selected from lists prepared by local electors and the legislative body. There is good reason to believe, however, that Sieyès did not have this plan in mind during the constitutional discussion of 1799, despite Bastid's assertion to the contrary. In 1789 the question at hand was how to make the monarchial administration more open and democratic, while in 1799 the problem was how to limit democracy in all aspects of government. That Sieyès associated his 1789 electoral plan with broadening rather than limiting popular participation in administration seems evident because his constitutional project of 1795 made no mention of this procedure. Most likely Roederer's suggestions along these lines convinced Sieyès to return to his original idea but for reasons vastly different from those of 1789. See Bastid, *Sieyès*, p. 413.

[108] Boulay de la Meurthe, *Theorie constutionnelle*, pp. 16–17.

the danger of uncontrolled elections was dealt with just as effectively as under Roederer's original system.

When Roederer took this plan to Bonaparte, the general was quite unhappy with the concept of the grand électeur.[109] Roederer then tried to make the office of grand électeur more appealing to Bonaparte by describing the honor and importance which would be attached to its holder, who would represent the national majority and be above party.[110] When it became obvious that Bonaparte would not accept the existence of this official in any form, Roederer came up with the plan of having three consuls with the First Consul serving as president.[111] Roederer did not envision a First Consul with unlimited power, but rather suggested that he have the approval of at least one other consul before taking any action or that if such approval was not forthcoming, the decision should rest with the Senate. Bonaparte, of course, refused to accept these limitations, but he did eventually accept the arrangement of a First Consul and two subordinate consuls.

In its completed form the Constitution of the Year VIII retained a good deal of the Sieyès-Roederer plan. Sieyès's extreme division of legislative power and Roederer's electoral and administrative ideas were incorporated in it.[112] Actually the final document eliminated the election of local officials by those on the communal list and returned to Roederer's original idea of appointment by the central government. Perhaps the greatest failure of the two men had been to create, as they had originally envisioned, an executive with some effective limitations on its power. Nevertheless, in a series of articles in the *Journal de Paris* Roederer had only praise for the new Constitution which he saw as the fulfillment of his own goals. He pointed out to his readers that the new electoral system had the virtue of being "a true representative system, exempt from the horrors of demagogy and the oppressions of aristocracy."[113] In addition the provisions allowing the government to choose its local administrators instead of relying on independent-minded elected officials would actually establish his long sought "gradual elections" with the advancement of individuals from the lowest offices to the highest. This system would ensure "not only the great respect for authority but also a great respect for public opinion" and advance the proprietors of the nation into "high places."[114]

While Roederer's influence on the drafting of the Constitution is clear, the extent to which the document fulfilled his desire for government based on social science may be less obvious. Did the Constitution create a gov-

---

[109] Ibid., pp. 47–48.

[110] This at least seems to be the purpose of a hastily written and untitled memorandum found in AN 29AP79.

[111] AN 29AP79 Untitled memorandum on the consuls; Boulay de la Meurthe, *Théorie constitutionnelle*, p. 48.

[112] For the Constitution of the Year VIII see John Hall Stewart, *A Documentary Survey of the French Revolution* (New York, 1951), pp. 768–79.

[113] JP 17 frimaire VIII (8 December 1799), in OR, 7: 394.

[114] JP 18 frimaire VIII (9 December 1799), in OR, 6: 394.

ernment which would respect the natural laws of economics, morals, and politics? Roederer believed that it would bring into office property owners who would surely enforce the natural laws of economics and provide political stability for the nation. The political organization contained elements that were thought to be scientific. The legislature as designed by Sieyès would be likely to satisfy Roederer's requirement that legislation be made through the use of reason rather than by inflammatory rhetoric, and the electoral system was almost certain to produce responsible legislators who could work harmoniously with the executive. Since the executive power had so much authority in proposing legislation and administering it, the legislature was not likely to interfere in the work of administration. Presumably with such a government in place laws could be passed to affect positively the morals of the citizenry. Admittedly Roederer's adaptation of Condorcet's social mathematics as they applied to legislation was not to be found in the Constitution, but then even Condorcet himself in drafting his constitution for the Convention in 1793 had been unable to include all of his theories in it.[115] While the Constitution of the Year VIII may not have completely fulfilled the requirements for rational government, it came close enough to satisfy Roederer. Events were soon to prove, of course, that social science and constitutions were to be of less importance than the personality of the First Consul, Bonaparte. This development, however, does not alter the fact that in 1799 Roederer believed that the document he had helped to shape would bring improved government to France because it was based on the most advanced theories of social science.

The coup d'état of brumaire brought to an end not only Roederer's search for stability, but also his political isolation as he was now on the winning side politically for the first time since 1791. Bonaparte had duly rewarded him for his support with the presidency of the Section of the Interior in the Council of State and even forced Corancez to relinquish control of the *Journal de Paris*.[116] Roederer's satisfaction with the events of brumaire also marked the extent of his disillusionment with his early ideals. In the hopeful days of 1788 Roederer had been full of enthusiasm for a democratically elected, representative government. By 1799 both democracy and true representation were to be avoided. Bonaparte might insure what Roederer had once called the "grand and durable results" of the Revolution through the imposition of order, but the noble ideals upon which Roederer had entered the Revolution were gone forever. His

---

[115] Keith Baker, *Condorcet: From Natural Philosophy to Social Mathematics* (Chicago, 1975), pp. 320–25.

[116] Bonaparte originally offered Roederer a seat in the Senate, but the latter preferred the Council of State. Bonaparte to Sieyès, 3 nivôse VIII (24 December 1799), in ed. John E. Howard, *Letters and Documents of Napoleon* (New York, 1961), I, 326. Also see Roederer, *Notice*, in OR, 3: 309. A memorandum of unknown origin declaring that the First Consul would not permit Corancez's name to appear on the *Journal de Paris* is found in AN 29AP91.

concern with the representation of the artisans of Metz had given way to his desire to see men of property in "high places." His distrust of the king and his Feuillant allies in the Constituent Assembly had been replaced by his support of a First Consul who had few limitations on his power. The Terror had destroyed these ideals, and Roederer had come to see stability and order as preferable to democracy and representative government. Nevertheless, Roederer's support for the Constitution of the Year VIII was not a cynical rationalization for the creation of authoritarian government. Roederer, like many of the brumarians, believed the Constitution would consolidate and insure the continuation of the rational reforms of the early Revolution which had been threatened by the political turmoil of the decade.

CONCLUSION

R oederer's political career is an interesting case study in the history of the French Revolution because the originality and depth of his thought was simultaneously a product of and a motivation for his practice of politics. The combination of the roles of politician and political theorist was not unknown during the Revolution (for instance Sieyès, Condorcet, Robespierre, and Daunou could all be so classified), but the number of such individuals was small. In Roederer's case he was not an abstract theoretician who tried to force reality to conform to his view of the world, but rather a thinker who developed his ideas in response to the environment in which he found himself. In many instances Roederer had proven to be a highly pragmatic practitioner of politics who did not let theory stand in the way of immediate accomplishment. There can be little doubt that he could have continued to function within the political system of the ancien régime. He might not have had the opportunities for effecting national policy that the Revolution provided; but by the late 1780s his contacts at court were growing, and it is not inconceivable that they might have eventually borne fruit in the form of some governmental post. However, the interrelated problems of tariffs and privileges in the foreign provinces and their conjunction with the political opportunities of the early Revolution brought into being his first important political theories. Once he had developed his ideas on democratic government, the political activities which followed were a product of the assumptions on which these theories rested. He won considerable repute as a patriot in the early Revolution: at Metz, on the Tax Committee, and in the Jacobins in the summer of 1791 he had demonstrated the qualities associated with patriotism and had acquired approbation, at least in part, for his success in the ventures he undertook.

Roederer's major political failure came in the summer of 1792. Here his political intuition seemed to have failed him as he remained loyal to constitutional monarchy long after the king himself had made it inoperable. This loyalty rested on the belief that the Revolution could be consolidated by revolutionary administrators like himself and his fear of allowing governmental authority to be dominated by the Parisian crowds. When the intent of the populace of Paris became clear, only two real alternatives existed: a forceful repression of the crowds or an alliance with them. Roederer, still considering himself a good revolutionary, could not contemplate repression; but as an administrator who had come increasingly to understand the problems of "government" as opposed to revolutionary

154

reform, he could not condone an alliance with crowds unwilling to accept the authority of their elected representatives. He instead opted for a path between repression and alliance with results that were hardly satisfying to him or France.

His rejection by the left after 10 August had a liberating effect on Roederer. No longer having to concern himself with maintaining his revolutionary credentials or justifying certain political actions merely to retain his position in the vanguard of the Revolution, he was able to regain his political balance. He reevaluated his former assumptions, rejected them, and established a new basis for political activity: social science. In the process he developed his important theories of economic liberalism. Practicality was not discarded, however; he was not so firmly wedded to his theoretical construct of society that he was unwilling to support any government which promised moderation and stability. In a clear indication of his pragmatism he accepted the basic work of the Thermidorian Convention and supported, though not without criticism, the Directory until after the coup d'état of fructidor. Only after fructidor did Roederer come to think that the Constitution of the Year III was totally inadequate and that the institution of stable, rational government required the total dismantling of the system of freely elected representatives.

From 1795 through 1799 Roederer's political influence was limited to his journalistic work. A persona non grata in political circles because of his actions on 10 August, Roederer did not take part in any of the political maneuverings during the Directory. He claimed to have no interest in political office although this claim may have been a way of saving face when he obviously could win none either through election or appointment. He also made no strong political commitments, perhaps for fear that they would lead to disastrous consequences for him personally such as those that had followed his behavior on 10 August. He contented himself with his association with Madame de Staël and her circle, his work at the Institute, and of course his newspapers. Yet when the opportunity to join the conspiracy of brumaire arose, Roederer, avoiding the indecision which had characterized his political activity since 1792, quickly opted for participation in the coup d'état. This seems to have been a result of his determination to bring about the definitive governmental reform he had so long advocated, his compatibility with the other conspirators (especially Sieyés and Talleyrand), and his confidence in the success of the project given the status of those involved. In 1799 Roederer's political instincts which had served him so well through 1791 finally revived after a long period of dormancy.

Roederer's final work of the revolutionary decade was compatible with both his political theories and pragmatic outlook. He believed, even if erroneously, that the new constitution would inaugurate an era of rational government based on social science, but he had been willing to accept significant modification in the document in order to win Bonaparte's approval, which was essential for its success. Roederer's political career, like all of the politics of the Revolution, had been a continual quest for a foundation upon which to build a new society for France. In 1799, believing that such a foundation had been established, he was filled with the self-satisfaction which follows success. But like all the previous political achievements of the Revolution, Roederer's were fated to be altered significantly, in this case by the character of the First Consul Bonaparte.

SELECTED BIBLIOGRAPHY

PRIMARY SOURCES

Manuscript Sources

Archives Nationales. Serie AP: Archives privées. 29AP1–119: Roederer Papers.
Archives Nationales. Serie AP: Archives privées. 284AP9: Sieyès Papers.

Documents

Archives parlementaires de 1787 à 1860. Iᵉ serie (1787–1799). Ed. M. J. Mavidal and M. E. Laurent. 86 vols. Paris, 1879.

AULARD, ALPHONSE. (ed.) *La Société des Jacobins: recueil de documents pour l'histoire du Club des Jacobins de Paris.* 6 vols. Paris, 1889–1897.

——. *Paris pendant la reaction thermidorienne et sous le directoire: recueil de documents pour l'histoire de l'esprit à Paris.* 5 vols. Paris, 1898–1902.

BRETTE, ARMAND. (ed.) *Recueil de documents relatifs à la convocation des Etats Généraux de 1789.* 4 vols. Paris, 1894.

DUVERGIER, J. B. (ed.) *Collection complète des lois, decrets, ordonnances, reglemens, avis du conseil d'état publie sur les editions officielles du Louvre de l'imprimerie nationale, par Baudouin et du Bulletin du lois.* Vol. I. Paris, 1834.

Revue rétrospective ou bibliothèque historique contenant des mémoires et documents authentiques, inédits et originaux pour servir à l'histoire de la litterature et des arts. Seconde serie. 12 vols. Paris, 1835–1837.

STEWART, JOHN HALL. *A Documentary Survey of the French Revolution.* New York, 1951.

Collected Works and Letters

BONAPARTE, NAPOLEON. *Correspondance de Napoleon I.* 32 vols. Paris, 1858–1870.

——. *Letters and Documents of Napoleon.* Ed. John E. Howard. New York, 1961.

BRISSOT, J. P. *Correspondance et papiers.* Ed. C. Perroud. Paris, 1911.

JEFFERSON, THOMAS. *The Papers of Thomas Jefferson.* Ed. Julian P. Boyd. Vols. 16 and 18. Princeton, 1961, 1971.

ROBESPIERRE, MAXIMILIEN. *Oeuvres complètes de Robespierre: Le Defenseur de la Constitution.* Ed. Gustave Laurent. Vol. 4. Nancy, 1939.

——. *Oeuvres de Maximilien Robespierre: Discours octobre 1791–Septembre 1792.* Ed. Marc Bouloiseau et al. Vol. 8. Paris, 1953.

ROEDERER, P.-L. *Oeuvres du comte P.-L. Roederer.* Ed. A. M. Roederer. 8 vols. Paris, 1853–1859.

ROLAND, J. M. *Lettres de Madame Roland.* Ed. Claude Perroud. 2 vols. Paris, 1902.

VERGNIAUD, P. *Vergniaud: Manuscrits, lettres, et papiers.* Ed. C. Vatel. Paris, n.d.

VERMOREL, A. (ed.) *Oeuvres de Vergniaud, Gensonné, Guadet.* Paris, n.d.

Memoirs

BARBAROUX, C. *Mémoires.* Ed. Alfred Chaubaud. Paris, 1936.

BARÈRE, B. *Mémoires.* Eds. H. Carnot and D. Angers. 4 vols. Paris, 1842–1844.

BARRAS, P. *Memoirs.* Ed. George Duruy. 4 vols. London, 1896.

BONAPARTE, Lucien. *Mémoires.* 3 vols. Paris, 1882.

BOUILLÉ, F.-C. AMOUR, MARQUIS DE. *Mémoires.* Eds. Berville and Barrière. 3rd. ed. Paris, 1823.

BOULAY DE LA MEURTHE, F.-J. *Théorie constitutionnelle de Sieyès.* Paris, 1836.

BOURRIENNE, L. *Mémoires.* Ed. Desiré Lacroix. 5 vols. Paris, n.d.

BRISSOT, J.-P. *Mémoires.* Ed. A. Lescure. Paris, 1887.

CLERY, J.-P.-L. "Journal," in *Mémoires de Clery, de M. le duc de Montpensier, de Riouffe*. Ed.
F. Barrière. 2 vols. Paris, 1856.
COUTEULX DE CANTELEU, J.-B. "Souvenirs," in *Mémoires sur les journées révolutionnaires et
les coups d'état*. Ed. A. Lescure. 2 vols. Paris, 1875.
DEJOLY, E.-L.-H. "Mémoires de Etienne-Louis-Hector Dejoly," ed. Jacques Godechot, *Annales
historiques de la Révolution francqise*, 1946, pp. 289–382.
DUQUESNOY, ADRIEN. *Journal*. Ed. Robert de Crevecoeur. Paris, 1894.
DUMONT, ETIENNE. *Souvenirs*. Ed. J. Benetruy. Paris, 1951.
FERRIÈRES, CHARLES-ELIE, MARQUIS DE. *Mémoires*. Ed. Berville and Barrière. 2nd. ed. 3 vols.
Paris, 1822.
FOUCHÉ, J. *Mémoires*. Ed. Louis Madelin. Paris, 1945.
LA REVELLIÈRE-LÉPEAUX, L.-M. *Mémoires*. Ed. O. Larevellière-Lépeaux. 3 vols. Paris, 1895.
LA ROCHEFOUCAULD, FRANÇOIS DE. *Souvenirs*. Paris, 1929.
LOUVET DE COUVRAY, J. B. *Mémoires*. Ed. Berville and Barrière. Paris, 1823.
MIOT DE MELITO, A. F. *Mémoires*. 3 vols. Paris, 1873.
MORRIS, GOUVERNEUR. *A Diary of the French Revolution, 1789–1793*. Ed. Beatrix C. Davenport.
2 vols. New York, 1939.
ROEDERER, P.-L. *Autour de Bonaparte: journal du comte P.-L. Roederer: notes intimes et politiques
d'un familier des Tuileries*. Ed. Maurice Vitrac. Paris, 1909.
——. "Chronique de cinquante jours du 20 juin au 10 août 1792 redigée sur pieces au-
thentiques," in *Mémoires sur les journées révolutionnaries et les coups d'état*. Ed. A. Lescure.
Vol. I. Paris, 1875.
ROLAND, J. M. *Mémoires*. Ed. Claude Perroud. 2 vols. Paris, 1905.
TALLEYRAND, C.-M. *Mémoires*. Ed. Adolphe Fourier de Bacourt. 5 vols. Paris, 1967.
THIBAUDEAU, A.-C. *Mémoires de A.-C. Thibaudeau 1799–1815*. Paris, 1913.
——. *Mémoires sur la Convention et le Directoire*. Ed. Berville and Barriére. 2 vols. Paris, 1824.

Newspapers

L'Accusateur public.
L'Ami du peuple.
Chronique de Paris.
Journal de Paris.
*Journal des débats et de la correspondance de la Société des Amis de la Constitution séante aux
Jacobins à Paris.*
Moniteur Universel. Réimpression de l'ancien Moniteur. 32 vols. Paris, 1847–1850.
Le Patriote français.
La Sentinelle.

SECONDARY SOURCES

ALLIX, EDGARD. "La Rivalité entre la propriété foncière et la fortune mobilière sous la Rév-
olution," *Revue d'histoire économique et sociale*, 6 (1913): 297–348.
BAKER, KEITH MICHAEL. *Condorcet: From Natural Philosophy to Social Mathematics*. Chicago,
1975.
——. "Scientism, Elitism and Liberalism: the Case of Condorcet," *Studies on Voltaire and the
Eighteenth Century*, 55 (1967): 129–165.
BARBER, ELINOR. *The Bourgeoisie in Eighteenth Century France*. Princeton, 1955.
BASTID, PAUL. *Sieyès et sa pensée*. 2nd ed. Paris, 1970.
BELLANGER, CLAUDE et al. *Histoire générale de la presse française*. 2 vols. Paris, 1969.
BERLANSTEIN, LENARD. *The Barristers of Toulouse in the Eighteenth Century (1740–1793)*. Bal-
timore, 1975.
BOSHER, J. F. *French Finances, 1770–1795: From Business to Bureaucracy*. Cambridge, 1970.
——. *The Single Duty Project: A Study of the Movement for a French Customs Union in the
Eighteenth Century*. London, 1964.
BOURDON, JEAN. *La Constitution de l'an VIII*. Rodez, 1942.
BOURGIN, GEORGES. "Un témoin de la Révolution: Roederer," *Revue historique*, 188 (1940):
259–270.
BRAESCH, FRÉDÉRIC. *La Commune de dix août 1792: étude sur l'histoire de Paris du 20 juin au
2 decembre 1792*. Paris, 1911.

BRETTE, ARMAND. *Les Constituants: Liste des députés et des suppléants élus à l'assemblée constituente de 1789.* Paris, 1897.

CHALLAMEL, AUGUSTIN. *Les Clubs contre-révolutionnaires: cercles, comités, sociétés, salons, reunions, cafés, restaurants, et librairies.* Paris, 1895.

CAVANAUGH, GERALD. "The Present State of French Revolutionary Historiography: Alfred Cobban and Beyond," *French Historical Studies,* 7 (1972): 587–606.

CHEVALLIER, J. J. *Histoire des institutions et des régimes politiques de la France moderne (1789–1958).* 3rd. ed. Paris, 1967.

CLAPHAM, J. H. *The Abbé Sieyès: An Essay in the Politics of the French Revolution.* London, 1912.

COBBAN, ALFRED. *Aspects of the French Revolution.* New York, 1970.

——. *The Social Interpretation of the French Revolution.* London, 1964.

DARNTON, ROBERT. *Mesmerism and the End of the Enlightenment in France.* Cambridge, 1968.

DAWSON, PHILIP. "The Bourgeoisie de Robe in 1789," *French Historical Studies,* 4 (1965): 1–21.

EGRET, JEAN. "L'Aristocratie parlementaire française à la fin de l'ancien régime," *Revue historique,* 208 (1952): 1–15.

——. *La Pré-révolution française, 1787–1789.* Paris, 1962.

ELLERY, ELOISE. *Brissot de Warville: A Study in the History of the French Revolution.* Boston, 1915.

FLAMMERONT, JULES. *Le Chancelier Maupeou et les Parlements.* Paris, 1883.

FORD, FRANKLIN. *Robe and Sword: The Regrouping of the French Aristocracy after Louis XIV.* New York, 1965.

FRYER, W. R. *Republic or Restoration, 1794–1797: The Politics of French Royalism with Particular Reference to the Activities of A. B. J. D'André.* Manchester, 1965.

FUGIER, ANDRÉ. *La Révolution française et l'empire Napoleonien.* Vol. IV of *Histoire des relations internationales.* Ed. Pierre Renouvin. Paris, 1954.

GALLOIS, LEONARD. *Histoire des journaux et des journalistes de la Révolution française (1789–1796).* 2 vols. Paris, 1845–1846.

GIESEY, RALPH. "Rules of Inheritance and Strategies of Mobility in Prerevolutionary France." *American Historical Review,* 82 (1977): 271–289.

GODECHOT, JACQUES. *La Contre-révolution: doctrine et action, 1789–1804.* Paris, 1961.

——. *Les Institutions de la France sous la Révolution et l'Empire.* Paris, 1951.

GRUDER, VIVIAN. *The Royal Provincial Intendants: A Governing Elite in Eighteenth Century France.* Ithaca, 1968.

GUYOT, RAYMOND. "Du Directoire au consulat: les transitions," *Revue historique,* 111 (1912): 1–31.

GWYNNE, G. E. *Madame de Staël et le Révolution française.* Paris, 1969.

HAHN, ROGER. *The Anatomy of a Scientific Institution: The Paris Academy of Sciences, 1666–1803.* Berkeley, 1971.

HAMPSON, NORMAN. *A Social History of the French Revolution.* Toronto, 1963.

HERTZBERG, ARTHUR. *The French Enlightenment and the Jews.* New York, 1968.

HOCQUARD, GABRIEL. *Metz.* Paris, 1961.

HYSLOP, BEATRICE FRY. *A Guide to the General Cahiers of 1789 with Texts of the Unedited Cahiers.* New York, 1936.

JAMES, MICHAEL. "Pierre-Louis Roederer, Jean-Baptiste Say, and the Concept of *industrie*," *History of Political Economy,* 9 (1977): 455–475.

KAISER, THOMAS E. "Politics and Political Economy in the Thought of the Ideologues," *History of Political Economy,* 12 (1980): 141–160.

KENNEDY, EMMET. *A Philosophe in the Age of Revolution: Destutt de Tracy and the Origins of "Ideology."* Philadelphia, 1978.

KNIGHT, ISABEL F. *The Geometric Spirit: The Abbé de Condillac and the French Enlightenment.* New Haven, 1968.

LACOUR-GAYET, G. *Talleyrand 1754–1838.* 4 vols. Paris, 1928–31.

LACOUR-GAYET, ROBERT. *Calonne: financier, reformateur, contre-révolutionnaire, 1734–1802.* Paris, 1963.

LA CROIX, SEGISMUND. *Le Département de Paris et de la Seine pendant la Révolution.* Paris, 1904.

LEDRÉ, CHARLES. *Histoire de la presse.* Paris, 1958.

LEFEBVRE, GEORGES. *The Directory.* Trans. Robert Baldick. New York, 1964.

——. *The French Revolution from its Origins to 1793*. Trans. Elizabeth M. Evanson. New York, 1962.

——. *The French Revolution from 1793 to 1799*. Trans. John Hall Stewart and James Friguglietti. New York, 1964.

——. *The Thermidorians*. Trans. Robert Baldick. New York, 1964.

LEITH, JAMES. *The Idea of Art as Propaganda in France, 1750–1799*. Toronto, 1965.

LESPRAND, P. "Election de député direct et cahier du tiers état de la ville de Metz en 1789," *Annuaire de la Société d'Histoire et d'Archéologie de Lorraine*, 15 (1903): 158–206.

LEVASSEUR, E. *Histoire du commerce de la France*. 2 vols. Paris, 1911.

LUCAS, COLIN. "The First Directory and the Rule of Law," *French Historical Studies*, 10 (1977): 231–260.

LUCAS, COLIN, "Nobles, Bourgeois and the Origins of the French Revolution," *French Society and Revolution*, pp. 88–131. Ed. Douglas Johnson. Cambridge, 1976.

LYONS, MARTIN. *France Under the Directory*. Cambridge, 1975.

MARGERISON, KENNETH. "P.-L. Roederer, The Industrial Capitalist as Revolutionary," *Eighteenth-Century Studies*, 11 (1978): 473–488.

MARION, MARCEL. *Dictionnaire des institutions de la France aux XVII et XVIII siècles*. Paris, 1923.

——. *Histoire financière de France depuis 1715*. 6 vols. Paris, 1927.

MARKHAM, FELIX. *Napoleon*. New York, 1963.

MATHIEZ, ALBERT. *After Robespierre: The Thermidorian Reaction*. Trans. Catherine A. Phillips. New York, 1965.

——. *Le Dix août*. Paris, 1931.

——. "Les Girondins et la cour à la veille du 10 août," *Annales historiques de la Révolution française*, 8 (1931): 193–212.

——. *The French Revolution*. Trans. Catherine A. Phillips. New York, 1964.

MATTHEWS, GEORGE, *The Royal General Farms in Eighteenth Century France*. New York, 1968.

MEYNIER, ALBERT. *Les Coups d'état du directoire: le dix-huit brumaire an VIII (novembre 1799) et la fin de la république*. Paris, 1928.

MICHEL, EMMANUEL. *Biographie du Parlement de Metz*. Metz, 1853.

MICHON, GEORGES. *Essai sur l'histoire du parti Feuillant: Adrien Duport*. Paris, 1924.

MIGNET, F. A. *Histoire de la Révolution francaise depuis 1789 jusqu'en 1814*. 3rd. ed. Vol. 2. Paris, 1826.

MITCHELL, HARVEY. *The Underground War Against Revolutionary France: The Missions of William Wickham, 1794–1800*. Oxford, 1965.

MORAVIA, SERGIO. *Il pensiero degli Idéologues: Scienza e filosofia in Francia, 1780–1815*. Firenze, 1974.

MORTIMER-TERNAUX, LOUIS. *Histoire de la Terreur 1792–1794*. 8 vols. Paris, 1863–1881.

OZOUF, MONA. *La Fete révolutionnaire, 1789–1799*. Paris, 1976.

PALMER, R. R. *The Age of the Democratic Revolution: The Struggle*. Princeton, 1964.

PAQUET, RENÉ. *Bibliographie analytique de l'histoire de Metz pendant la Révolution*. Paris, 1926.

PARISET, G. *Histoire de France contemporaine depuis la Révolution jusqu'à la paix de 1919*. Ed. E. Lavisse. Vol. 2. Paris, 1920.

PICAVET, F. *Les Idéologues: essai sur l'histoire des idées et des théories scientifiques, philosophiques, religieuse, etc. en France depuis 1789*. Paris, 1891.

PFEIFFER, LAURA B. "The Uprising of June 20, 1792," *The University Studies of the University of Nebraska*, 12 (1912): 197–343.

POPKIN, JEREMY D. "The Newspaper Press in French Political Thought," *Studies in Eighteenth-Century Culture*, 10 (1981): 113–133.

——. *The Right-Wing Press in France, 1792–1800*. Chapel Hill, 1980.

PRICE, JACOB. *France and the Chesapeake: A History of the French Tobacco Monopoly 1674–1791, and of its Relationship to the British and American Tobacco Trade*. 2 vols. Ann Arbor, 1973.

RENOUVIN, PIERRE. *Les Assemblées provinciales de 1787: origines, développement, résultats*. Paris, 1921.

REYNAUD, JEAN. *Vie et correspondance de Merlin de Thionville*. Paris, 1860.

ROEDERER, A.-M. *La Famille Roederer*. Paris, 1849.

ROELS, JEAN. *La Notion de représentation chez Roederer*. Heule, 1968.

RUDÉ, GEORGE. *The Crowd in the French Revolution*. London, 1959.

SAINTE-BEUVE, C. A. "Roederer," *Causeries du lundi*, Vol. 8. 3rd. ed. Paris, n.d.

SCOVILLE, WARREN, G. *Capitalism and French Glassmaking 1640–1789*. Berkeley, 1950.

Sée, Henri. *L'Evolution commerciale et industrielle de la France sous l'ancien régime.* Paris, 1925.

Seligman, Edmund. *La Justice pendant la Révolution.* Paris, 1901.

Soboul, Albert. "L'Historiographie classique de la Révolution française: sur des controverses récentes," *Historical Reflections/Réflexions Historiques,* 1 (1974): 141–167.

Staum, Martin. *Cabanis: Enlightenment and Medical Philosophy in the French Revolution.* Princeton, 1980.

——. "The Class of Moral and Political Sciences, 1795–1803," *French Historical Studies,* 11 (1980): 371–397.

Suratteau, J. "Les élections de l'an V aux conseils du Directoire," *Annales historiques de la Révolution française,* 154 (1958): 21–63.

——. "Le Directoire: points de vue et interpretations d'apres des travaux récents," *Annales historiques de la Révolution française,* 224 (1976): 181–214.

Sydenham, M. J. *The First French Republic, 1792–1804.* Berkeley, 1974.

——. *The French Revolution.* New York, 1966.

——. *The Girondins.* London, 1961.

Tallandier, M.-A.-H. *Documents biographiques sur P.C.F. Daunou.* Paris, 1847.

Taylor, George. "Noncapitalist Wealth and the Origins of the French Revolution," *American Historical Review,* 82 (1967): 469–491.

——. "Types of Capitalism in Eighteenth-Century France," *English Historical Review,* (1964): 478–497.

Thompson, J. M. *Robespierre,* 2 vols. New York, 1968.

Tonnesson, Kare D. *La Défaite des sans-culottes: movement populaire et reaction bourgeoisie en l'an III,* Oslo, 1959.

Vandal, Albert. *L'Avènement de Bonaparte.* 2 vols. Paris, 1902–1907.

Van Duzer, Charles. *Contribution of the Idéologues to French Revolutionary Thought.* Baltimore, 1935.

Wicks, Daniel, "The Court Nobility and the French Revolution: The Example of the Society of Thirty," *Eighteenth-Century Studies* 13 (1980): 263–84.

Woloch, Isser. *Jacobin Legacy: The Democratic Movement Under the Directory.* Princeton, 1970.

INDEX

Amar, André, 93
Ami du peuple, 90, 138
Amnesty of 4 brumaire, 136
Anthoine, François, 64
Artois, Charles-Philippe de Bourbon, comte de, 21

Babeuf, François-Noel (Gracchus), 137
Baker, Keith, 108
Barbaroux, Charles-Jean-Marie, 91
Barère, Bertrand, 63, 119
Barnave, Antoine-Pierre-Joseph-Marie, 49, 62, 63, 65, 70, 72
Barras, Paul-Jean, 140
Barthélemy, François, 144
Bastid, Paul, 130, 150n107
Bayle, Pierre, 146
Beauharnais, Josephine, Madame, 115
Beauvau, Charles-Juste, Marshal, 17, 19, 23
Bechet de Lehautcour, 12, 15
Bénézech, Pierre, 143
Bernard, Madame, 93
Billaud-Varennes, Jean-Nicholas, 119
Bonaparte, Napoleon, 133, 139, 143, 147, 151, 152; and Roederer, 147–48
Bosher, J. F., 32n96, 54
Bouillé, François-Claude-Amour, marquis de, 30, 63
Boulay de la Meurthe, Antoine-Jacques-Claude-Joseph, 148, 149n103, 149n104
Bourdon, Jean, 148
Bourgin, Georges, 1
Brissot, Jacques-Pierre, 66, 68, 74, 75, 86, 90, 132
Brottier, André-Charles, abbé, 136
Buzot, François, 65, 66, 70, 71, 74

Caisse patriotique de la Maison de secours, 87
Calonne, Charles Alexandre de, 13–14, 17, 18, 19, 21, 23; and Maupeou reform, 4; and stamp tax proposal of 1787, 35–36
Caraman, comte de: and surtax on the gabelle, 10–11; intermediary for Saint-Quirin, 18
Carnot, Lazare-Nicholas-Marguerite, 141, 143, 144
Champ de Mars, massacre of, 66
Champion, 88
Chenier, Marie-Joseph, 121
Choiseul, comtesse de, 17
Chronique de Paris, 76, 90

Class of Moral and Political Sciences of the National Institute, 110
Clichy Club, 138
Club de l'Evêché, 75
Cobban, Alfred, 32
Cochon de Lapparent, Charles, 143
Collot d'Herbois, Jean-Marie: attack on Roederer, 83–84
Combe, 92
Comité contentieux of Paris, 78, 80
Commission of eleven of the National Convention, 125, 129
Committee of General Security of the National Convention, 115
Committee of Thirty, 60
Committees of the Constitution and Revision of the Constituent Assembly, 68
Condillac, Etienne Bonnot de, 95, 100, 110
Condorcet, Marie-Jean-Antoine-Nicolas Caritat, marquis de, 2, 76, 90, 95, 103, 108, 110, 125, 152; and social science, 94
Constant, Benjamin, 141, 148
Constitution of the Year VIII, 2, 151
Constitutional Club of the Hotel de Salm, 138
Contribution foncière, 79, 81
Contribution mobilière, 79, 81
Corancez, Olivier de, 115, 133n1, 134–35, 147, 152
Cordelier Club, 65, 67
Coroller du Moustoir, Louis-Jacques-Hippolyte, 65, 66
Coup d'état of 18 brumaire, 2, 147–48

D'André, Antoine, 57, 72, 75, 76
Daunou, Pierre-Claude, 148, 149n104
Défenseur de la Constitution, 84, 89
Dejoly, 88, 91
Delacroix, J.-P., 85
Delahante, Jacques, 43, 45, 47, 49
Delly d'Agier, Claude-Pierre, 50, 51, 58
Demarest, 43, 45, 49, 50, 51
Démeuniers, Jean-Nicholas, 141n54
Destutt de Tracy, Antoine-Louis-Claude, comte de, 101, 110
Ducos, Jean-François, 131, 132
Dumas, Mathieu, 141
Dupont de Nemours, Pierre-Samuel, 34, 35, 55, 56, 58, 59, 111, 126, 129; and the tobacco monopoly, 45, 45n52, 46, 54; view of financial reform in the Constituent Assembly, 33

www.ingramcontent.com/pod-product-compliance
Lightning Source LLC
Chambersburg PA
CBHW080926100426
42812CB00007B/2382